CLIVE CUSSLER

Stuart Leuthner

Copyright © 2017 by Stuart Leuthner .All rights reserved. No part of this book may be reproduced, stored in a retrieval system, or transmitted in any form or by any means, electronic, mechanical, photocopying, recording, scanning, or otherwise except as permitted under Section 107 or 108 of the 1976 United States Copyright Act, without either the prior written permission of New Word City. Requests for permission should be addressed to the **editors@newwordcity.com**. For more information about New Word City, visit our Web site at
www.newwordcity.com

INTRODUCTION 7
PRELUDE 13
1
BYZANIUM 19
2
BEGINNINGS 27
3
HERR, ICH BIN EIN KLAVIER SPIELIER! 31
4
WHEN MY BABY SMILES AT ME 35
5
A MAN WHO MADE FUNNY FACES 39
6
THE END OF THE RAINBOW 45
7
THE VILLAIN OF THE LIGHTHOUSE 53
8
I STILL KNOW HOW TO MILK A COW 59
9
CALL LLOYDS OF LONDON 63
10
THE INSTIGATOR OF OUR ADVENTURES 69
11
JUST DRIVE IT UNTIL IT BREAKS 75
12
THIRTY DAYS ON THE ROAD GANG 81
13
FIFTY-SIX SPARK PLUGS 87
14
FIX ME UP 95
15
CLIVE CUSSLER ENGINE CHIEF 101
16
RAGAMUFFIN 109
17
DIVING FANATICS 115
18
NO GOOD DEED GOES UNPUNISHED 121
19
THE FLYING RED MULE 127
20
A PERFECT FIT 133
21
BESTGEN & CUSSLER 141
22
A LITTLE PAPERBACK ADVENTURE 147
23
HORACE P. QUAGMIRE 155
24
THE CHARLES WINTHROP AGENCY 163
25
ESTES PARK 169
26
A HOTSHOT FROM THE WEST COAST 175
27
SOUR FACED BIDDY 183

28 ARMPIT, TONSIL & GROIN 191
29 CLIVE CUSSLER WASN'T GOING ANYWHERE 197
30 WHO THE HELL IS CLIVE CUSSLER? 201
31 QUIT YOUR JOB 207
32 LOOKOUT MOUNTAIN 213
33 THE BOOK TOUR FROM HELL 221
34 I WANT TO DO A DEAL 227
35 IF YOU LET THEM PUBLISH THAT RAG, YOU'RE RUINED! 235
36 A PLATTER OF CHEESE: ONE KIND 243
37 BECAUSE IT'S INCONVENIENT 249
38 TOUCHED BY A CAR 255
39 IT'S A DUESY 263
40 PARADISE VALLEY 269
41 THE REAL CLIVE CUSSLER 275
42 THE HAND ROUTINE 281
43 HUMBLE HERBERT I AIN'T 287
44 HUNTING THE HUNLEY 293
45 FISH BOAT FOUND 299
46 CUSSLER GAVE GOOD QUOTE 307
47 THE BOOK NOBODY WANTED 315
48 LET'S BREAK NEW GROUND 323
49 THE CUSSLER THING 333
50 JUST CALL ME DAD 341
51 THE INVISIBLE TYCOON 349
52 SHE WALKS WITH THE ANGELS 355
53 THE SON ALSO RISES 361
54 A SQUEAKY WHEEL 371
55 SAND STORM 379

56 BOMBS AWAY 387
57 I'LL PAINT THEM ANY COLOR I WANT 395
58 VIN FIZ 401
59 PLEASE PASS THE SALT 407
60 HARDBALL 413
61 THE $100 MILLION QUESTION 421
62 CHATTED WITH CLIVE 429
63 A SLOSH OF JOSHUA SLOCUM 435
64 THE HOLY GRAIL 443
65 SOCIETY OF CUSSLERMEN 449
66 A GENEROUS MAN 453
67 THE KEYS TO THEIR FERRARI 461
68 THE NEXT BIG ADVENTURE 469
69 EPILOGUE 475

INTRODUCTION

The Bug was the giveaway.

On a warm summer afternoon in 1968, my father pulled up to the house in a new car. Well, new to us anyway. At its heart, it was a used Volkswagen Beetle, the ubiquitous road dog of Southern California in the day. This one had been chopped and diced, however, by a local hot-rodder bent on making it an off-road desert rambler. They were called Baja Bugs back then, weekend playthings for the semi-adventurous. My father's selection was not for the faint of heart. Painted red and yellow, it had a flattened snout covered in silver mesh and an exposed rear engine compartment complete with a roaring open exhaust.

The first time my father pulled up to the house in it, my sisters and I piled in with glee. I remember it had a folding sunroof, and we took turns standing on the front seat with our arms extended like British royalty, buffeted by rushing air as we got a quick ride around the block. It was a crazy car, and my sisters and I absolutely loved it.

I suppose it was only in my subconscious that I realized all my friends' fathers were driving nondescript sedans or station wagons. I am quite certain that none of my playmates ever saw their father leave the house in the morning dressed in a three-piece suit, only to climb into a hot VW for the commute to work. Yet that was my father.

In hindsight, that Baja Bug says a lot about Clive Cussler. He's a man who's never been keen on conformity and, in fact, relishes rattling the gates of authority. He's always had a high regard for having fun and still carries a childlike joy about him. The Bug was certainly an intimation of his lifelong love affair with the automobile, as well as his thirst for adventure. But most of all, I think that car represented the mark of his irrepressible creativity.

My father has always shined in the creative department, whether it was spray-painting the family Christmas tree gold, just to be different, or inserting a hand-carved totem pole in the living room of his mountain home. Yet it was in his professional life where his creativity paved the way to success. His first real enterprise, running a two-bit gasoline station in suburban Los Angeles in the 1950s, was a marvel of creative marketing. Old family photos show a tiny gas station emblazoned with signs and promotions that would have impressed P.T. Barnum. His subsequent years in advertising revealed his clever knack for humor in product promotions for print, radio, and television. My sisters and I fondly recall watching him produce TV commercials for a local Denver bank in the 1970s, where he hired classic Hollywood character actors and inserted them into humorous situations for memorable effect.

But he has left his most indelible mark in fiction writing. He started with a minor thriller about an apocalyptic cult living in a seamount near Hawaii, introducing a lanky protagonist named Dirk Pitt. Rather than create a prototypical sleuthing detective or undercover spy, my father made Pitt a marine engineer and pilot who operated in and around the seas. When he completed the manuscript for *Pacific Vortex*, I'm sure he had no inkling Pitt would still be sailing the literary seas some forty-five years later.

Pitt, of course, is the quintessential American hero, a tough and intelligent man's man who also makes the women swoon. But there's a little more to the heart of the character. Like his creator, he stands six feet three inches and has wavy black hair. He has a like fascination with historical mysteries and a passion for antique cars. And he charges through life on his own terms. I always thought it a bit redundant when my father started writing himself into the books, à la Hitchcock, as his alter ego was already swashbuckling through the nearby pages.

Though *Pacific Vortex* was not initially published, my father was undaunted, writing two more adventure stories featuring the heroic Pitt that did make it to print. They were similar to *Pacific Vortex* in structure, linear mysteries that followed Pitt from beginning to end. But things changed with his next book, *Raise the Titanic!* The story featured a historical prologue, followed by multiple subplots that ultimately intertwined in a tense climax. It became his patented form of writing adventure fiction and has since been copied by dozens of successful writers.

The book was written when nobody knew what the wreck of the *Titanic* looked like, and there were serious doubts about it ever being located. Yet in typical creative boldness, my father didn't just rest at fictionally locating the *Titanic*; he raised it to the surface and completed its maiden voyage to New York. *Raise the Titanic!* was the breakthrough novel that secured his career as a writer and paved the way for his dominance in the genre of adventure fiction. In the dozens of books written since, he's held to a common theme: creative stories that are fun to read. A similar theme has followed his personal life. He's often said over the years that if it ain't fun, then it ain't worth doing. It's a mantra that describes both his life and his work. Since his days as a youth, he's blazed a path of fun and creativity that few men can match.

I've been blessed to be able to carry on the literary adventures of Dirk Pitt and introduce him to a new generation of readers. It's a daunting challenge to add to another's lavish body of creative work, but I do have a slight advantage. When it comes to writing about Pitt, at least, I've got a ready source of inspiration into the heart and soul of the character. One that started, perhaps, with a long-ago ride in a Baja Bug.

- Dirk Cussler

PRELUDE

Six-year-old Clive Cussler stared wide-eyed at the placid blue Pacific Ocean. It was the boy's first encounter with the Southern California shoreline since his family's recent move from the frozen suburbs of Minneapolis. Stretching as far as he could see, the dazzling tableau of sand, water, and azure sky were interrupted only by the Huntington Beach Pier and a smudge of smoke trailing behind a haze-blurred liner.

Suddenly, as if commanded by an inner voice, Clive began to run towards the water. His parents, busy unpacking beach gear, looked up in astonishment. Clive's mother, Amy, called after him, "Wait, Clive, wait!" But her son, his lanky legs churning like pistons, continued his mad dash across the sand. Splashing into the water, he was ambushed by a foaming breaker and dumped back onto the beach.

Undaunted, the youngster jumped up and charged back into the pounding surf. On his second attempt, Clive's timing was better, and he soon found himself in over his head. Opening his eyes, Clive was transfixed by his first glimpse of the underwater world. Peering at several tiny fish darting across the sun-dappled bottom, he momentarily forgot he didn't know how to swim. Suddenly, a large hand plunged through a froth of bubbles. Eric Cussler had sprinted into the water and after a few frantic thrusts, managed to grab his son's arm and haul him back to the beach. A few days later, Amy enrolled Clive in swimming lessons.

That abbreviated dip in the Pacific Ocean at Huntington Beach marked the beginning of Clive Cussler's life-long love of the sea. Growing up in Southern California he spent long, lazy days on the beach, body-surfing and swimming. Stationed in Hawaii during the Korean War, Clive and his air force buddies strapped on an aqualung when few amateurs would venture into the depths. During the late 1960s, Clive managed a dive shop for a year, an experience that expanded his knowledge of the underwater world and honed his diving skills.

The allure of the sea beckoned again when Clive slid behind a typewriter one night and dove into writing action adventure tales. Clive's first novel's action is set against a backdrop of the world's oceans - mysterious, beautiful, unpredictable, uncharted, and treacherous. His hero, a marine engineer, works for the fictional National Underwater and Marine Agency (NUMA), an oceanographic research organization. Little did he realize the "pot boiler," as he called his first effort, would spawn a globally popular adventure series still going strong more than forty years later.

In 1979, Clive joined a select group of "aquanauts," spending three days in Hydrolab, an underwater habitat on the sea floor, fifty feet below the surface near St. Croix. Providing Spartan accommodations for four divers, the habitat served as a research station from 1970 to 1985. "We dove in the morning, noon, and in the evening when it was dark," Clive recalled. "I felt like a true denizen of the deep."

"I felt like a true denizen of the deep." The same year he visited Hydrolab, Clive elevated his fascination with the sea to a new level when he founded the real-life NUMA, a nonprofit organization dedicated to preserving maritime and naval history. Funded primarily by Clive's book sales, NUMA's crew of dedicated marine experts and volunteers have discovered more than 100 significant underwater wrecks, including the Civil War submarine, *H.L. Hunley*.

Jacques Cousteau was the first explorer to provide the general public a glimpse into the underwater world. Educating and inspiring with his films and books, Cousteau was a staunch believer in marine conservation. Clive, through the adventures of eco-warrior Dirk Pitt and his associates, communicates the same message - the oceans are not a convenient dumping ground or an infinite source of food and energy. They are a priceless, fragile resource and it is crucial for all of us to understand how our activities affect the sea.

Today, Clive is the keystone of a publishing empire Forbes described as, "the literary equivalent of a theme park." In addition to the flagship Dirk Pitt novels, co-written since 2004 with his son, he oversees four spinoff series, co-written with a team of outstanding authors. In the pages of his bestselling novels, Clive's intrepid heroes fight injustice and punish those who would exploit and pollute the world's oceans, while NUMA's dedicated explorers continue to search for the mysteries hidden beneath their restless waves.

The seeds for Clive's accomplishments may well have been planted on that brilliant summer day at Huntington Beach in 1937 when six-year-old Clive Cussler hit the water running. More than three-quarters of a century later, he is still diving headfirst into adventure.

1
BYZANIUM

In January 1973, Clive retreated to his unfinished basement and took stock. It was not a pretty picture. Forty-one years old, he had a wife, three children, a mortgage, and was unemployed. As far as his writing career, all Clive had to show for nearly ten years of labor were three unpublished manuscripts.

Common sense suggested he should concentrate his efforts on finding another job, but Clive was determined to follow his dream. Surviving on unemployment, occasional freelance jobs, and Barbara's salary, he spent the majority of his time in the basement working on his new novel. "Thing's might have been tight," he recalls, "but nobody was looking over my shoulder while I worked on a boring campaign, adding their two cents, bitching at me to control costs and trying to stab me in the back. I was now doing what I loved to do - write."

On Clive's desk, made of two sawhorses and an unfinished door, the pages of his next book were piling up - the working title: *Titanic*. Although Clive cannot pinpoint the moment of his inspiration, he realized an attempt to raise the world's most famous shipwreck would provide a thrilling challenge for Dirk Pitt and his NUMA associates. "My original inspiration was based on fantasy and to see *Titanic* brought up from the seabed and towed into New York Harbor, completing her maiden voyage begun three quarters of a century before. Fortunately, it was a fantasy shared by millions of her devoted fans."

Raising the *Titanic* was not a new idea. Only a few months after the ship went down, the wealthy Astor, Widener and Guggenheim families (all lost relatives in the disaster) contacted the Merritt and Chapman Derrick and Wrecking Company (MCD&W) to investigate the feasibility of locating and raising the ill-fated liner. With headquarters in New York City, MCD&W was one of the world's largest marine salvage operations. Since the technology did not exist to find the wreck, much less hoist the 46,000-ton ship from a depth of two and a half miles, MCD&W graciously declined.

The entire world was stunned by the *Titanic* disaster. Within days of the liner's sinking, films, poems, books, songs, plays, postcards and memorabilia commemorated the liner and her tragic end. Released only twenty-nine days after the disaster, *Saved from the Titanic* was a silent film starring Dorothy Gibson, an actress who was aboard the ship and left on the first lifeboat. Gibson appeared in the same outfit she was wearing on the night of the catastrophe.

During the years after the sinking, there were more urgent issues than a shipwreck lying in the frigid depths of the North Atlantic. World War I, the Great Depression, and another world war demoted the *Titanic* to a footnote. Interest in the *Titanic* began to gather momentum in the mid-1950s, with the publishing of Walter Lord's highly successful book, *A Night to Remember*, followed by the film adaptation in 1958. Over the years, dreamers and crackpots had proposed a series of outlandish schemes to resurrect the *Titanic* involving electromagnets, balloons, turning the ship into a giant ice cube by freezing the water around the hull with liquid nitrogen, millions of Ping-Pong balls, 180,000 tons of molten wax, and manned deep-sea submersibles.

During the early 1980s, flamboyant Texas oilman Jack Grimm, who had already hunted for Noah's Ark, the Loch Ness Monster, Bigfoot and the hole in the North Pole providing access to the mythical hollow earth, sponsored three serious expeditions to locate the *Titanic*. Several prominent scientists were hired as consultants, but the expeditions came up empty due to bad weather and technical problems.

In 1985, a joint French-American venture set sail for the North Atlantic. Led by oceanographer/engineer Jean-Louis Michel and Dr. Robert Ballard, a marine geologist working for the Woods Hole Oceanographic Institute and the U.S. Navy, the secret expedition was funded by the Navy to photograph the wreckage of a sunken nuclear submarine. Once the primary mission was completed, the Navy said Ballard and his team could spend twelve days searching for the *Titanic*.

During the early morning of September 1, 1985, a boiler appeared out of the gloom on one of the search ship's monitors, followed moments later by port holes and pieces of a ship's hull and railings. It was the *RMS Titanic*. Instead of being intact, the stern and bow sections lay almost 2,000 feet apart, facing in opposite directions.

Since Clive wrote his book ten years before the wreck was discovered, Dirk Pitt's fictional *Titanic* is in one piece. Wayne Valero, co-founder of the Clive Cussler Collector's Society has been reading and writing about Clive's work for almost forty years. In his book, *From the Mediterranean Caper to Black Wind*, Valero describes the process Clive uses to make the raising of the *Titanic* believable. "Cussler will take a premise like what if you could raise the *Titanic*? . . . How would they do it? Who would do it and for what purpose?"

Known as alternate or counterfactual history, the "what if" style of writing first appeared during the 1880s. Based on actual historical events, writers presume a few alterations could result in a significantly different world. Ward Moore's *Bring the Jubilee* depicts a United States in which the Confederacy has won the Civil War. In Len Deighton's *SS-GB*, Operation Sea Lion is successful and England is occupied by Nazi Germany. When big game hunters travel back in time to hunt Tyrannosaurus rex in Ray Bradbury's "A Sound of Thunder," one of them accidentally kills a butterfly. Returning to the present, the adventurers are dismayed to discover a number of disconcerting changes.

In his adventure thriller, Clive recounts the disaster in a short, but stirring prelude. He also provides clues as to why the U.S. government would want to raise the liner. The action shifts to the 1980s when U.S. and Soviet relations have reached a low point. Byzanium, an extremely rare element, is desperately needed to complete the "Sicilian Project," a defensive system designed to destroy attacking missiles before they reach North America. When a search for the element on a Russian island runs into trouble, Dirk Pitt comes to the rescue, but it turns out the mine had been played out in 1911. Believing the only Byzanium in the world is in the *Titanic's* vault at the bottom of the Atlantic Ocean, the government commissions NUMA to raise the ship.

While American and Russian spies and counterspies go about their clandestine business, Pitt and his NUMA team find the *Titanic*. Robots are sent down to seal the damaged hull with "Wetsteel." Pliable until it comes in contact with water, the substance "can bond itself to a metal object as though it were welded." When the hull is sealed, compressed air is pumped in and the *Titanic* "leaps out of the waves like a modern submarine blowing its ballast tanks."

Once the *Titanic* is refloated, Clive lulls the reader into believing the novel is headed for a happy ending, but a hurricane threatens to send the resurrected ship back to the bottom. When the *Titanic* finally reaches New York, Pitt opens the vault. Nothing! A surprising climax connects the dots of the multiple story lines, and Pitt locates the missing Byzanium. America is safe until the next Dirk Pitt novel.

Clive finished the novel on June 25, 1974. While he carefully packed the manuscript, his mind was racing. *Titanic* was not only an exciting story, it was his best writing so far; still, there was no guarantee Peter Lampack could find a publisher. And, if he did, would the advance be enough for him to pursue a career as a writer? He drove to the post office and sent the parcel to New York. After a quick stop for a quart of milk, Clive was back in the basement, launching Dirk Pitt's search for *Vixen 03*.

2
BEGINNINGS

During the early twentieth century, Aurora, Illinois, was home to a vigorous collection of industries, including three corset factories, six manufacturers of heavy equipment, numerous foundries and machine shops, and the Chicago, Burlington & Quincy Railroad's car works, a sprawling, smoky complex employing more than 1,200 men. Located forty miles west of Chicago, the "City of Lights" - Aurora was one of the first Midwest cities to illuminate its downtown with electric lights - could also lay claim to the title, "World Center for Steel Cabinetry." Seven businesses, including Lyon Metal, Aurora Metal, All-Steel, Equipto, and The Durabilt Steel Locker Company fabricated steel shelving, desks, lockers, and cabinets.

When Eric Cussler reported for work at the Durabilt factory on the morning of July 15, 1931, he was exhausted. The twenty-nine-year-old German immigrant had spent the night in the waiting room at St. Joseph's Hospital, managing at most an hour of fitful sleep. At a little after 2 a.m., a nurse woke him with a gentle tap on the shoulder. He was the father of a healthy baby boy who would be named Clive Eric Cussler. The newcomer's mother, Amy, was enamored with Clive Brook, the suave actor whose smoldering good looks made him a matinee idol in both his native England and the United States. Best remembered for playing opposite Marlene Dietrich in *Shanghai Express*, his film credits also include *The Return of Sherlock Holmes* and John Huston's *The List of Adrian Messenger*.

Although elated by the birth of his son, Eric was troubled. Aurora, like the rest of the nation, was in the depths of the Depression. Wages had been steadily cut - Eric was taking home less than $15 a week — and rumors had been circulating for several weeks that Durabilt was planning major layoffs. The machines had only been running for a few minutes that morning when they ground to a halt and a supervisor ordered the men to assemble on the plant floor. After a few conciliatory remarks about the gloomy economy and how much the company regretted such extreme measures, he read off a list of more than 100 employees, including Eric, who were no longer on the payroll. After a few quick goodbyes, Eric cleaned out his locker and walked out of the plant into a cheerless dawn.

3
HERR, ICH BIN EIN KLAVIER SPIELIER!

The Cussler clan's origins can be traced to a band of gypsies who roamed Spain during the fourteenth century. Migrating to France, they continued their nomadic wanderings until the outbreak of the War of Austrian Succession in 1740. At that time, the name was spelled "Cussiliere" (pronounced Coos-lair). When the war ended, several families settled in Prussia and the name was Germanized to Cussler.

Eric Cussler's childhood was extremely grim. The youngest of three children, he grew up in Neunkirchen, an industrial town located in southwest Germany. His father, a career soldier, was a bad-tempered tyrant who verbally and physically abused his family. Shipped off to a military academy when he was eleven, Eric was assigned to an infantry brigade during World War I. Wounded, he would always walk with a limp, described by Clive as, "More like Grandpa McCoy on *The Real McCoys* than Deputy Chester Goode on *Gunsmoke*."

After graduating from the University of Heidelberg, the handsome, barrel-chested young man worked in a Frankfurt bank and joined one of the underground groups determined to evict the occupying French troops. When his political activities came to the attention of the French authorities and he realized Germany was setting out on a dark adventure, Eric booked a cabin on the *SS Ohio*. He arrived in New York on May 11, 1925.

A limp was on the list of medical symptoms that could result in exclusion. After spending six miserable days in a crowded dormitory on Ellis Island, Eric was allowed to plead his case before the Board of Special Inquiry. Facing a one-way ticket back to Germany, he announced, "Herr, Ich bin ein klavier spielier!" ("Sir, I am a piano player!"). An official escorted him to Ellis Island's third-floor recreation room and pointed to an upright piano.

Eric's sister, Francis, an accomplished pianist, had taught him to play an old German march. Eric sat down and played the song fast and slow, soft and loud. Standing on the "forte" pedal, he ended his extemporaneous concert with a thundering crescendo. As the melody faded, the official shrugged, "Mr. Cussler, it appears you are a piano player." Thankfully, he did not request an encore, and Eric was allowed to pass through the "golden door." As far as his family or friends recall, Eric never played the piano again.

Francis had arrived in the United States several years before her brother married an American. Eric was living on a farm in Plano, Illinois. After a year in Plano, laboring in the fields and learning English, he moved to Chicago, pressing pants in a laundry for a nickel a pair, before landing a job as a bookkeeper for a large auto parts store. Clive recalls his father's often told stories of the frenetic Roaring Twenties: "Driving his roommate's Stutz Bearcat, making bathtub gin, seeing 'Al Scarface' Capone on the courthouse steps, walking by bullet-riddled gangsters sprawled in the street and meeting my mother, Amy Hunnewell."

4
WHEN MY BABY SMILES AT ME

Amy Hunnewell's lineage can be traced back to Roger Hunnewell, an English fisherman who arrived in Boston in 1654. As the American frontier moved west, the Hunnewells followed. William "Will" Hunnewell, born in 1887, grew up on a farm in Idaho. Hired on as a fireman for the Minneapolis, St. Paul and Sault Ste. Marie Railroad, Will married Amy Bigalow in 1887, and their daughter, Amy Adaline, was born in St. Joseph, Missouri in 1901.

A rolling stone, Will left his job on the railroad, tried farming and managed several resorts in Iowa and Minnesota, before opening a saloon and distillery in Monticello, a small town located thirty miles west of Minneapolis. In a fortuitous move, he sold the saloon in 1919, two weeks before Prohibition went into effect, and went back to work for the railroad.

In 1921, Amy, now twenty, moved to Minneapolis and worked as a receptionist in a medical office. Evenings and weekends, she played the piano at a Minneapolis theater, providing background music for silent movies. During a weekend jaunt to Chicago with a girlfriend, Amy met Eric. "My parents," Clive says, "always told everybody they were properly introduced by mutual friends. Only when they were in their seventies did they admit they actually met when my father asked my mother for a dance at the Trianon Ballroom."

Located on Chicago's south side, the Trianon Ballroom was extremely popular during the Jazz Age. Ted "Is Everybody Happy" Lewis and his orchestra were on the bandstand the evening Eric and Amy met, and the star-crossed couple spent the night fox-trotting to "It's Only a Shanty in Old Shanty Town" and "When My Baby Smiles at Me." Eric and Amy were married on June 10, 1930, at the bride's parent's home. They rented a small apartment in Aurora, Illinois, and Eric was hired by Durabilt - a job that would prove to be short-lived.

5
A MAN WHO MADE FUNNY FACES

By 1931, the Depression had tightened its grip on America and unemployment reached more than 20 percent. With no possibility of finding another job in Aurora, Eric, Amy and baby Clive moved in with Will Hunnewell. Amy's mother had died in January and Will was living in Minneapolis. Thanks to his seniority, Will's job with the railroad was secure and he was fortunate to have a steady paycheck.

Unwilling to sponge off anybody, especially his in-laws, Eric immediately looked for work. For a short time, he sold refrigerators. "Selling refrigerators," Clive says, "door-to-door in Minneapolis, in the Depression, in the middle of the winter! He might as well have tried to sell them to Eskimos." Clive chuckles, "Dad always insisted he actually sold one, but nobody believed him."

In late winter 1932, Eric's luck took a turn for the better. He was hired, with a salary of $23 a week, as a traveling auditor for the Jewel Tea Company. Founded in 1899, the Jewel Tea Company was a home delivery service, offering housewives an assortment of coffee, tea, spices, laundry and toilet products. At one time, the company's brown and yellow vans and their friendly drivers were a familiar sight in much of the U.S.

During the Depression, it was not unusual for a company to give a new employee an advance on their wages. When Jewel Tea advanced Eric $8, he brought the check home and proudly laid it on the dining room table. Clive remembers his mother's story about the entire family standing around the table, staring in awe at the check, while she burst into tears.

Traveling by train or car, Eric was constantly on the road. To maximize his time with his family, the Cussler's rented a series of apartments in Terre Haute, Indiana and Louisville, Kentucky, before moving back to Minneapolis in 1937. When they lived in Louisville, Clive recalls leisurely walks with his grandfather along the banks of the Ohio River. "We would watch the steam boats on the river and pass by the Seagram's distillery. Seagram's big water tank was shaped like a jug and I thought it was amazing. One of those things that always stays with you."

Now six, Clive was enrolled in kindergarten, but soon became desperately ill and was diagnosed with pneumonia. Before the development of antibiotics, pneumonia, known as the "captain of the men of death," was often fatal, especially for children. Treatment consisted of simply placing the patient in an oxygen tent and waiting for recovery or death. Much to his family's relief, Clive chose the former.

After more than a week in the hospital, Clive's condition began to improve and another patient was moved into his room - an elderly derelict named Wendell, who had been found half frozen in an alley. Bored to tears, Clive was happy to have somebody to talk to, especially a character as colorful as Wendell. "That old guy," Clive says, "taught me card games, made funny faces, performed tricks with his false teeth and told me stories no six-year-old should have heard."

One morning, a nurse came into Clive's room to check the boy's vital signs. Clive pointed to his new friend and asked why Wendell had turned an unhealthy shade of blue. The nurse took one look at the old-timer, gasped, and whisked the curtain around the bed. Shortly after, two orderlies appeared, covered Wendell with a sheet, and quickly rolled him out of the room. When Eric was informed a "street bum" died in the bed next to his darling son, Clive remembers his father's fury. "I could hear him yelling in the hall with his German accent and was afraid he was going to tear the hospital down."

With Clive on the mend, Eric and Amy wanted him home for Christmas. Ignoring the medical staff's objections, they extricated Clive from the hospital and soon tucked him into his own bed. Although money was still scarce, Clive discovered later his parents sacrificed their small savings to insure he had a merry Christmas.

On Christmas morning, Eric and Amy helped half carried Clive to the living room where a shiny black Lionel steam locomotive and three bright-red passenger cars were racing around the Christmas tree. As the train passed a little white shanty, a switchman would spring out, swing his lantern, and pop back inside. Clive spent Christmas morning stretched out on the floor, entranced with the mechanical switchman. Amy suggested he give him a name. Clive thought for a moment and nodded. "I'll call him Wendell."

"That's an odd name," Amy said, "Where did you come up with that?"

As he continued to watch the switchman, dutifully swinging his lantern to protect imaginary motorists from the thundering express, Clive replied, "Oh, from a man who makes funny faces."

In late January 1938, the Jewel Tea Company notified Eric there were two available positions he might want to consider. One, a promotion, would require him to relocate to Chicago. The other, in the Los Angeles office, was a lateral move - his salary would remain the same. The temperature in Minneapolis was hovering near zero and Clive, still recuperating, was as white as the snow piled eight feet deep around their apartment building.

With his son's health paramount, Eric elected to apply for the job in California. Within a week, the Cusslers packed everything they could fit into their 1937 Ford Victoria and hit the road. The first day they managed only twenty-six miles. Road maintenance was almost nonexistent, and Eric often had to plow through a foot and a half of snow. The Ford slid off the icy roads three times; on two occasions, they were pulled out of a ditch by sympathetic truckers. After spending the night in a motor court, conditions improved and when they reached Omaha, the snow, much to Clive's amazement, was beginning to disappear.

In Texas, Eric turned west onto Route 66, and a few days later, they crossed the Colorado River on the Old Trails Arch Bridge and entered California. For Clive, "Our trip west was a great adventure. I, of course, knew absolutely nothing about California, but realized my parents were excited about the move.

As the town of Needles receded in the Ford's rearview mirror, Eric concentrated on his driving while Amy busied herself with a map. Sitting in the back seat, Clive, his face pressed against the window, stared at the desolate desert stretching forever in all directions. What kind of future, he wondered, waited for him in the Golden State?

6
THE END OF THE RAINBOW

It was February 1938, when the dusty Ford rolled into San Bernardino. The seemingly endless desert had given way to groves of citrus trees marching into the distance, framed by the picture postcard San Gabriel Mountains. California, the Cusslers decided, might actually be a nice place to live.

In Pasadena, Eric turned left on San Gabriel Boulevard and headed for Alhambra, a small city ten miles northeast of downtown Los Angeles. Amy's cousin and her husband lived in Alhambra and Eric rented a small Spanish-style house on their block. A year later, he bought a brand-new bungalow in the same neighborhood. Except for the four years Clive spent in the Air Force, he would live at 2101 Winthrop Drive until his marriage in 1955.

When Eric and Amy made the decision to relocate to California, the ramifications went far beyond simply moving to another state. For much of its history, California has been seen as a mythical paradise, standing apart from the rest of the nation - a place of new beginnings and realized dreams, where baseball-size gold nuggets were free for the taking and a future movie star could be discovered waiting tables.

Writer John Gunther, who toured the United States in the 1940s, described California as, "A whole great world of its own" inhabited by "the outside fringe." Carey Williams, a writer who reported extensively on the land and people of California, titled one of his books, *The Great Exception*. "The profound transformation of California," Williams wrote, "economic, social and physical, are difficult to emphasize sufficiently." Historian Merry Ornick called Southern California, "the end of the rainbow."

Growing up in Alhambra had a significant effect on Clive. Although born in the Midwest, he quickly adopted Southern California as his inherited spiritual destination. In the land of perceived unlimited opportunity, Clive developed imagination, confidence, and optimism - qualities that have served him admirably in business and in his writing career.

Amy enrolled Clive at Fremont Elementary School, a nine-block walk from their house. Alhambra had grown so rapidly there were insufficient classrooms, and a group of large, army surplus tents (wooden walls with sturdy canvas roofs) were erected next to the school. Clive will never forget the smell of sunbaked canvas, but he remembers most his anemic appearance those first few weeks. "I was still recuperating from my bout with pneumonia," he says, "and looked like something that had crawled out from under a rock. Sickly pale, so skinny you could count my ribs and wearing short pants."

The local youngsters were tanned, strapping, and wore grown-up pants. Although the kid next door felt it his duty to beat Clive up on several occasions, the combination of southern California's sunshine and Clive's youthful resilience quickly restored his health and he was soon out on the playground with newfound friends. "I was very fortunate," he says. "There were five or six other boys in the neighborhood who were my age and we were always up to something."

Clive's "gang" scavenged scrap lumber from construction sites and built multi-room tree houses. Holes dug in the ground, covered with boards and lit with candles, became trenches of the Great War. A fanciful twenty-foot long pirate ship, complete with a crow's nest and plank to walk, was "anchored" in a vacant lot. When a local farmer harvested his crop of hay, the boys would stack up the bales and defend their Foreign Legion fort against marauding Bedouin hordes.

On most evenings, the boys played football or baseball, but Winthrop Drive would grow silent when they dashed inside and gathered around the glowing radios occupying a place of honor in their living rooms. Sitting cross-legged on the floor, Clive and his friends thrilled to the exploits of *Dick Tracy*, *Jack Armstrong, the All-American Boy, Captain Midnight,* and *Red Ryder*. When they listened to *Inner Sanctum*, Clive would turn off the lights to make the tales of assorted ghosts, ghouls, and lunatics even scarier.

Like most Americans of their generation, Clive's family was addicted to the silver screen - maybe more so. When Eric was attending college in Germany, he worked as a projectionist in a movie theater. According to Clive, "Dad was a real movie nut." Hollywood's wholesale dream therapy helped audiences of the 1930s temporarily forget the hardships of the Depression. Two or three times a week, Clive and his parents would catch a show at the Alhambra Cinema or Academy Theater in Pasadena. A thirty-five cent ticket delivered a lot of entertainment: short subject, cartoon, newsreel, and travelogue followed by the B film and finally, the feature. By the time the Cusslers arrived home, it would often be close to midnight. "I had school the next day," Clive says. "Our neighbors and my teachers thought it was scandalous."

The ocean was only a half-hour's drive from Alhambra and Clive's parents would regularly take their son and his friends to spend a fun-filled day at the beach. They would frequently ride the legendary Cyclone Racer at The Pike amusement park in Long Beach.

The Japanese attack at Pearl Harbor on December 7, 1941, was especially terrifying to citizens on the west coast. Hawaii's proximity to California convinced the state's residents it would only be a matter of time before swarms of bloodthirsty Japanese soldiers charged through their front doors. Wild rumors suggested a massive Japanese battle fleet lurking near Catalina Island, clandestine Japanese air bases hidden in the California deserts, and turncoat Japanese fishermen covertly mining San Francisco harbor.

Beaches were strung with miles of barbed wire, coastal cities were blacked out, anti-aircraft guns guarded defense plants with roofs disguised to look like suburban neighborhoods, and sandbags ringed businesses and homes. On February 23, 1942, a Japanese submarine attacked an oil field near Santa Barbara. Although the shelling only resulted in minor damage, the ship's optimistic captain radioed home he left the entire city in flames.

Eric Cussler signed up as a volunteer air raid warden. Wearing a white helmet and armed with a nightstick, he would walk through the neighborhood admonishing negligent citizens to close their curtains so an errant light would not provide a Japanese bombardier with a target. Incendiary bombs were one of the most feared weapons in the Japanese arsenal and many homes were equipped with so-called spare pumps. Hooked up to a large can of water, the hand-powered pumps could be used to extinguish fires set by the bombs. Although the attacks never materialized, Clive and his friends found a use for the pumps after the war, installing them in the back seats of their cars and gleefully squirting unsuspecting pedestrians walking on Alhambra's sidewalks.

World War II was a major event for Clive and his friends. Old enough to comprehend their parents' anxiety, they eagerly followed the radio broadcasts, newsreels, newspaper and magazine articles describing the monumental battles raging in Europe and the Pacific. Clive built squadrons of model airplanes, friend and foe, and hung them from his bedroom ceiling. He also began his lifelong passion for collecting, filling his room with bottle caps, matchbook covers, and baseball cards. On the wall, he taped two paintings by Peter Helck clipped out of *Esquire* magazine: Jimmy Doolittle winning the 1932 Thompson Trophy air race in his red and white Gee Bee and Ralph DePalma and a mechanic pushing their Mercedes across the finish line after the car broke down with less than a mile to go at the 1912 Indianapolis 500.

7
THE VILLAIN OF THE LIGHTHOUSE

In 1943, Eric Cussler left Jewell Tea and went to work as the credit manager for the Cudahy Packing Company in the company's Los Angeles office. He had only been on the job for a short time when a Hollywood producer called and asked if Cudahy would donate a ham for a door prize at a charity event. Wartime rationing had elevated the gift of a ham to the level of a Cadillac, but somehow Eric managed to deliver the goods.

To show his appreciation, the producer arranged for Eric's family to tour the Paramount lot, an event Clive recalls as "one of my biggest thrills." He watched Gary Cooper shoot a scene from *The Story of Dr. Wassel*, based on the actual exploits of a heroic World War II physician in the Philippines, and was introduced to its director, Cecil B. DeMille. "He reached down from his lofty director's chair," Clive says, "and patted me on the head."

The Cusslers also attended live radio shows. Eric and Amy's favorite was the *Lux Radio Theater*. Hosted by DeMille, the shows recreated popular films, often with original cast members. Clive preferred the homespun antics of *Fibber McGee and Molly*.

Clive read the family's copies of *Grimm's Fairy Tales* and Hans Christian Andersen's *The Little Mermaid* so often they ultimately fell apart. When Amy and Eric did their weekly grocery shopping, they would drop their son off at the local library, picking him up several hours later. Clive gravitated to historical novels: World War I, C.S. Forester's *Horatio Hornblower* series and Joseph Altsheler's harrowing adventures of two cousins, one a Confederate, the other fighting for the Union.

Clive also enjoyed the Tom Swift books, a series starring a boy-genius inventor who uses up-to-date technology, often not yet in existence at the time, to save the world and defeat villains. Among Clive's favorites, *Tom Swift and His Electric Runabout: The Speediest Car on the Road*. Clive laughs, "I always thought it was pretty nifty that he painted the car purple."

Amy Cussler belonged to the Book-of-the-Month Club, and Clive used several of his mother's selections as subjects for school book reports. When he was nine, Clive turned in a report on *Gone With the Wind* and his teacher doubted the assignment's authorship. Amy assured her, not only had her son read the book, he had written the report by himself with no help from his parents.

Clive's classmate and longtime friend, Felix Dupuy, remembers him as, "boisterous, outgoing and creative. Clive loved to dress-up in costumes and make-believe he was that character. When we were in seventh grade, Clive wrote and produced a series of skits he called his Dr. Doolittle plays. They were really clever and the teacher allowed him to perform several for the class."

One of the skits, *The Villain of the Lighthouse,* featured Clive, who was always taller than everybody else, playing the part of the lighthouse. "He would stick his arms out, swinging them back and forth to simulate the light beams," Dupuy says, "while all sorts of villains, damsels in distress and brave heroes chased each other around his legs. Clive always liked to be the center of attention. He had the ability to get everybody laughing."

Clive's friends would spend afternoons at the Cussler's house, often being invited to stay for dinner. Dupuy remembers Amy Cussler, "as a wonderful, gentle-hearted woman who made us feel welcome. Amy never had a bad word for anybody, and she was constantly fussing over us, setting out a plate of cookies or some other treats."

As much as they liked Amy, Clive's friends admit being somewhat intimidated by Eric's thick accent, burly physique and trademark limp. "I think my friends thought my mother and I lived in fear of Dad's wrath," Clive says. "Nothing could have been further from the truth." On the rare occasions when Clive and his father did get into a row (usually provoked by Clive's teenage automotive adventures) Eric could work up a head of steam, but that was as far as it went. Much to his credit, Eric was able to overcome the toxic memories of his unhappy relationship with his abusive father.

"Despite the lingering effects of the Depression, and the necessary sacrifices and shortages during the war," Clive says, "my childhood was ideal. If there were ever two people who cherished each other, it was my mother and father. We were always doing things together and having fun. I loved them, and I knew they loved me. I have always considered myself extremely lucky to have such wonderful parents."

8
I STILL KNOW HOW TO MILK A COW

When Clive was in the eighth grade, he had two paper routes. Getting up with the birds, he delivered the *Los Angeles Times*. After school let out, Clive would climb back on his Schwinn and sling copies of the *Daily News*. When Amy realized the grueling routine was affecting her son's health, she insisted he relinquish the afternoon route, but Clive continued delivering the *Times* until he was a freshman in high school.

Once a week, Boy Scouts of America Troop Six would meet in a large log cabin built with telephone poles donated by the local phone company. Clive became a member of its Cobra Patrol shortly after his twelfth birthday. The troop would spend one weekend a month and several weeks during the summer at Camp San Antonio in the San Gabriel Mountains. With some assistance from his father, Clive earned the twenty-one merit badges required to achieve the rank of Eagle Scout before he was fifteen. "The hiking and camping," Clive recalls, "Thursday night meetings, wonderful friendships and working on my merit badges with my father - those marvelous experiences will always be with me."

After he gave up his paper route, Clive toiled at a succession of after school and summer jobs: sanding and polishing pianos in a music store's basement, grinding water pump impellers, and loading trucks at a commercial laundry. "It was a wonder the job at the pump company didn't kill me," Clive says. "The air was so thick with metal grindings I'd have to wash my hair with Old Dutch Cleanser."

When he was sixteen, Clive spent the summer at his uncle's dairy farm in Monticello, Minnesota. His friends thought he was crazy for passing up the beach, chasing girls, and hanging out at the drive-in, but Clive would not have missed it for the world. It was not only Clive's first trip East since his family moved to California, he would also have the opportunity to spend two months at a real, working farm. "That summer at my aunt and uncle's farm was one of my best summers ever," Clive recalls. "I worked in the fields, pitched hay, fed horses from my hand, went fishing on the lake behind the barn, and attended county fairs. Believe it or not, I still know how to milk a cow."

9
CALL LLOYDS OF LONDON

"When I was fifteen, I didn't just *want* a car," Clive says. "I *had* to have a car!"

Walking home from school, Clive spotted a 1923 Jewett languishing in the back row of a used car lot owned by Joe Servais, a sympathetic confidant of Alhambra's car-crazed adolescents. Built by the Paige-Detroit Motor Company and named for H.M. Jewett, the company's president, Jewetts were produced from 1922-26. Post-war America was zooming into the rocket age, and a boxy sedan built in the 1920s was considered positively prehistoric. Servais informed Clive the Jewett could be driven off the lot for $15.

Whenever Clive brought up the subject of a car, Eric would tell his son he needed insurance, effectively ending the discussion. On his own initiative, Clive called several insurance companies, but when he told the agents he was fifteen, they told him to call back in a few years, laughed at him or hung up.

Dejected, Clive went to see Servais and explained the obstacle between him and the Jewett. Servais, working under a car, hollered, "Call Lloyd's of London, they'll insure anything." Although Servais was obviously joking, Clive only heard, "they'll insure anything."

When Eric came home from work that evening, a large, black touring car was parked in the driveway. Charging into the house, he yelled, "Damn it, Clive! You've been told a hundred times you couldn't have a car without insurance." Faced with his father's fury, Clive blurted out his carefully rehearsed response. "Dad, Lloyd's of London will insure anything." Clive still remembers the look on his father's face. "It was one of the few times I really got to my old man."

Although the Jewett was never insured, Eric allowed Clive to keep the car after he promised to limit his driving to the immediate neighborhood. Stripping the car to its bare bones - removing the fenders, hood, top, and trunk - Clive added a truck-style flatbed and painted a large number "12" on the doors and radiator. He had transformed the staid Jewett into what is known today as a "beater" or "rat rod."

Clive had owned the Jewett for only a short time when the car's vacuum fuel pump gave up the ghost. A volunteer had to perch on the cowl in front of the windshield and pour gasoline directly into the vacuum canister. One afternoon, Clive was descending a hill when the car hit a bump. The youngster holding the gas can lost his grip, fell back into the car, and Clive, blinded by a face full of gas, lost control. Jumping the curb, the car skidded into a vacant lot. It had rained earlier and the Jewett's brakes (mechanical, rear wheels only), questionable under the best of conditions, were useless in the mud. Crashing through a rail fence into a neighbor's yard, the runaway jalopy careened across the lawn, down the driveway and back into the street. Clive kept going. Afraid the Jewett and its daredevil driver were probably on the Alhambra police department's "most wanted list," Clive sold the car to a junk dealer.

Returning to Servais's back row, Clive bought a 1925 Auburn for $22. A pair of silver flower vases in the spacious back seat was a reminder of the car's genteel heritage. Now insured, Clive recalls, "We had a lot of fun in the Auburn. My buddies and I would drive to football games, dressed like gangsters. We'd wear overcoats, old fedora hats pulled down over our eyes and clamp big stogies between our teeth."

In an attempt to expose her son to the arts, Amy had signed Clive up for violin lessons when he was ten. After three years of suffering for all involved, the instrument was relegated to the garage. Clive salvaged the violin's case and the school's security guards never figured out it was filled with beer and wine instead of an imaginary Tommy gun.

Felix Dupuy has fond memories of their escapades in Clive's Auburn. "After dark, we'd sneak onto an abandoned country club and drive around the fairways." During one of their nocturnal outings, Clive, Felix, and another friend, Dick Klein, were watching a motorcyclist jump over a sand trap. Determined to emulate the stunt, Clive managed to get the Auburn airborne, but the heavy car quickly ran out of airspeed and buried itself in the sand. The engine expired in a cloud of steam, and all four wheels fell off.

"Clive made a typical Cussler move," Dupuy says. "He doused the car with gas and set it on fire. When the fire department showed up, the three of us were sitting on a hill, watching all the excitement and laughing like hell."

The Jewett and Auburn had been good for laughs, but Clive, now seventeen, wanted a hot rod. Born in California, the stripped down, modified vehicles first appeared in the 1930s on the dry lakes located northeast of Los Angeles. During the 1940s, drag racing grew in popularity and hot rodders were often seen as rebels, a viewpoint perpetuated by films like *Hot Rods to Hell* and *Dragstrip Riot*.

Clive bought a 1936 Ford sedan, a car with first-class hot rod potential, but soon discovered the car had a major drawback. "Most of our gang," Clive says, "drove sporty roadsters with room for one passenger. My Ford had a back seat, and I usually wound up chauffeuring everybody around."

During the next year, Clive transformed the Ford into a classic California hot rod - lowered, teardrop fender skirts, custom hubcaps, and a dark, metallic green paint job. Under the hood, the warmed-up flathead V-8 was equipped with milled heads, oversize pistons, a three-quarter cam, and a pair of Stromberg 97 carburetors.

The Ford was Clive's daily driver until he joined the Air Force. "I invested a huge amount of time and at least $1,000 fixing the car up, which at that time was a hell of a lot of money. As soon as I joined the Air Force, my father wanted the car out of the driveway and sold it some kid for $69."

10
THE INSTIGATOR OF OUR ADVENTURES

Clive's success might suggest he was an excellent student. "Not so," Clive concedes, "I was average, at best."

While his teachers lectured on the fine points of transposing fractions or transient verbs, Clive would be "staring out the window, lost in another time, manning a cannon on John Paul Jones's ship, the *Bonhomme Richard*, charging up Cemetery Ridge with Pickett's division, or reversing the tide at Little Big Horn, saving Custer and his 7th Calvary. When called upon to recite, I would look at the floor and mutter an answer so out of context that the teacher thought I wandered into her class by mistake."

His report cards were filled mostly with Cs and Ds, and Clive's teachers would invariably tack on the admonishment familiar to generations of perceived underachievers: "Clive seems bright enough, but he doesn't apply himself."

In their senior year, Clive and his friends discovered they

could choose several electives. The boys immediately signed up for typing and home economics, believing the classes would provide an opportunity to meet girls. Clive learned how to type, a skill that would ultimately prove extremely useful, but chances for romance vanished when the girls became annoyed because the boys' cakes consistently rose higher than theirs.

With his afternoons and weekends occupied by a job or wrenching on his hot rod, Clive had little time to pursue girls. "Why," he says, "would I spend money on a date when I needed a new carburetor? I did have a steady girlfriend in grammar school, but we split up in high school. Years later, I received a letter from her. She was living in Tucson and wrote. 'You probably don't remember me, my name's Joy Marshall.' I wrote her back: 'You have to be kidding. How could I ever forget the first girl I ever kissed?'"

Organized sports were also out of the question, but Clive taught himself to play golf. When his grandfather managed the resort at Lake Okoboji in Iowa, Clive's mother took lessons and her dusty bag of antique clubs hung in the corner of the Cussler's garage. Clive borrowed Byron Nelson's book, *Winning Golf*, from the library, dusted the spider webs off his mother's golf bag, and spent his evenings in the backyard working on his short game.

Felix Dupuy's family belonged to the posh San Gabriel Country Club. The two boys would often play together and Dupuy, impressed with his friend's performance on the fairways, convinced him to compete in one of the club's tournaments. On the day of the event, Clive, who now owned a respectable set of clubs, arrived in his hot rod, wearing his customary costume: a leather jacket, white T-shirt, and jeans with the cuffs rolled up. He recalls the day with obvious satisfaction. "I went out on the course, shot a sixty-nine and shocked the hell out of the stuffy country club crowd."

Students entering their freshman year at Alhambra High School were allocated 100 merits. During the next three years, the number would go up or down, determined by a convoluted formula based on grades, attendance, and behavior. Graduation required a minimum of seventy merits. At the end of his freshman year, Clive was comfortably in the black with 116. By the time he was a senior, his score had plummeted to the low forties. To make up for the deficit, Clive was required to stay after school for a month and work with the groundskeeper, mowing, trimming hedges, and edging "miles of sidewalk with that miserable tool with the teeth."

Clive's quick wit and personality made up for his less than stellar performance in the classroom. "Clive was usually the instigator of our adventures," Felix Dupuy says. "He never seemed to run out of new ideas, and always seemed to be living a little closer to the edge than the rest of us. Clive was an only child, and I always felt he got away with things my parents would have really come down on me for."

Dick Klein agrees with Dupuy's assessment. "Clive has always been a real character, and ever since I've known him, he has always been coming up with some new scheme." Klein remembers a conversation with his father: "For some reason, Dad and I ended up discussing the qualities, positive and negative, of my friends. When Clive's name came up, my father told me, 'Of all the guys you hang around with, that Cussler kid knows how to work the system. He will probably be the guy who makes the most money without having to do a lot of hard work.'"

Under Clive's picture in his high school yearbook, it simply states, "College Prep." However, leafing through the pages of the 1949 *Alhambran*, Clive, in his leather jacket, white T-shirt and cuffed jeans, slouches nonchalantly among the members of the Senior Council, Spanish Club, German Club, Latin Club, Varsity Track Team, Scholarship Society, and

Chemistry Team. One of Clive's friends happened to be the yearbook photographer.

On June 16, 1949, Clive Eric Cussler strode across the stage in the Alhambra High School auditorium and was awarded his diploma. When he and parents got home, Eric presented him with a wristwatch, while Amy, close to tears, beamed proudly. Later that evening, Clive and several friends, "drove around, just goofing off. We stopped at a drive-in, had a hamburger, and that was about the extent of our celebration. I think we were all just glad to be finished with high school."

11
JUST DRIVE IT UNTIL IT BREAKS

During the summer of 1949, Clive was hired as a delivery driver for an auto parts store. Not only did he get to drive the company truck, but he was eligible for an employee's discount, a perk that helped him and his friends keep their cars running.

Clive's high school academic record ruled out a four-year college, but he knew his parents expected him to continue his education. Pasadena Junior College (now Pasadena City College), a twenty-minute drive from Alhambra, offered a two-year associate's degree and Clive, along with friends Felix Dupuy, Dick Klein, and Jack Hawkins applied for the fall semester. All four were accepted. Since English was the one subject in which Clive had shown promise, he majored in journalism and surprised his parents and himself by earning above average grades.

As their first year wound down, Clive and Felix began to plan a cross-country road trip. "The idea to take the trip," Dupuy says, "like most ideas, was Clive's. Our goal was to visit the four corner states - California, Washington, Maine and Florida - and as many others in between before we had to be back for school in the fall."

Today, kids graduate from high school and think nothing of spending several months backpacking across Europe, New Zealand, or South America. In the early 1950s, it was highly unusual for two eighteen-year-old boys to set off on a grand tour of the United States. There was no question about their transportation. Not only was Felix's 1939 Ford more dependable than Clive's car, it was a convertible. During Easter break, they plotted their route and practiced packing and unpacking the car. If economical lodging was not available, they would camp out on folding cots or, in bad weather, sleep in the car.

During the first week of June 1950, Clive and Felix waved goodbye to their parents and headed north on Route 101. Amy and Eric were convinced the duo would be lucky if they got as far as San Francisco. Felix's parents were a little more optimistic, predicting they might make it to Seattle.

When they left Alhambra, Clive and Felix had a total of $200 between them, but they planned to seek out temporary work along the way. In Oregon, the boys spotted a sign advertising for raspberry pickers. "The job," Felix remembers, "paid fifty cents per lug, a tray that holds four wooden baskets. How hard, we thought, could it be to fill a bunch of those up?"

After a few hours in the hot sun, Clive and Felix were reduced to hiding rocks and sticks under the fruit - anything to fill the cursed baskets. That night, burnt to a crisp and aching, they calculated ten hours of backbreaking labor had netted each of them $2.20.

Back on the road, the car's driveline began to make a strange noise and Felix pulled into a gas station. "I'll never forget that station," Clive says, "It looked like something right out of the *Gasoline Alley* comic strip. Instead of a lift, there was a grimy pit where the mechanic climbed down and worked on the underneath of the car. This old guy appeared out of the gloom, dressed in greasy overalls, a Quaker State hat and wiping his hands on an oily rag. An old yellow hound just laid there, mustering up an occasional half-hearted 'Woof.' After a ride around the block, the mechanic told us it was a problem in the transmission or rear end. But without pulling them apart, it was impossible to say which. He then offered some advice I have adhered to ever since, 'If I were you boys, I'd just drive it until it breaks.'"

In Seattle, the boys stayed with Clive's aunt and uncle. The strange noise, now localized in the rear of the car, had escalated to the point where something had to be done. Jacking the car up, they discovered a pin had worked its way out of the sleeve on the drive shaft where it entered the differential - a quick fix for two California hot rodders.

With their cash running low, it was time to look for real work. Clive was hired by Federal Pipe & Tank, the only company in the United States still producing wooden pipes and tanks for the railroads, to unload lumber from box cars for $1.55 an hour. Felix, who had worked in his father's tire store since he was six, went to work at a Goodyear Tire store.

After almost a month in Seattle, their funds replenished, the boys bid farewell to Clive's relatives, and several days later, crossed into Canada over the Ambassador Bridge in Detroit and drove to Niagara Falls. After marveling at the mighty cataracts, they pushed on to Maine, turned south, and two days later, arrived in New York City. After checking into the YMCA on West 63rd Street, they visited Grant's Tomb, strolled through Central Park, rode the elevator to the top of the Empire State Building, and drove across the Brooklyn Bridge.

On Flatbush Avenue, they spotted a pool hall and decided to check it out. "Felix and I were dressed in our leather jackets and jeans," Clive says. "The locals were wearing dress shirts and pleated pants. One guy got right in my face, 'What gang are you guys with? What block are you from?' After I explained we just arrived after driving from southern California, they looked at us like we stepped out of a spaceship. One dashed to the front window and pointed at Felix's car. 'That's a real hot rod. You guys are California hot rodders.'"

The two tourists now found themselves surrounded by new friends who insisted on paying for their drinks. "Those guys," Felix says, "didn't have a driver's license, much less a car. They lined up in front of the pool hall, and I gave them a ride around the block."

After a quick stop in Philadelphia, Clive and Felix were soon in Washington, D.C. Rather than spending money on a hotel, they slept in the bushes next to the Capital building. "We crawled out in the morning, dragging our sleeping bags," Felix says. "I can only imagine what would happen if somebody attempted to sleep in those bushes today." Felix also recalls spending a great deal of time at the Smithsonian and Civil War battlefields. He smiles, "Clive has always liked that kind of thing."

12
THIRTY DAYS ON THE ROAD GANG

It was well after midnight, with a thunderstorm raging, when the boys arrived in Kingsland, Georgia, a small town close to the Florida border. Seeking shelter, they set up their cots on the front porch of a schoolhouse. In the morning, Clive woke up squinting at the business end of a large revolver brandished by the local sheriff. Accusing them of vandalizing the school, the sheriff ordered them to accompany him to the town's barber shop.

On the way, Clive tried to explain they were just passing through, but the provincial lawman cut him off and pointed to his car. "It's real fast, so don't think you guys can get away." Clive laughs, "That hick sheriff was bragging about a 1941 Ford four-door with fox tails, jeweled mud flaps, and blue dot tail lights. To us, a car loaded down with that gooker junk was a clown car."

To us, a car loaded down with that gooker junk was a clown

car." Wearing an apron, and in the middle of a haircut, the barber was also the town's justice of the peace. Clive and Felix thought the situation was rather comical until the barber/justice of the peace jabbed his scissors at them and declared, "You boys are going to spend thirty days on the road gang." Clive, uncharacteristically quiet up to that point, was fed up with hillbilly justice. "We're two red-blooded American college boys, touring the great United States," he snapped. "What kind of welcome do we get in Kingsland, Georgia? Threatened with a month on a chain gang for getting in out of the rain!"

Threatened with a month on a chain gang for getting in out of the rain!" Caught off guard by Clive's outburst, the sheriff told the boys to stay put while he and the barber/justice of the peace walked to the post office and checked out the wanted posters. As soon as the two men were out of sight, Clive and Felix looked at each other, nodded, and sprinted to Felix's car. A short time later, they were safely across the Florida state line.

After three days in Miami, they drove to New Orleans. "It was late August," Clive says. "A large percentage of the population had fled the heat and humidity. The city looked like a ghost town." Departing the Crescent City, the boys slept in a boxcar, toured Carlsbad Caverns, and spent two days at a dude ranch owned by Felix's uncle in Arizona. The temperature was now reading in the low 100s. When the Ford's engine began to overheat, a quick look under the hood revealed a cracked block. A liberal coat of liquid solder was smeared on the fracture - a makeshift fix that Clive and Felix hoped would get them home.

Driving at night, when it was cooler, they crossed from Arizona into California at three in the morning. Clive was at the wheel; Felix was sleeping in the back seat, and more than 100 miles of deserted highway stretched ahead. Although he did his best to ignore it, Clive kept glancing at the temperature gauge. Its needle, slowly, but certainly was inching toward HOT!

"True story," Clive says. "A few miles from Indio, it began to rain. As the engine cooled down, Al Jolson came on the radio singing 'California, Here I Come.' That old Ford got up and flew, and I knew we were home free."

Three months and 13,600 miles after they left, Clive and Felix arrived in Alhambra. "Our parents were so glad to see us back in one piece," Felix says, "they came completely unglued." Clive describes their cross-country pilgrimage as, "a life changing experience. The trip gave both of us an entirely new appreciation for our country and its citizens. It certainly expanded our horizons."

Little did Clive and Felix know their horizons were about to be expanded beyond anything they could have imagined.

13
FIFTY-SIX SPARK PLUGS

During their three months on the road, Clive and Felix had paid scant attention to the news and were surprised to learn the "police action" in Korea had escalated into a full-blown war.

The boys registered for the fall semester at Pasadena Junior College, but when the government ratcheted up the draft, they decided it might be wise to enlist. Clive, who had always wanted to drive a tank, was ready to join the army. Felix convinced him they should consider a branch of the service offering more options than a perilous ride into combat in a steel coffin. On October 10, 1950, Clive and Felix, accompanied by several friends, drove to Los Angeles and were sworn into the United States Air Force.

A few days later, the recruits departed from Union Station in Los Angeles headed for basic training at Lackland Air Force Base in San Antonio, Texas. A sergeant, undoubtedly swayed by the fact Clive towered over his fellow recruits, announced he would be in charge during the trip to Texas.

When the train stopped in Alhambra, family and friends were waiting on the platform to see the boys off. One of Clive's friends slipped him a large bottle of cheap bourbon, and when the train was once again underway, Clive and Felix headed for the club car. The bottle was passed around; somebody produced a banjo, and the congregation was soon singing "Good Night Irene" at the top of their lungs. One thing led to another, and several car windows were broken. Word of the fracas was wired ahead, and a squad of MPs climbed aboard at El Paso. Clive, relieved of his short-lived command, recalls the remainder of the trip was, "extremely subdued."

At Lackland, marching and drills took up most of the recruit's day. Clive and Felix were assigned to the same seventy-man squadron. Their commander, a corporal named Franklin, constantly reminded the squad that basic training culminated with an inter-company marching contest he expected them to win. When the squad realized how obsessed Frankin was with winning, they went out of their way to screw up. One man, on Clive's signal, would suddenly break ranks and march off at a ninety-degree angle, or the first two ranks would take longer steps, and an awkward gap would appear between the lines. Felix often played the part of the spastic marcher. "Clive figured out all kinds of goofy maneuvers," he says. "We drove Franklin nuts."

Unknown to Corporal Franklin, the squad was planning a coup d'état. During their hour of free time before evening chow, the men would sneak off and practice marching by themselves. When the day of the big contest arrived, the squad marched to victory. Clive laughs, "Franklin couldn't believe it. We didn't know if he was going to burst with pride or go into cardiac arrest."

A few weeks into basic, the recruits were required to fill out a form listing three choices for technical training and report for career counseling. Clive's first choice was aerial photography. The sergeant interviewing him informed him aerial photography was not a realistic option. His second choice, Clive explained, would be military intelligence since it involved spies. Military intelligence, the sergeant advised him, was even less of an option.

Realizing his training might have more to do with the air force's needs than his preferences, Clive asked about opportunities in the motor pool. Leaning back in his chair and clasping his hands behind his head, the sergeant drawled in a fatherly tone, "No way. A sharp guy like you doesn't want to work in a greasy motor pool. All you end up doing is changing spark plugs. You want A&E - Aircraft and Engine."

A&E school (now called Aircraft and Powerplant), consists of sixteen specialized branches of intensive instruction including hydraulics, electronics, engine theory, propellers, airframe fabrication, and fuel systems.

"That sergeant was good," Clive says. "I bought his line and walked out of the office convinced that working on aircraft engines was far more glamorous than the motor pool. Instead of changing six spark plugs on a Dodge truck, I ended up changing fifty-six spark plugs on a Pratt & Whitney airplane engine. Real glamorous!"

After completing basic training, Clive received orders to report to the Department of Aircraft Maintenance Training at Sheppard Air Force Base in Wichita Falls, Texas. Felix Dupuy remembers the day they parted company. "Clive left Lackland at the end of November. We said goodbye, shook hands and he walked out the door. Just like that. We had known each other since we were kids and didn't know if we would ever see each other again."

Felix never received his orders. After sitting in the barracks for two weeks, he suggested if the air force had no need for his services, he would like to go home. After reviewing his test results, the air force sent Dupuy to electronics school in New Mexico where he studied the workings of the atomic bomb. After two years at a SAC base in Maine, Dupuy returned to California, graduated from UCLA with a business degree and eventually took over his father's tire business.

Clive reported to Sheppard Air Force Base in November. He was not impressed with the Texas Panhandle. "Wichita Falls was the absolute pits," he says. "When I attempted to find the falls, I discovered they had been destroyed by a flood in 1886. If you were looking for some real excitement, there was Archer City, the dismal little burg where they shot *The Last Picture Show*."

A&E school lasted six months. Clive graduated in the upper 10 percent of his class, and he was ordered to report to advanced engine school at Chanute Field, near Rantoul, Illinois. Since the train was scheduled to depart on Memorial Day weekend, Clive and another airman, Bill Flaherty, decided it would be foolish to pass up a once-in-a-lifetime opportunity to attend the 1951 Indianapolis 500. When the train stopped in Indianapolis's Union Station, they got off and hitched a ride to the track. After watching Lee Wallard take the checkered flag in his blue and gold Belanger Motors Special, they hurried back to the depot. "When we finally arrived at Chanute," Clive says. "Bill and I gave them a lame story about getting off the train to call our parents and being left behind."

At Chanute, Clive worked on the Pratt & Whitney R-4360 Wasp Major, a powerful beast nicknamed the "corncob" due to its intertwined arrangement of four staggered rows of twenty-eight cylinders.

He graduated from advanced engine school in August 1951.

After a tedious train ride, he arrived in San Antonio and found his way to Kelly Air Force Base.

Clive describes his three months at Kelly as, O.J.T. - on the job training. Working with experienced mechanics, he learned the ins and outs of the C-97.

In October 1951, Corporal Clive Cussler was ordered to an ATS Squadron at Hickam Air Force Base in Oahu, Hawaii. When he read ATS, Clive was thrilled, believing he had been assigned to an attack squadron. His joy was short-lived - ATS is Air Transport Squadron.

14
FIX ME UP

Shortly before he shipped out to Hawaii, Clive was given a two-week leave. After a few days in Alhambra, he asked Dick Klein's girlfriend, Caroline Johnston, if she could find him a date. Caroline said her neighbor was available but definitely not Clive's type. Envisioning the next two weeks sitting on his parent's couch, Clive remembers telling Caroline, "I don't care if she has two heads. Fix me up."

On October 10, 1951, Dick and Caroline, with Barbara Knight in the back seat, arrived at Clive's house in Dick's 1942 Ford. Clive, smoking a cigar, sauntered down the sidewalk attired in a white T-shirt, Levis, flight jacket, and white scarf. The foursome attended a football game, during which Clive and Barbara sat as far away from each other as possible. "Our first date," Clive says, "was a disaster. Barbara not only looked rather dowdy, she was the most introverted girl I ever met. We might have exchanged a total of ten words." Equally unimpressed, Barbara confided to Caroline she thought Clive looked like a hoodlum member of a motorcycle gang.

While Dick and Caroline waited in the car, Clive walked Barbara to her front door. As they stood awkwardly on the porch, Clive did something he still cannot understand. "I asked her if she would like to go out again and couldn't believe it when she said yes. Barbara always told me she never understood why she agreed to see me again."

The next night, driving his mother's Pontiac, Clive arrived at Barbara's house. When she answered the door, they looked at each other in disbelief. Barbara, wearing a pretty party dress, was radiant. Squared away in his dress uniform, Clive was the picture of decorum. They spent the evening at several clubs in Hollywood, dancing to the cool sounds of Stan Getz and Nappy Lamare. Clive and Barbara went out two more times before he reported back to Kelly; although he might not have realized it at the time, Clive was in love.

Barbara Knight's father grew up on a farm in Paige, North Dakota. During the Depression, Ted Knight climbed into a box car and ended up in Los Angeles. He enrolled at U.S.C. and majored in business. On a boat trip to Catalina, Ted met Helen Casale, a comptometer operator for the A&P supermarket chain. They were married in August 1931, and Barbara Claire Knight was born in Oakland on June 14, 1933.

When Barbara was thirteen, Ted decided to move back to North Dakota and bought a farm near the small town of Buffalo. Barbara graduated from Buffalo High School in 1951 and moved back to Los Angeles. She was living with her grandmother and working at the Department of Motor Vehicles when she met Clive.

Following a short stay at Camp Stoneman in San Francisco, Clive sailed to Hawaii on the USS *General D.E. Aultman*, an aged troop carrier that had served in World War II. Even before the ship had reached the Golden Gate Bridge, Clive was disconcerted by the *Aultman*'s rolling from side to side. He went to the sick bay and told the medic he needed some pills. The corpsman suggested he wait until they had at least left San Francisco Bay, but Clive insisted and walked out with a large bottle of Dramamine.

"I wasn't sick," Clive says, "but the way that ship was rolling, I wanted to be prepared." Three days out of San Francisco, the *Aultman* sailed into a typhoon and almost everybody on board was soon in bad shape. The bunks were six tiers high and the men, unable or unwilling to move, would simply lean out and vomit onto the deck. Thanks to his visit to the sick bay, Clive never got sick and sold his surplus pills to distressed shipmates for $1 a pill.

Arriving at Hickam, Clive was assigned to a bunk in an ancient barracks, scarred with shrapnel hits from the Japanese attack on Pearl Harbor. "There were more than a hundred men living in one large room," Clive says. "It was worse than the ship. The guy in the bunk next to me would stagger in at two or three in the morning and throw up on the floor. The character on the other side would wobble in just as smashed and piss on the wall."

During an orientation lecture, an officer told the assembled airmen they were very lucky - Hawaii was a paradise and the duty was choice. He explained that their tour would be three years and anyone wanting to spend leave in the U.S. would have to fly commercial and pay for it. A short, stocky fellow sitting near Clive growled, "Three stinking years in Hawaii! No leave in the States unless we pay our own way! Hell, this isn't World War II! This is pure bullshit!" Clive leaned over and told him he agreed completely.

On the way out of the auditorium, the two men introduced themselves. Al Giordino, a native of Vineland, New Jersey, and fellow R-4360 mechanic, was employed as an apprentice stone mason when he enlisted. Instead of basic training, Giordino was sent to Embry-Riddle, a civilian aviation school in Miami. After four months at advanced engine school, he also shipped out on the *General D.E. Aultman*. Giordino concurs with Clive's assessment of the passage. "They wouldn't let us up on the deck because they knew damn well we'd probably jump off and take our chances in the ocean." Although Clive and Al came from diverse cultures - Southern California and New Jersey - the two men developed a deep and lasting friendship.

Unhappy with the prospect of three years duty, even in paradise, Clive and Al presented themselves at the base commander's office and volunteered for combat duty in Korea, a nine-month tour. An obviously annoyed officer informed them C-97s, for which they had been trained, were not serviced in Korea. "He had the nerve," Giordino says, "to repeat the same bullshit - we were lucky to be spending three years in paradise."

15
CLIVE CUSSLER
ENGINE CHIEF

Resigned to three years at Hickam, Clive and Al's first order of business was finding better quarters. Exploring the base, they discovered a barracks with two vacant rooms. After stowing their gear, they tacked phony names on the doors. Al has forgotten his pseudonym, but he remembers Clive's was, "C. Potvin." (Chuck Potvin was an innovative California manufacturer who designed aftermarket speed equipment for hot rods).

The ruse worked until the two squatters were assigned to KP. Going out of their way to avoid the squadron office, Clive and Al never got the word. After they neglected to show up, notes were posted on their doors ordering them to report to the first sergeant. The two squatters packed up and beat it back to their old quarters, but it was too late. Realizing he never saw them except on the flight line, the sergeant had Clive and Al busted to private first class.

Originally, the maintenance of the C-97s was carried out with a system left over from World War II. A team of twenty men, under the supervision of a crew chief, were responsible for one airplane. Each member of the team was a specialist - engines, airframe, electronics, propellers, instruments, etc. When their airplane was gone, the team had nothing to do, but when the C-97 returned, they would have to work round-the-clock shifts and get it back in the air. With no idea when their airplane would arrive, it was almost impossible for the mechanics to make extended plans.

Clive had been working on the line for a short time when the air force introduced the "dock system." Crews were now assigned scheduled shifts, working on whatever airplane happened to be parked in their dock. Al Giordino considers the dock system to be, "One of the rare intelligent decisions the air force made."

"Charlie Davis was a member of my crew," Clive says. "One of the few real characters I have met in my life." Growing up on a farm in Tecumseh, Oklahoma, Charles Davis took flying lessons and earned his private pilot's license while he was in high school. In 1950, he enlisted in the air force, but there was a surplus of pilots, and Davis found himself in engine school. A big, gruff fellow, with a voice that matched, Davis stenciled "I.H.T.F.P." (I Hate This Fucking Place) on the back of his overalls. Prudent officers tended to leave him alone.

One afternoon, a "fireball" (an airplane that has to be serviced, fueled, and back in the air ASAP) landed at Hickam. Fireballs were usually C-97s delivering wounded soldiers from Korea to military hospitals in California. Conditions aboard the aircraft were grim. Clive was often the first aboard, opening the cargo doors for ventilation and asking the nurses if they required anything.

"When they were on the ground," Clive says. "It was frightfully hot inside the airplanes, and the smell was horrible. There would be seventy-five men on stretchers - legs and arms missing, guys you knew were going to die before they got to the U.S. I don't know how those nurses did it."

The crew of this particular C-97 refused to take off because the wing flaps, essential during takeoffs and landings, were making an awful racket when activated. Perched on ladders, a troupe of mechanics was working feverishly, but nobody could figure the problem. By the time Clive and Charlie arrived, a large crowd of onlookers had gathered, including a number of officers. "Charlie," Clive relates, "dressed in his greasy overalls, with I.H.T.F.P. on the back, looked at the airplane, then at the officers. In that big voice of his, he bellowed, 'Any dumb son-of-a-bitch knows all you have to do is oil the flap tracks,' and walked away, leaving me standing there. A colonel looked at me, looked at the airplane, and immediately ordered, 'Do what the man says. Oil the flap tracks.' A few minutes later, the airplane was on its way to San Francisco."

During his three years in Hawaii, Davis joined a flying club and spent his spare time accumulating hours and ratings. After he was discharged, Davis spent eleven years as a corporate pilot for a construction company. In 1966, he was hired by Eastern and was a 727 captain when the airline folded in 1990. Currently, Davis lives in Ranchester, Wyoming, "doing a little flying and whatever else old farts do."

"Working with Clive," Davis says, "was a lot of fun. He was an excellent mechanic. We all knew people's lives depended on what we were doing and took it very seriously, but we had very little patience with the old soldier types. Clive really knew how to get under their skin. I didn't know what it would be, but I always had the feeling Clive would end up doing something special."

A few weeks after the flaps incident, Clive had his own

moment in the sun. A C-97 was en route from California to Hickam with a plane load of military dependents. After passing the point of no return (not enough fuel to return to San Francisco), they lost an engine. After flying another 400 miles, a second engine failed. A C-97 with a full load of passengers could fly on two engines, but when the plane was fifty miles out from Hawaii, the third engine had to be shut down. The crew red-lined the remaining engine, but the airplane was rapidly losing altitude. Ten miles from Hickam, they managed to start one of the ailing engines and brought the aircraft in for a safe landing. Word had spread quickly that an airplane was in trouble, and everybody, including Clive, was at the airstrip when the C-97 landed. The undersides of the aircraft's wings were coated with soot and hot oil was raining down from the engines. Looking up at the R-4360 that saved the day, Clive realized, "it was one of my engines."

According to the manual, an R-4360 was good for 800 hours before overhaul. In the real world, they never came close. Each engine was fitted with a thirty-gallon oil tank, with a fifty-five-gallon oil drum in the airplane's belly. If an engine ran low, oil could be pumped into the tank from the drum. Oil may have been the life blood preventing the engines from suffering kinetic destruction, but oil also created carbon buildup. Known as "coking," the carbon would eventually cause extensive damage. When one of Clive's engines was nearing 700 hours, he would schedule an immediate oil change since clean oil helped reduce coking.

The day after the C-97's brush with disaster, Clive was ordered to report to the base commander's office. On the way, he had visions of a soul-stirring award ceremony. As a medal was pinned to his chest by a smiling officer, Clive's family, friends, colleagues and invited VIPs would give him a standing ovation. His reverie was quickly shattered when the officer ordered him to stand at attention and proceeded to chew him up one side and down the other.

A general happened to be a passenger on the crippled airplane. After it landed, he walked under the wing and noticed something on one of the engine nacelles. Peering closer, the officer saw, painted in large block letters, CLIVE CUSSLER-ENGINE CHIEF, surrounded by an assortment of hot rod decals - Iskendarian Cams, Edelbrock Manifolds, Stromberg Carburetors, and Moon Equipment. The general did not think this was the appropriate way to decorate one of the air force's C-97s.

After the colonel finished unloading on him, Clive managed to get the last word. "I politely reminded him, if I hadn't insisted on having my engine's oil changed regularly, the general, along with everybody else on that airplane would have ended up in the Pacific Ocean."

16
RAGAMUFFIN

A year after they arrived in Hawaii, Clive and Al Giordino moved out of the barracks. Al was married before he enlisted and his wife, Connie, joined him in Hawaii. They rented an apartment in downtown Honolulu and bought a new Chevrolet convertible. Clive, who was driving a very large, luxurious 1941 Packard limousine, moved into a small apartment on Waikiki Beach.

Although the mechanics were more than 4,000 miles from a combat zone, the air force required every enlisted man to qualify once a year with a weapon. Al considered the trips to the firing range, "Another classic example of air force bullshit. Mechanics were not issued a weapon, and when it was time to qualify, we had to hike over to supply and check one out for the day."

At the range, the men were divided into teams of two. While one man was shooting, his partner would be down in a pit, operating the targets. During one trip to the range, Al was shooting, and Clive was in the pit. "I'm concentrating on the bull's eye," Al says, "when I noticed Clive's hat hanging on the corner of the target and immediately started shooting at the hat. It wasn't long before everybody was trying to hit it. When we got done, Clive's hat looked like a piece of Swiss cheese and he wore it back to the base with tufts of hair sticking out of the holes."

"The entire time we were in Hawaii," Al says, "Clive had one civilian outfit - a pair of blue jeans and a red gaucho shirt that I don't think were washed unless he got caught in the rain. He was so tall and skinny, his fatigues hung on him like they were still on a clothes hanger."

One afternoon, Clive and Al were walking across the base when they encountered an approaching major. Al immediately smelled trouble. "Clive was wearing his funky fatigues, argyle socks, brown loafers and his shot-up hat. After ordering Clive to stop, the officer looked him up and down and snapped, 'What the hell are you? Your hat is a disgrace, and those socks are ridiculous. You're a ragamuffin!' From then on, Clive would walk into the squadron, strike a silly pose, and proudly announce, 'Hey everybody, I'm a ragamuffin.'"

When a friend's car broke down, Clive volunteered to drive to the Ford dealer and pick up a part. Cruising through the back lot, he spotted a 1941 Ford. Seeking out a salesman, he asked the car's price. Taken in on trade, the car's motor was shot, and Clive could have it for $10. After checking the dipstick and finding it dry, Clive poured in five quarts of oil. The engine was soon running, and Clive towed the car back to the base behind his Packard.

A hanger, well stocked with tools, was provided by the air force for airmen to work on their personal vehicles. After some cursory cosmetics and a tune-up, Clive sold the Ford for $75. He was soon operating an enterprising used car business, scouring the island for cast off vehicles he would clean up and peddle for a profit.

17
DIVING FANATICS

During the war, aircraft maintenance was paramount, while the hangers and ground equipment had been badly neglected. "Ground equipment," Al Giordino explains, "was anything that didn't fly - ladders, generators, tools, tool boxes and APUs, auxiliary power units." Tired of working in the oily bowels of an R-4360, Clive, Giordino, and two other mechanics, Dave Anderson and Don Mercier, went to see their line chief. "We told Sargent Birch," Giordino says, "If we were relieved of our duties on the line, we could fix up the hanger and the ground equipment."

Much to their surprise, Sargent Birch told them to go for it, and they were soon scraping, painting, and overhauling. Several APUs, "requisitioned" from other squadrons, were quickly repainted and stenciled with their new home's designation. After a month's labor, the hanger and its contents were in such great shape that the four airmen could complete their assignments by ten o'clock and spend the rest of the day at the beach.

During their first year and a half at Hickam, Clive and his friend's entertainment - like most young servicemen far away from home for the first time - consisted of going downtown, getting drunk, attempting to pick up girls, getting drunker, and after the bars closed, bumbling back to the base. When Clive and his friends finally got around to exploring the island's magnificent beaches and surrounding water, he declares, "We became diving fanatics."

In the early 1950s, equipment available for amateur divers was scarce, rudimentary, and sometimes dangerous. "My first mask," Clive says, "was a rather strange affair with two snorkels equipped with Ping-Pong balls to keep the water out. My fins looked like bedroom slippers with big flaps." Giordino recalls, "If we couldn't find a piece of gear, or it was too expensive, we would make it ourselves. I turned an aircraft instrument case into an underwater camera housing and Dave Anderson assembled a pretty respectable spear gun from some parts he scrounged in the engine shop."

Having explored the limits of snorkeling, the four friends pooled their resources and ordered an "Aqua-Lung" directly from Jacques Cousteau's Spirotechnique factory in France. Costing $75, plus freight, the tank and double hose regulator are believed to be among the first of its kind shipped to Hawaii.

Two months later, the gear finally arrived. After picking up the crate, the four airmen rushed to their hanger, fired up a compressor, filled the tank with 200 pounds of stale air, and drove straight to the beach. Taking turns, one man would cautiously descend to twenty or thirty feet, while the other neophyte frogmen floated on the surface, ready to come to his aid if he got in trouble. Clive is amazed they survived the experience. "Air embolisms and decompression times were vague terms for most sport divers in 1951. It was a wonder we didn't suffer any number of ghastly diving maladies."

In early June 1952, a C-97 maintenance flight, which required a mechanic onboard, provided Clive with paid transport and two work-free weeks in California. He was thrilled with the opportunity to see Barbara Knight.

Clive and Barbara had been writing to each other, but his arrival on her birthday was a complete surprise, and the couple was inseparable for the next two weeks. Flying back to Hickham, Clive recalls listening to the Ames Brothers singing, "You, You, You" on the radio and making up his mind to ask Barbara to marry him.

Clive might have been determined to win Barbara's hand, but he had also fallen under the spell of another lady. When he saw a poster announcing sports car races at an abandoned airport near Honolulu, he and Al Giordino drove over there. Clive struck up a conversation with a driver who owned a Jaguar XK 120. Invited to sit in the car, Clive says, "I was instantly, completely hooked. I had to have my own Jaguar."

If he was going to pursue two classy ladies - Barbara and a Jaguar - Clive needed a bankroll. Instituting an austerity program, he gave up his apartment and moved back into the barracks, expanded his used car business, and replaced the gas-guzzling Packard limo with a 1939 Fiat Topolino ("little mouse"). Recalling their last year in Hawaii, Al said, "Clive was so tight he would beg pennies from his friends so he could go to the movies at the base theater."

In August 1954, after almost three years in Hawaii, Sargent Clive Cussler received his orders to ship out. Sitting in the barracks girding himself for another torturous boat ride, he was informed there was a seat available on an airplane leaving within the hour for San Francisco. Grabbing his duffle bag, he shook a few hands and hurried to the flight line. As the C-97 winged east, Clive was lulled to sleep by the muffled roar of the four R-4360s.

18
NO GOOD DEED GOES UNPUNISHED

Clive's flight touched down at Travis Air Force in August of 1954. After spending two days at Camp Stoneman, a Greyhound delivered him to the downtown Los Angeles bus station where he caught another bus to Alhambra. It was six o'clock in the morning when Clive, after dragging his duffle bag and diving gear for six blocks, arrived at 2101 Winthrop Drive. When his parents answered the door, Clive spread his arms and announced, "I'm through with the air force!"

After a flurry of hugs, kisses, and tears, Amy cooked breakfast while Clive and his father discussed plans for the future. Clive wanted to do marry Barbara Knight and buy a Jaguar. Eric doubted he could help with his son's love life, but if Clive was serious about a Jaguar, that could be arranged.

In 1946, Eric had left the Cudahy Packing Company and gone to work for an accounting firm specializing in car dealerships. Four years later, Eric opened his own office and was now managing the books for sixty-five dealerships. One of his clients was Peter Satori, the largest foreign car dealer in the western United States, with showrooms in Pasadena, Glendale, and San Francisco. In addition to Jaguar, Satori sold Rolls-Royce, Bentley, Rover, Hillman Minx, Austin Healey, Aston Martin and MG. Amy drove her son to Pasadena, and an hour later, Clive drove out of the dealership in a brand new, gun-metal gray, XK 120 roadster. With a sticker price of $3,600, the sleek sports car was tricked out with red spoke wheels and a red leather interior.

With his Jaguar parked in the driveway, Clive was ready to pursue Barbara. After she had met Clive, Barbara had majored in art at the University of North Dakota in Grand Forks. Returning to Los Angeles, she spent several semesters at El Camino College in Torrence, before transferring to UCLA. Clive and Barbara were soon dating on a regular basis and, in late January 1955, Clive drove up to Mulholland Drive in the Hollywood Hills and proposed. Clive and Barbara were married on August 26, 1955, at the Chapel of the Roses in Pasadena. Dick and Caroline Klein were best man and matron of honor and Felix Dupuy served as an usher.

After a week's honeymoon in Ensenada, Mexico, the couple rented an apartment in Alhambra on Hellman Boulevard. To raise the money needed to outfit the apartment, Clive sold the Jaguar and replaced it with a used Nash Rambler station wagon. "Barbara never forgave me," Clive says. "She claimed she would have cooked dinner on a camp stove, eaten on the floor, and decorated the place with wooden crates rather than part with the Jaguar."

After they were married, Barbara left UCLA and went to work in the personnel department at the Southern California Gas Company. Clive was hired as a salesman at Peter Satori Motor's Pasadena store. One afternoon, Dick Klein stopped at the dealership to say hello. "Clive was eating his lunch in the back seat of a Rolls-Royce in the service area," Klein says. "He looked absolutely miserable. When I asked him how he liked selling cars, he confessed, 'I couldn't sell a glass of water to a man dying of thirst in the desert.' Clive was always such a go-getter, and I had never seen him that down." Sliding into the seat next to his friend, Klein admitted he was also unhappy.

Klein had enlisted in the air force a few weeks before Clive and spent three years running a printing press at a base in St John's, Newfoundland. He was currently preparing zinc plates used for offset printing, a tedious process involving a slimy, abrasive solution and acid. On weekends, Clive would sometimes help Dick clean the residue out of the catch tubs, a job he remembers as, "Very labor intensive, very hot, and very dirty."

"Here we were," Klein says, "the two of us, sitting in the back of a Rolls-Royce, stuck in jobs we loathed. Clive asked me, 'What do you think we should do?' Since we both knew how to work on cars, off the top of my head, I suggested we open a service station. Clive thought about it for a few minutes, flashed the familiar Cussler grin and told me it was the best idea I'd ever had."

Union Oil Company's headquarters in downtown Los Angeles was their first stop. When the company's representative inquired about their experience, Clive and Dick explained they had been working on cars since they were teenagers. The rep informed them there was more to operating a service station than changing a spark plug or replacing a head gasket. If they were serious, he would arrange it so they could spend a day working at a station in Glendora. The owner, who wanted to retire, could provide the rep with an evaluation of their performance.

After Clive and Dick put in a ten-hour day at the station,

the owner invited them to a local watering hole where he proceeded to hammer the beers. When it was time to leave, he was in no condition to drive. Clive and Dick volunteered to drive their new friend home, but after spending the evening listening to him rant about how much his wife disapproved of his drinking, they propped him up in a chair on the porch, rang the doorbell, and made a hasty escape.

No good deed goes unpunished. When Clive contacted Union Oil, the rep informed him, "You guys are going to hate me now, but someday you will appreciate what I'm telling you. The station owner says you guys would be lucky to stay in business for six months. Get some experience and come back and see me." Despite his initial disappointment, Clive agreed they had a lot to learn, and the rep offered to make a few calls on their behalf - Clive reported to a Union Oil station in Los Angeles, and Dick was hired by a station in Monterey Park.

19
THE FLYING RED MULE

Clive and Dick had been working in their respective stations for six months when a "For Lease" sign appeared in the window of a Mobil station in Alhambra. Clive contacted Mobil and heard a familiar refrain - you don't have enough experience. However, when the company learned Clive and Dick had lived in Alhambra for twenty-plus years, the lease was approved. Dick laughs, "Mobil figured our families, friends, and neighbors would buy enough gas, oil changes, and lube jobs to pay the bills."

"Clive and Dick's Petrol Emporium" opened for business in November 1955. Located at the corner of Garvey Avenue and Ramona Boulevard, adjacent to the San Bernardino Freeway, the station was similar to countless red and white Mobil stations scattered across America in the 1950s. The office was separated by a wall from the two service bays, each equipped with a hydraulic lift - restrooms were around back. A pair of pumps, regular and ethyl, along with air and water hoses, were located on an island. Close to the street, a large, free-standing sign was crowned with Pegasus, Mobil's famous red flying horse. "Clive," Dick remembers, "always got a kick out of referring to Pegasus as, 'the flying red mule.'"

This was the era of gas wars. The partners purchased a 1926 Chevrolet truck. Painted red and white, and emblazoned with "Clive and Dick's Petrol Emporium," the colorful vehicle parked next to the busy freeway, displaying the station's gas prices. As soon as a competing station dropped their price, Clive or Dick would hurry down to change the price on the truck. "Clive," Dick says, "was always coming up with clever promotions. We did weekly mailings, offering a free brake adjustment or lube job. The majority of the customers who came in for the free deal would end up spending money on a tune up, wipers or tires."

Rather than buying their tires from Mobil, Clive and Dick were able to negotiate a better price from Felix Dupuy. Clive persuaded Felix to wrap 100 bald tires in striped paper. The impressive piles of tires gave customers the impression Clive and Dick's Petrol Emporium was a major tire outlet and therefore able to offer the best price.

When they opened the station, Clive and Dick worked fifteen hours a day, seven days a week, closing only for Christmas and New Year's. A year later, two employees were hired and the partners were able to take some time off. They bought a 1948 Mercury convertible, stripped it - similar to the job Clive had done on his Jewett - and outfitted it with oversized truck tires. Weekends, they would explore Southern California's deserts, searching for ghost towns, Spanish antiquities, and lost gold mines. Although they never found anything of value, the treasure hunters took along several vintage rifles and amused themselves, plinking at rocks.

A Harley-Davidson Servi-Car was added to the station's

roster. The three-wheeled motorcycle, fitted with a cargo box behind the seat, would be towed behind a car being delivered to a customer, unhitched and ridden back to the station. The trike was also used to respond to accidents. "The majority occurred on the San Bernardino Freeway," Dick says. "We would often get there before the cops or ambulance, pry off the doors and perform first aid." During the four years they owned the station, Clive and Dick testified in eighteen accident investigations.

Dick and Caroline were renting an apartment in a triplex next door to the station. After their son was born, they bought a house in La Puente. Clive and Barbara were living in the apartment on Hellman Boulevard they shared with a basset hound named Sam. When their landlord informed the couple they were not allowed to have a pet, they moved into the Klein's vacated apartment. A few months later, Clive purchased the triplex. The extra room came in handy after the arrival of Clive and Barbara's daughter, Teri Lynn Cussler, in January 1958.

When Clive and Dick's Petrol Emporium opened, Mobil estimated the station should pump 27,000 gallons a week. Two years later, Clive and Dick were averaging 36,000 to 40,000 gallons a week. Their success convinced the partners it was time to expand. Another Mobil station, also located in Alhambra, had gone broke, and Clive and Dick were confident they could turn it around. Once the second station was making money, they would add a third, then a fourth, and so on.

When the plan was presented to Mobil, the company responded with an emphatic "No!" Dick recalls the stalemate. "Mobil insisted we were doing just fine and should forget about buying another station. Clive and I both knew we would never make any real money with a single station. When the company refused to even discuss our proposal, we sold the business in the fall of 1959."

Six months later, construction began on the Long Beach Freeway. Garvey Avenue was closed to through traffic, and the station's new owners were lucky if they pumped 11,000 gallons a week. Eventually, the station was torn down and replaced by an apartment building.

20
A PERFECT FIT

After they sold the station, Clive and Dick went their separate ways.

Clive remembers feeling, "kind of lost and up in the air." With only one year of junior college, three years wrenching on aircraft engines and four years pumping gas, his options were limited. One thing he was sure of, any future employment would have absolutely nothing to do with spark plugs.

A headhunter contacted Clive and told him a Newport Beach supermarket was looking for an advertising manager. The job - requiring neither a college degree nor experience - sounded like something to consider. Willing to try almost anything, Clive called and scheduled an interview.

Richard's Lido Market was a forerunner to today's boutique supermarkets. Located near the waterfront in Newport Beach, the upscale market opened in 1956. "The store's plush interior, muted color scheme, and dramatic lighting," Clive says, "was something you might expect to find in a nightclub, not a supermarket. I have never seen another food store with a comparable degree of sophistication."

When Clive arrived for his interview, he was ushered into the store manager's office. "He asked me if I had a background in advertising," Clive says. "I lied, of course, telling him I had worked on all sorts of campaigns for some very large accounts." Impressed, the manager asked Clive to return with a sample of his work. Leaving the store, with nothing to show, and worried a more qualified candidate might arrive at any minute, Clive bought a newspaper, a large piece of cardboard, a ruler and a pencil. Sitting in his car's passenger seat - he was now driving a Volkswagen bug - Clive studied the supermarket advertising in the newspaper and roughed out an ad. "Honestly," he admits, "it wasn't very good."

Returning to the market, he presented it to the manager who agreed with Clive. "I think the word he used was 'mediocre.'" With any hope of being hired slipping away, Clive told him it was the best he could do sitting in his car. After looking at the ad again, the manager laughed. "If you managed to do this sitting in a Volkswagen, I guess it isn't that bad."

Clive would later write, "Advertising and I were meant for each other. You need a devious mind, combined with an industrious talent for innuendo, duplicity, and hokum. It was a perfect fit."

Clive had only been on the job for a few hours when he faced a crisis. His first assignment was a full-page newspaper ad announcing the market's weekly specials. After doodling for several hours, with a deadline looming, he had nothing to show. Hustling to the store manager's office, Clive casually mentioned how impressed he was with the store's recent ads. The manager was responsible for the ads before Clive arrived. Explaining he operated under the premise, "If it ain't broke, don't fix it," Clive asked if he could look over the manager's shoulder while he "worked his magic."

The manager took the bait. Within six months, Clive not only developed his own style, the store's ads were winning awards from the Orange County Advertising Club and the Ladies Home Companion Supermarket Competition.

In the fall of 1960, Clive sold the triplex and rented an apartment in Newport Beach. In the morning, he would get up early and spend an hour running, swimming, and body surfing, before riding his bicycle to the market. Teri was now three. "Living so close to the ocean was wonderful," she recalls. "I was convinced the beach was simply an extension of our front yard."

Clive and Barbara, now expecting their second child, purchased a three-bedroom house on Primrose Street in Costa Mesa. Located a few miles east of Newport Beach, the small town was known as the lima-bean-growing capital of the world. Dirk Eric Cussler was born in January 1961.

"Our backyard in Costa Mesa had a wild jungle feeling," Teri says. "Dad built an oriental garden with a fish pond and planted all sorts of trees, bushes and flowers. Our playhouse was built on stilts, and the roof and sides were covered with bamboo. It had one of the tricks Dad has always been famous for - a sandbox hidden under the floor. The kids on our block were always coming over to play in our yard."

April 12, 1961, marked the 100th anniversary of the first shots fired during the Civil War. Clive decided the centennial provided a wonderful opportunity to promote Richard's Lido Market. Assisted by Leo Bestgen (a part-time employee who was studying art at Orange Coast College), Clive pulled out all the stops.

Enlarged images by noted Civil War photographers decorated

the store, and Clive rented period costumes from Knott's Berry Farm and MGM's costume department - the market's employees looked like they just walked off the set of *Gone with the Wind*. Products still being produced by companies dating back to the Civil War - including H.J. Heinz, Arm & Hammer, Van Camps, and Underwood Deviled Ham - were advertised at their 1860s' prices. "That one," Clive says, "almost caused a riot."

Customers who brought in a vintage photograph of an ancestor dressed in a Civil War uniform qualified for a free pound of hamburger. By the time the promotion ended, the market had given away more than 200 pounds of meat. A few years after he left Richard's, Clive ran into the store manager who hired him. Clive's Civil War extravaganza, he acknowledged, was the most successful promotion in the market's history.

Clive liked his job, but his relationship with owner Dick Richard was never harmonious. "Dick," Clive says, "was a peppery, short-tempered control freak with a Napoleon complex. He stood a little over five feet, and we were convinced he was threatened by anybody taller than him. I was constantly fighting with him over the design and content of the store's advertising."

Things came to a head when Clive and Leo's work was noticed by several local retailers. Asked if they would consider freelancing, Clive went to see his supervisor who had no objections as long as it did not interfere with their duties at the market. During a Chamber of Commerce meeting several of the duo's freelance clients cornered Dick Richard. After relating how delighted they were with his employee's creative efforts, they told him he was lucky to have such talented fellows on his payroll.

For reasons only he understood, Richard called Clive and Leo into his office the next day and fired them. "Not only had I gotten permission from the manager," Clive says, "None of our freelance clients were in competition with the market. We didn't even get two weeks' notice. The ungrateful S.O.B. simply showed us the door."

21
BESTGEN & CUSSLER

Clive and Leo's unpleasant departure from the market convinced them they should combine their talents and work for themselves. The Bestgen and Cussler Agency opened for business in October 1961. "We rented an office in Newport Beach," Clive says. "It was small, only two rooms, but after we painted, wallpapered, and decorated the place with a few antiques, it looked pretty good."

Leo set up his drawing board in one room, and Clive knocked out copy in the "conference room" on a large table purchased at a Railway Express damaged goods sale. Initially, business was slow and Clive had to augment his income by working nights in a liquor store. Less than a year after the agency opened, Bestgen and Cussler's cash flow had improved to the point where Clive was able to quit the liquor store, and the agency moved to a larger office, also in Long Beach.

One of the agency's clients owned a large yacht. Following an evening of merrymaking aboard, the owner headed for shore in his runabout. On the way, the tipsy mariner collided with several moored vessels but managed to run his boat up on the beach before it sank. Rather than salvaging the craft, he gave it to Clive. With the help of several friends, Clive pulled the boat off the beach and towed it home. After repairing the damage, he painted the hull red, white, and blue, replaced the tired inboard engine with a potent 100 horsepower outboard, and lettered *First Attempt* on the transom.

Teri remembers the family's weekends on the water. "After speeding around Newport Harbor, Dad would find a secluded beach on one of the islands and park the boat. Mom and Dad would whip up a wonderful picnic lunch while we kids played in the water."

The runabout was fun, but Clive, like most boat owners, lusted after something bigger. He traded up to a twenty-six-foot navy whaleboat, previously owned by a Swedish carpenter, who had added a deck and cabin. By the time Clive finished with his own refinements, including another multicolored paint job, the vessel was, according to Clive, "A 'character boat.' I naturally christened the craft *Second Attempt*, and we had great times entertaining friends and rubbing gunnels with yachts costing millions of dollars. But, I learned the ageless lesson - a boat is a hole in the water you shovel money into. Except for a little eight-foot Sabot sailboat, she was the last craft I ever owned."

In the fall of 1963, Bestgen and Cussler, with a client waiting list, was thriving, but the partners were bored. Tired of laying out mundane ads, Leo wanted to concentrate on a career as an illustrator. Clive was ready to see if he had the stones to cut it at a major advertising agency. After selling the accounts, office equipment, and furniture, the two men shook hands and set out on their new callings.

Searching the *Los Angeles Times* want ads, Clive learned that D'Arcy - the agency responsible for the famous phrase, "Coca Cola," the pause that refreshes" - was seeking a copywriter. The account executive who interviewed Clive asked him if he would be willing to create a sample ad for one of his clients, Aerojet-General, a major space and defense contractor that was branching out into nuclear technology. Clive still remembers the headline that won him the job: "The Spectrum of Nuclear Diversity."

Clive was soon writing copy for several of D'Arcy's top accounts, including Budweiser, Royal Crown Cola, Ajax Cleanser, Bank of America, and General Tires. His 110-mile, round-trip commute to downtown Los Angeles provided Clive with lots of time to think. "I came up with some of my best campaigns," he says. "While I was stuck in those horrendous traffic jams."

When his campaigns began to win awards and attract new business, Clive was promoted from copywriter to copy chief, and ultimately, to creative director.

Clive's success in advertising is a testimony to his imagination and creativity, but it also has something to do with the nature of the beast. With no formal training in advertising or marketing, Clive happened to drift into a profession that places more emphasis on life experience than a stack of college degrees. In his insightful book, *Advertising, Its Use and Abuse,* author Sir Charles Higham describes the "advertising genius." Although the book was published in 1925, the qualifications Sir Charles set down for the successful ad man are still pertinent: "He must have a knowledge of the psychology of every class; and sufficiently quick perceptions to be able to grasp, if only superficially, the processes and uses of every kind of manufactured article and serviceable idea . . . he must be able to arouse interest on any occasion and for every legitimate end. By virtue of their natural qualities they possess the flair for making known in a manner that arrests attention instantly."

Sir Charles would no doubt agree, Clive Cussler has *flair*.

22
A LITTLE PAPERBACK ADVENTURE

C live and Barbara's second daughter, Dayna Gayle Cussler, was born in March 1964. Seven months later, Barbara was hired by the Costa Mesa police department. Working from six in the evening until two in the morning, she filled in for the dispatcher and female prisoner's matron.

"Before she left for work," Teri says, "Mom would prepare dinner. When Dad got home from work, he would warm it up and the four of us, with Dayna in her high chair, ate dinner. After supper, we would get into our pajamas, and once we were tucked in, Dad would tell us fantastic bedtime stories. He has always been a fabulous father because he was like a big kid himself." She laughs, "He still is."

After the children were asleep, Clive had nobody to talk to. Weary of spending his evenings on the couch watching mind-numbing television programs, he decided to try his hand at writing fiction. "I didn't have the great American novel burning inside me," he says, "or an Aunt Fanny who came across the prairie in a covered wagon to chronicle. I just thought it would be fun to produce a little paperback adventure series. I have always been partial to old-fashioned blood-and-guts adventure and wanted to write the same kind of tales."

Clive grew up during the heyday of pulp fiction and the Saturday matinee serials. The pulps (named for the cheap paper on which they were printed) and serials featured a wide range of larger-than-life heroes, ravishing femmes fatales, fiendish villains, exotic locales, and non-stop action. Doc Savage dominated the pulps. Known as "The Man of Bronze," Doc combined a mixed bag of talents - surgeon, scientist, inventor, musician, master of disguise, and philanthropist - with a statuesque physique and a steadfast pursuit for justice.

Residing on the eighty-sixth floor of a Manhattan skyscraper, he maintained a fleet of automobiles, airplanes, and boats in a secret hanger on the Hudson River. Aided by a troupe of trusted sidekicks, Doc's sworn duty, as summarized by his creator, Lester Dent, was to "right wrongs and punish evildoers."

Saturday movie serials were divided into ten or fifteen episodes, each running approximately twenty minutes. Episodes would always end with the hero in a perilous situation, a cliffhanger, with no apparent avenue of escape. This guaranteed the youthful audience would return the following Saturday and plunk down another fifteen cents to watch the hero somehow manage to stay alive until the next climax. Popular serials during the 1930s and 1940s included *Flash Gordon, Dick Tracy, Secret Agent X-9, Captain Marvel, The Green Hornet,* and *Don Winslow of the Coast Guard.*

Searching for a writing style to emulate, Clive gravitated to the work of bestselling novelist Alistair MacLean, the author of *H.M.S. Ulysses, The Guns of Navarone, Where Eagles Dare,*

South by Java Head, and *Ice Station Zebra*. Clive considers MacLean to be "the master" of the genre and credits the writer for the format and success of his first books.

One critic described a MacLean plot as, "A hero, a band of men, hostile climate, a ruthless enemy . . . The pace of the narrative consists in keeping the hero or heroes struggling on in the face of adversity." MacLean's heroes are calm, cynical, multitalented men who, in their single-minded quest to complete the mission, are pushed to the limits of their physical and mental endurance.

McLean provided Clive with an archetype, but, with one exception, he did not use his characters in more than one book. In an effort to discover the secret of sustaining an ongoing cast of characters, Clive analyzed Edgar Allan Poe's Parisian detective Auguste Dupin, Sir Arthur Conan Doyle's Sherlock Holmes, Herman McNeile's Bulldog Drummond, Raymond Chandler's wisecracking Philip Marlowe, Mickey Spillane's hard-boiled Mike Hammer, and Ian Fleming's dashing James Bond.

"I used my experience in marketing to design my protagonist," Clive explains. "What would be different about him? What can I do that nobody else has done? Since James Bond was really hot, I knew any similarity to him would be a dead end. I was also determined not to write about a private detective, cop, or secret agent."

Clive drew upon his real-life diving experiences and fascination for the sea to create a marine engineer working for the fictional National Underwater and Marine Agency (NUMA) who is, according to Clive, "Cool, courageous, and resourceful - a man of complete honor at all times and an absolute ruthlessness whenever necessary." Having created his hero's identity, Clive had to give him a name.

Flipping through an encyclopedia, Clive came upon an entry

for William Pitt. "Pitt the Elder," as he was known, served as England's prime minister during the 1700s and is considered the architect of the British Empire. In his book, *The Adventure Writing of Clive Cussler*, Wayne Valero explains, "'Pitt not only has a nice ring to it, he [Clive] also wanted a one-syllable name because it was easier to say something like, 'Pitt jumped over the wall,' rather than 'Shagnasty jumped over the wall.'"

Having settled on Pitt, Clive needed an equally strong first-name. "Pitt's first name was right there in front of me," Clive says, "sleeping in the crib. My desk and typewriter were in my son's room, and Dirk likes to tell the story how he fell asleep listening to the sound of my typewriter."

Laboring nights and the occasional weekend for three years, Clive finished writing his first novel, *The Sea Dweller* (later published as *Pacific Vortex*) in 1967. On the opening page, he introduces the character who has gone on to entertain millions of readers in a series of bestselling novels featuring state-of-the-art technology, sojourns to the past, dastardly villains, classic automobiles, and beautiful women. The non-stop action is set against the world's oceans and the search for sunken ships and the secrets they embrace in their underwater graves.

> . . . A six-foot-three-inch deeply suntanned man, clad in brief white bathing trunks, lay stretched on a bamboo beach mat. The hairy, barrel chest that rose slightly with each intake of air, bore specks of sweat that rolled downward in snail like trails and mingled with the sand. The arm that passed over the eyes, shielding them from the strong rays of the tropical sun, was muscular but without the exaggerated bulges generally associated with iron pumpers. The hair was black and thick and shaggy, and it fell halfway down a forehead that merged into a hard-featured but friendly face.

> Dirk Pitt stirred from a semi-sleep, and raising himself up on his elbows, stared from deep green glistening eyes at the sea. Pitt was not a casual sun worshipper; to him, the beach was a living, moving thing, changing shape and personality under the constant onslaught of the wind and waves...

Even the most stalwart hero needs a sidekick, and Pitt's is Al Giordino, a character based on Clive's air force partner-in-crime. Providing a stoic and burly contrast to Pitt's lean sophistication, Giordino made his first appearance in chapter fourteen of *The Sea Dweller*.

> ... Giordino held his hands aloft and stretched. He was short, no more than five feet four in height, his skin dark and swarthy, and his Italian ancestry clearly evident in his black curly hair. Complete opposites in appearance, Pitt and Giordino were ideally suited to one another: one of the primary reasons why Pitt had insisted that Giordino became his Assistant Special Projects Director.

The plot kicks off with Pitt discovering a communication capsule containing pages from the logbook of the *Starbuck*, a missing nuclear submarine. The last time the sub was heard from, it was in the Pacific Vortex, an area near the Hawaiian Islands with the same ominous reputation as the Bermuda Triangle - thirty-eight ships have vanished in the Pacific Vortex since 1956. The search for the answer to the missing ships leads Pitt into a life-and-death struggle with Delphi, a giant madman with "bestial yellow eyes." Convinced the world is headed for nuclear destruction, Delphi has been praying on Pacific shipping to finance an underwater fortress where he plans to avoid the apocalypse. During the attack on Delphi's lair, Giordino sacrifices his pinky finger, jamming it into the barrel of a gun to save Pitt's life.

23
HORACE P. QUAGMIRE

In 1966, D'Arcy merged with another agency, Johnson-Lewis. Based in San Francisco, Johnson-Lewis had recently landed the prestigious Bank of America account, and after the merger, it was obvious to everybody at D'Arcy, including Clive, Johnson-Lewis's management was now calling the shots. "Dan Lewis was put in charge of our office," Clive says. "The guy was a jerk. We were working our hearts out, picking up new accounts for D'Arcy, winning all kinds of awards, and Lewis sacks thirty-two of us simply because he wanted to bring in his own people."

Job hunting again, Clive interviewed with J. Walter Thompson and was offered a senior creative position on the Prudential Insurance account. The job not only offered him an opportunity to work on a prestigious account, he would be taking home $2,500 a month (roughly $223,000 a year in 2016 money). Clive was on the verge of accepting the job when Barbara showed him a classified ad she cut out of the local newspaper - the Aquatic Center dive shop in Newport Beach was seeking a retail clerk, a job paying $400 a month. Puzzled, Clive asked her what she had in mind. "If you're determined to write sea stories," Barbara replied, "don't you think you should go to work in a dive shop?" Barbara was undoubtedly more concerned with her husband's health than perpetuating Dirk Pitt's future adventures. The stress of Clive's job, plus the grinding daily commute, would not only end up taking a toll on him, it was bound to impact his family.

"Barbara never pushed or inspired me," Clive says. "She certainly wasn't my inspiration. I never let her forget what she said when I first began to write - 'Don't get your hopes up. Nothing will ever come of it.' Barbara may have read *Mediterranean Caper*, but she never really liked my books. She didn't have to. What Barbara did, which in the long run was much more important, was take care of me."

Curious, and with nothing to lose, Clive interviewed with the owners of the dive shop: Ron Merker, Omar Wood, and Don Spencer. After hearing a brief summary of his employment history, Merker blurted out what all three were thinking. "Mr. Cussler, don't you think you're a little overqualified?" Clive explained he was writing a series of novels focused on diving and working in the shop would provide him with the research he needed to make his plots ring true. Clive's cause was bolstered by Spencer, a commercial photographer who labored in Hollywood before following his dream.

There were three Aquatic Center dive shops: Newport Beach, Laguna, and Santa Anna. Clive arrived at the Santa Anna shop during the summer of 1968, and immediately began to shake things up. On the large marquee sign in front of the shop, Clive replaced WET SUITS 20% OFF with KEEP AMERICA GREEN - BAN LOBSTERS FROM THE HIGHWAY and DIVERS DO IT DEEPER! A surplus aircraft belly tank, painted fluorescent orange and filled with bikini-clad mannequins, was installed on the store's roof. Another mannequin, also outfitted with a bikini, was positioned in front of the store where "she" could be seen by driver's approaching from both directions. Clive recycled old air tanks gathering dust in the store room. Painted candy apple red, a vivid color favored by hot rodders, the tanks were *en vogue* with younger divers, and the store had a hard time keeping up with the demand. A month after he was hired, Clive was promoted to manager. Within six months, the store's sales had increased by 20 percent.

The dive shop had a phone for information about water conditions. A disembodied voice would drone, "This is the Aquatic Center dive report. The surf is three to four feet; the water temperature is seventy-five degrees, and visibility is ten feet." Clive became the voice of a salty dog named Horace P. Quagmire, "daredevil darling of the dismal depths." In addition to water conditions, callers would now be entertained by Quagmire's jokes, sea tales, and recipes for abalone, along with a list of items currently on sale at the Aquatic Center dive shop. Even today, divers who remember the reports will often show up at Clive's book signings and ask him to sign their copies, "Horace P. Quagmire."

When business was slow, Clive would set up his portable typewriter on a card table behind the counter. After a little more than a year at the store, he finished *Chase a Teaser by the Fin* (later published as *The Mediterranean Caper*). Definitely more polished than *The Sea Dweller*, the book opens with an attack by an archaic World War I fighter on a contemporary air force base. Pitt and his NUMA associates, searching for a prehistoric fish called the Teaser, are soon on the trail of an ex-Nazi who is running a vast smuggling enterprise out of an underwater cavern off the coast of Greece. The indomitable Pitt not only thwarts the bad guys, he bags the elusive Teaser.

Having completed his two goals - a second novel and collecting research - Clive realized it was time to return to the real world, and gave his notice. "Working in the store," Clive says, "was a wonderful experience. I met some very special people and learned what diving was all about." Although he had been diving since 1953, Clive had never been certified. Ron Merker not only helped him get his card, he selected Clive to serve as dive master on the store's expeditions to Santa Catalina. Although unhappy to see him go, Clive's employers wished him well and presented him with an orange-face Doxa dive-watch, a treasured memento he - and Dirk Pitt - still wear today.

Resigned to another advertising job, Clive was not keen about climbing back into the Los Angeles pressure cooker. A compromise presented itself when a friend told him Ralph Yambert & Associates, an agency located in nearby Newport Beach, was looking for a creative director. The shop's small-town atmosphere would not only reduce Clive's stress level, working close to home would allow him to spend more time with his family. Yambert was more than happy to score somebody with experience, and Clive was soon back in the saddle, extolling the virtues of U-Haul trailers and Chris-Craft boats.

Even as Clive worked out the plot for his third book, he was questioning if his writing would ever amount to anything more than a hobby. After he finished *The Sea Dweller,* the manuscript had been sent to a number of publishers. All Clive had to show for his efforts was a pile of rejection slips. The majority were form letters and the few who sent him a personal response informed Clive he was wasting his time - publishers were not buying adventure books. Among his papers, Clive has a page torn out of a Girl Scout calendar. Dated March 13, 1969, he scribbled: "Almost gave up writing today, but talked myself out of it. Had a cup of coffee and pushed on."

"That note," Clive concedes, "represents the lowest point in my writing career."

If he hoped to have any success, Clive knew he had to find an agent.

24
THE CHARLES WINTHROP AGENCY

C live's quest to land an agent is a publishing legend. "I've been asked to tell the story," he acknowledges, "more times than Judy Garland sang 'Over the Rainbow.'"

Clive had been writing and producing television commercials for more than ten years, but his day-to-day dealings were with theatrical and talent agencies, not literary agents. After talking to several colleagues and making a trip to the library, Clive compiled a list of more than twenty prospects with offices in New York, but all the lists in the world would not guarantee success. Convincing an agent to represent an unpublished author can be as difficult, or more so, than finding a publisher.

Clive needed an angle.

Enlisting the talents of one of the agency's art directors, Clive concocted a letterhead and envelope for the "Charles Winthrop Agency." "I grew up on Winthrop Drive," Clive says, "and always thought it sounded classy." The dignified letterhead featured a classic typeface, printed in black, on gray Strathmore paper. Clive used his parent's address - they were now living in Laguna Hills - because "it sounded tonier than Costa Mesa." Clive purposely neglected to include a phone number. Anticipating a prolonged search, he ordered 1,000 sheets of stationery and matching envelopes.

Selecting the name at the top of his list, Clive sent his first query to Peter Lampack at the prestigious William Morris Agency in New York:

> Dear Peter: As you know, I primarily handle motion picture and television screenplays. However, I've run across a pair of book-length manuscripts which I think have a great deal of potential. I would pursue them, but I am retiring soon. Would you like to take a look? Charlie Winthrop.

A week after he mailed the letter, Clive's father, who had been alerted to the ruse, called and told him a letter had arrived addressed to Charlie Winthrop. After setting what was probably a record for the twenty-mile drive to Laguna Hills, Clive tore open the letter:

> Dear Charlie: On your say-so, I'll take a look at the manuscripts. Send them to my office. Sincerely, Peter Lampack.

After mailing the agent copies of *The Sea Dweller* and *Catch A Teaser By The Fin*, Clive tried to concentrate on a campaign introducing a new El Toro lawnmower. Several weeks later, another letter resulted in another mad dash to Laguna Hills:

> Dear Charlie: Read the manuscripts. The first one is only fair, but the second one looks good. Where can I sign Cussler to a contract? Sincerely, Peter.

Clive read the letter a second time, and then a third. "I was dumbfounded," he recalls. "Could finding an agent possibly be that easy?" Clive dispatched his address to Lampack. The agent responded, introducing himself and including a contract Clive signed and sent back. The remaining Charles Winthrop Agency envelopes ended up in the trash, and Clive wrote his next novel on the back of the stationery.

Lampack is often asked why he was willing to take Clive on as a client. "Not only was I intrigued by the idea of an ongoing adventures series, I found Dirk Pitt to be an attractive and compelling protagonist. Clive is a natural storyteller, an extremely important attribute if he hoped to maintain the reader's interest throughout a series. I was pretty sure I could find a publisher for *Catch a Teaser by the Fin*, but I was not impressed with *The Sea Dweller*. The science fiction elements not only interfered with the adventure genre, it was also his first attempt and I did not think it was as accomplished as his second manuscript."

With a legitimate New York agent in his corner, Clive began to believe he might be able to pull off what had seemed a fading dream a few months earlier. "When Peter took me on as a client," Clive says, "it was the inspiration for me to believe someday I might actually be able to make a living writing novels, It was also time to get out of Los Angeles."

25
ESTES PARK

In May of 1970, Clive, arriving home from work, walked into the kitchen and announced, "The time is right. We should leave." Barbara, busy preparing dinner, dried her hands on a towel and smiled, "Fine, let's go."

Disenchanted with Southern California's urban sprawl, clogged freeways, and smog, Clive and Barbara had been considering a move to another part of the country for some time. In short order, Clive sold the house and boat, put the furniture in storage, and bought a new Mercury Monterey station wagon, fitted with a hitch to pull a tent trailer. The couple had absolutely no idea where they would end up. Clive's utopian vision saw his family settled in a picturesque resort town. Barbara would work in a crafts store, and he would drive a school bus. His part-time duties would provide him with the time to write Dirk Pitt adventures.

"I figured," Clive says, "wherever we landed, it would be

almost impossible to starve in the United States."

The Cusslers hit the road in early June. Driving up the coast, they arrived in Coss Bay, Oregon. Delighted with the area's stunning natural beauty, Clive deposited his family in a campground and drove to the state employment office. The fellow behind the desk was a volunteer who worked at the local television station. After looking over Clive's resume, he almost begged him to apply for a job at the station. Clive was tempted. "Coos Bay is a beautiful place, and the job sounded interesting. But we were only two weeks into our trip, and I wanted to see more of what the country had to offer. I thanked him, and we headed east."

Teri Cussler looks back on the odyssey as a wonderful adventure. "Even though my sister, brother, and I had a lot of fights in the back seat, we have always considered that summer to be the best three months we ever spent together. We camped out a lot, but every three or four days we would stay in a motel. Dad was always great about finding one with a pool. He also stopped at a lot of historic sites because Dad has always liked that kind of thing. It got a little old after a while because a young girl couldn't care less about battlefields."

Dirk describes the trip as, "Probably the closest our family has ever been. I was nine, an age when a trip across America was a major event. There were so many great things to see along the way, but it seemed like it took us forever to get there."

Dayna, only six, thought they were on, "a very long vacation. I don't think I had any realization we were leaving our house in California forever and moving to someplace new."

One stop Clive had included on their itinerary was Aspen, Colorado. "From everything I read, I had created this fantasy that Aspen was a Rocky Mountain Shangri-La. It ended up being a terrible letdown. The entire town was overrun with hippies and dogs." Leaving Aspen's bohemians and canines behind, the Cusslers drove to Denver. Unimpressed with the "Mile High City," Clive and Barbra decided it was time to return to Coos Bay.

Stopping at a camp site in Boulder, Clive struck up a conversation with a fellow traveler parked next to them. He suggested Clive would regret it if he failed to drive through Rocky Mountain National Park on their way west. The park's gateway is the picturesque town of Estes Park, nestled against a backdrop of snowcapped peaks. Among the towns attractions were herds of elk, charming Victorian homes, and the stately Stanley Hotel, where Stephen King penned part of *The Shining*.

As they rolled into town, Clive and Barbara realized Estes Park was exactly what they were looking for. After Clive parked the car and trailer on Elkhorn Avenue, Barbara and the kids set out to explore the town's shops and galleries. Clive bought a copy of the local newspaper, the *Trail* (now the *Trail Gazette*). A listing under "Houses for Rent" caught his eye: "*Pretty Swiss chalet, well maintained with marvelous views, $200 a month.*" Clive hurried to a phone booth, and a half hour later, the owner met him at the property.

"It was exactly like the ad described," Clive remembers, "A pretty place out in the woods, with a great view of Longs Peak. We signed a lease for a year."

During their first year in Estes Park, the children were enrolled in school, Barbara was hired as a secretary at the University of Colorado in Boulder, and Clive finished his third book, *Hermit Limited* (later published as *Iceberg*). A missing yacht - its crew incinerated at their posts - is found inside an iceberg. Sinister industrialists, planning to take over South America try to stop Dirk Pitt from discovering the yacht's connection to their nefarious conspiracy. The book's supercharged climax has Pitt foiling the attempted assassination of the presidents of French Guiana and the Dominican Republic at Disneyland.

Hermit Limited introduced Clive's now familiar use of multiple, interlaced plots. "My first two books," Clive explains, "were basic potboilers, what I call formula A - the reader walks beside the protagonist from chapter one to the last page. In *Hermit Landing*, I began to use Formula B. Convoluted plots and subplots are going on that not even Pitt and Giordino are always aware of."

Clive also moved the action into the future, something he came up with while researching the James Bond books. "The gadgets Bond had at his disposal," Clive says, "were usually dated five years after the books were published. By placing Dirk Pitt in the future, it allows me to introduce technology scientists and engineers predict will be available in ten or twenty years from now."

Although Clive was pleased with *Hermit Limited*, Barbara's salary was insufficient to cover the bills; the family's savings were dwindling. It was once again time for him to look for a day job. Since consolidating their commute would cut expenses, Clive began his job search in the Boulder Yellow Pages. A few days later, he parked in front of the Barry Cossette Advertising Agency, the first listing under "Advertising Agencies & Counselors."

Walking in the door, he stuck out his hand and announced to the young man sitting behind a desk, "Hi, I'm Clive Cussler your new partner."

26
A HOTSHOT FROM THE WEST COAST

Once Barry Cossette concluded the tall, brash visitor was not dangerous, demented or worse, a salesman, he offered him a chair. Clive gave him a quick summary of his experience and Cossette decided this might be the best thing that had walked in his front door since he opened the agency. The two men shook hands and agreed to join forces.

Their first order of business was to pitch new accounts. In addition to a Dodge dealership, they picked up Deep Rock Water, a bottled water company dating back to 1896. When the city of Denver refused to run city water to druggist Stephen Kostich's property, he drilled his own well and began to bottle and sell the crystal clear water that flowed from the aquifer. The company was purchased by Merrill and Dorie Fie in 1967, and a few years later, Deep Rock Water was supplying drinking and distilled water to the entire state of Colorado.

The market for bottled water in the early 1970s was a far

cry from what it is today. Deep Rock's customers, with few exceptions, were commercial accounts and advertising was limited to radio spots during the spring and summer months. Clive created "Drinkworthy," a character who resided in Deep Rock's well and praised the water's attributes with an enigmatic Maine accent. Although it was never clear if Drinkworthy's girlfriend, Ida Mae, lived in the well with him, she provided a sarcastic foil to his good-natured sales pitch. Both character's voices were provided by "Little Johnny" Harding, a local radio personality.

Although Clive was working with tight budgets, he added occasional cameo appearances by character actors whose voices would be instantly recognized by the public - Andy Devine, Dennis Day, and Harry Morgan helped Drinkworthy sell Deep Rock Water. In addition to western themes aimed at the local audience, Clive's commercials featured story lines inspired by current topics. In one spot, Drinkworthy uses Deep Rock water to cure a young girl during an exorcism. In another, Ida Mae threatens to burn her bra because Drinkworthy is paying more attention to his precious water than to her.

Merrill Fie remembers Clive as "a very colorful character who helped us sell a lot of water. You never knew what he was going to come up with, but it always worked." Dorie Fie concurs - "Although it has been a lot of years since the Drinkworthy spots were on the radio, our friends still tell us they were some of the most unforgettable advertising done in Denver."

Clive and Barry Cossette's relationship was amicable and the agency was profitable, but Cossette, inspired by Clive's tales of Los Angeles advertising, picked up and moved west in late 1970. Although Clive inherited the agency's accounts, without somebody to share the load, he decided it was time to look for a steady paycheck.

In the *Denver Post*'s classifieds, he discovered three downtown Denver agencies were seeking a copywriter. After setting up appointments with all three, Clive dusted off his portfolio and resume, put on his best suit, and drove to Denver, confident he would be working by the end of the week. At his first interview, the agency's owner began their conversation by telling Clive he was extremely overqualified. Clive countered, telling him he was getting a good deal. Dismissing Clive's argument with a wave of his hand, he ended the interview, adding, "The last thing we need is a hotshot from the West Coast coming in here and telling us we're doing everything wrong."

Assuming he had simply run into a small-minded yokel with a cow-town mentality, Clive was still upbeat when he arrived for his second interview. "It was like listening to a tape recording of the first guy," he says. "After telling me I was overqualified, he - this is a true story - told me, 'We don't need hotshot from the West Coast coming in here telling us how it's done.'" Walking out of the office, Clive was tempted to drive to the city limits and check to make sure the sign read, "Welcome to Denver," and not "Pumpkin Corners."

It was now Friday. Clive's third interview was scheduled for the coming Monday. He used the weekend to prepare a signature Cussler gambit.

Wadding up his oldest suit, he tossed it in a corner. Next, he eradicated the word "creative director" and any mention of awards from his resume and portfolio. The reels of his television commercials were deposited in a drawer. As an added touch, he skipped shaving for two days.

At the appointed time, Clive, looking like a lanky version of Willy Loman, was sitting in the reception area of Hull/Mefford Advertising. Looking around, he noticed the furniture had seen better days; the walls were past due for a paint job, and the solitary framed award was four years old. He was ushered into Jack Hull's office, and after some small talk, with as much humility as he could muster, Clive explained he was very happy to be in Denver, far away from those know-it-all hotshots in California who made his life miserable. Hull ended up offering him the job for $10,000 a year. Clive talked him up to $12,000.

Reporting for work the next morning, Clive was shown to his office. "It was an alcove," he says, "next to the restrooms. I was given a beat-up desk and an ancient Royal typewriter. There wasn't even a phone, and everybody had to practically crawl over me to go to the john." Clive's assignments included writing copy for a trucking company, a real estate firm, and an insurance agency. "I had to come up with this saccharine prose," he says, "congratulating gangs of grinning agents for selling a million dollars' worth of homes or life insurance."

On the job, Clive went out of his way to cultivate the image of a quiet, dedicated family man. If his co-workers noticed him at all, they were impressed by his work ethic. From the minute he walked into the office until quitting time, Clive pounded away at his typewriter. They had no way of knowing Clive could usually finish his assignments before noon, spending the rest of the day working on the next Pitt adventure.

In January 1971, Clive purchased a new house on West 72nd Street in Indian Tree Village - a development located in Arvada, a bedroom community ten miles northwest of Denver. "When my father got done with the house," Teri says, "it was really something." Dad built a sundeck in the back yard, installed overhead track lighting and a freestanding fireplace in the family room, and paneled the bathroom so it looked like a railroad caboose."

The house backed up to a municipal golf course, a feature the Cussler children considered "our big backyard." When no golfers were in sight, Dayna would go out and look for golf balls, selling them to the same duffers who originally lost them. Dirk and several of his friends found a golf cart stuck in a sand trap and spent the rest of the night driving around the fairways until the battery went dead. "I heard my father's stories about growing up in California," Dirk says. "He thought the forts and tree houses we built were fine, but we also cobbled together a boat. It wasn't very seaworthy, and when Clive found out I had been out on the golf course lake, he flipped out."

Juggling the demands of his family and job, Clive managed to put aside as many hours as he could spare to write. One of his cohorts at Hull/Mefford remembers Clive giving him a tour of his home office. "We went down the stairs to his unfinished basement and had to duck under the damp clothes hanging on the line. Tucked back in a corner, next to the cement brick wall, were two sawhorses with a door across them and this old manual typewriter. After he made it big, we always laughed about Clive's classy office in his basement."

27
SOUR FACED BIDDY

In the spring of 1971, Hull/Mefford was in big trouble. Empire Savings Bank, the agency's most important client, was unhappy with the shop's lackluster television commercials. The bank's president put it on the line - if Hull/Mefford did not come up with something better by the end of the week, he would look for a new agency.

Pandemonium reigned. Burning the midnight oil only resulted in a series of uninspired storyboards quickly shot down by the client. By Wednesday afternoon, the situation was on the verge of panic. Up until now, Clive had been ignored, but with the heat on, somebody suggested the tall guy sitting next to the john might have some ideas.

Clive was called into Jack Hull's office and given a quick briefing. Could he come up with something by Friday? "I flashed my best Machiavellian smile," Clive remembers, "and said I would give it some thought. Jack didn't know I had been listening to what was going on and already had a campaign laid out in my head."

Early Friday morning, everybody involved with the account was assembled in the conference room. When it was his turn, Clive began his pitch by explaining all savings and loans were basically the same. By law, they had to pay the same interest, offer the same premiums, mortgages, etc. What convinces a customer to choose one bank over another? Service! Empire Savings had to be promoted as a friendly place to do business. Managers and tellers should know their customers' names and treat them like friends - not an account number. The answer, Clive repeated for emphasis, was service.

Clive unveiled his storyboard. The hand-drawn frames followed a bad-tempered old lady who is avoided like the plague. When she arrives at Empire Savings Bank, the teller's friendly demeanor wins her over, and she leaves smiling. Empire's president loved the idea and Clive was no longer the quiet guy sitting next to the john.

After he had been working on the "mean lady commercial" for a few days, Clive was discussing the project with Barbara over dinner. "If only Margaret Hamilton was alive," he lamented. "She would be perfect for the spot." Barbara informed him Hamilton was definitely alive, having recently appeared in *The Anderson Tapes*. (Hamilton is best known for her role as the evil, cackling Wicked Witch of the West in *The Wizard of Oz*.)

A script was sent to Hamilton's agent and the actress flew to Denver. "Margaret," Clive says, "was a sweetheart. She not only regaled the production crew with stories about the making of *Oz*, everybody brought their kids to meet her, and Margaret signed photographs for all of them."

Clive's commercial opens with Hamilton hurrying down the street, wearing a severe black dress, a little black pillbox hat, and tightly clutching her purse. Homeowners pull their shades down, men cross the street, and mothers, clutching their children to their bosoms, dash into their houses. In the bank, the teller greets the sour-faced biddy with a radiant smile. "Hello, Mrs. Jones. How are you today?" Hamilton looks puzzled. After finishing the transaction, he flashes another smile and exclaims, "Now, Mrs. Jones, you have a wonderful day." Hamilton pauses, turns to the camera, and breaks into an unexpected smile, as the voice-over announces: "Just when you thought you hadn't a friend in the world, isn't it nice to know somebody cares enough to remember your name. Empire Savings cares."

The "mean old lady" commercial was so successful, Clive went on to produce a series, featuring well-known character actors from film and television, including: Mike Mazurki, one of Hollywood's outstanding tough guys; Charlie Dell, best known for playing Nub Oliver on *Evening Shade*; Joe E. Ross, the rotund Gunther Toody of *Car 54, Where Are You*; *Laugh-In*'s Dennis Allen; and Ted Knight, the pompous news anchor on *The Mary Tyler Moore Show*. "Character actors," Clive states, "are the finest people in the entertainment business. They're professional, incredibly cooperative, and a pleasure to work with."

In addition to several Clios (advertising's answer to the Oscars) and International Broadcasting Excellence Awards, Clive's commercials were prize winners at both the Venice and Chicago Film Festivals. Winning awards of this caliber is a major accomplishment for a writer working in New York, Chicago or Los Angeles, but Clive was bringing home the gold in a market inhabited by clients with small budgets and even smaller imaginations.

In 1972, Hull/Mefford merged with a Boulder agency owned by two women, Mary Wolff and Jan Weir. Jack Hull left for a job with Empire Savings Bank, and the agency's name was changed to Mefford, Wolff & Weir. Having been elevated to vice president and creative director, Clive was making $17,000 a year and driving a company car.

Clive's creative team included art director George Yeager and assistant art director Errol Beauchamp. Yeager, who studied graphic design at the Carnegie School of Fine Arts, worked in Pittsburgh before moving to Denver. "When I was hired," Yeager says, "Jack Mefford, myself, another art director, the production manager, and a secretary were located in one office. The writers worked in another office." Shortly after he arrived, the secretary asked Yeager for his portfolio, explaining it would be sent over to the other office and reviewed by the writers. A few days later, Yeager was stunned when a tall fellow strode into his office, tossed his portfolio on his desk, declared, "Worst stuff I've ever seen," and stalked out. "I'm thinking," Yeager says, "Who the hell is this fool," and was starting to get mad when the secretary, who had been watching everything, laughed and asked how I liked meeting Clive. The whole thing was a typical Cussler set up."

Yeager remembers Clive as, "A hard worker who made everything look easy. He was a great teacher, a good friend, and a wonderful family man. At the office, he always made us feel like we were part of the process and respected our input. At home, he was always building something or working with Dirk on his car."

Errol Beauchamp graduated from North Texas State, (now the University of North Texas). "The three of us," he recalls, "Clive, George, and myself would eat lunch together, go drinking after work, and attend events organized by the advertising community. Clive was older than we were and always acted as our champion with management. If he thought we weren't getting decent benefits or deserved a raise, he would tell them to take care of us because we were the guys doing the real work."

Both Yeager and Beauchamp agree Clive had little patience with anybody he thought was not pulling his weight. During one especially hot spell, the window-mounted air conditioner in Clive's office broke down. He reported the problem to the office manager, but several days went by, and it had not been fixed. "I walked by Clive's office," Yeager says. "Clive was sitting there, calmly typing away, wearing nothing but his underwear. Word soon got around, and everybody found an excuse to walk by and sneak a peek."

28
ARMPIT, TONSIL & GROIN

Clive was offered the position of Mefford, Wolff & Weir's executive vice president in early 1972. "I appreciated their faith in me," Clive says, "but I politely turned them down. Management has never interested me. Creative was what I enjoyed, and creative was where I wanted to stay."

Shortly after Clive turned the offer down, the agency hired Mel Warren, an account executive who had been working in New York. From the moment the two men met, they took an instant dislike to each other. "To this day," Clive says, "I can't explain it. He would come in the room, and the hair just stood up on the back of my neck. Mel did have one talent. He was good at corporate in-fighting. I wasn't."

The animosity between the two men can be traced to the "creative revolution" in advertising. Where the account executive once reigned supreme, creative directors were now the agency stars. Famed ad man David Ogilvy referred to his creative directors as "trumpeter swans." Clive was still wearing a suit, but his hair was longer, and he was sporting a neatly trimmed beard. In his office, he installed wooden beams on the ceiling, draped cloth in swooping whorls between the beams, and positioned lights behind the cloth.

Earl Beauchamp laughs, "I always felt like I was walking into a cocktail lounge. That office was pure Clive. He had star quality. Not only was he responsible for the agency holding onto their important clients, he was hiring movie stars and winning major awards. All of the attention Clive received really got on Mel Warren's nerves."

Warren had been working at the agency for three months when he scheduled a meeting. George Yeager remembers, "None of us could believe it. Mel announced none of the work produced by Clive and myself was good enough to enter in the Denver Advertising Federation's (DAF) annual awards show." Founded in 1891, the DFA is the world's oldest advertising club. Nicknamed the Alfalfa Club, in honor of the plant introduced in Colorado in the late 1800s to feed livestock, the organization's awards were called, "Alfies."

After the meeting, Clive showed up in Yeager's office. Visibly upset, he flopped in a chair. "I had never seen him so upset," Yeager says. "The two of us had been freelancing, and Clive told me, 'The hell with Warren. We should split the entrance fee and enter our freelance work.' I was just as mad as Clive and told him to go for it." On the entry form, Clive listed the agency name as, "Armpit, Tonsil & Groin." When the DAF contacted Clive, they informed him his "agency" had won several "Alfies," but they would not be allowed to use the bogus name because it would demean the organization.

At the awards dinner, Clive and Yeager, wearing sunglasses and smoking big cigars, played their parts to the hilt. "When we were called up to accept our awards," Yeager says, "everybody in the room, including us, couldn't believe it when they announced the winner was the 'Yaeger & Cussler Agency.'" For the remainder of the evening, Jack Mefford, Mary Wolff, Jan Weir, and Mel Warren were besieged with questions regarding Denver's award-winning new agency. Although Clive tried to explain it was simply a misunderstanding, the majority of those present assumed the two men had opened their own agency on the sly and planned to walk away with Mefford Wolff & Weir's best accounts.

During the next few months, Clive assumed the brouhaha was forgotten until, busy planning a new campaign, he was summoned to Jack Mefford's office. "Jack fired me," Clive says. "When I asked him why, all he could mumble was some crap about my two-hour martini lunches and showing up late for work. Mel Warren had been looking for an excuse to torpedo me and the mix-up with the DAF awards ultimately gave him what he needed."

As he cleaned out his desk, Clive looked around the agency. "The nice new offices, the awards hanging on the walls, all because of my hard work," Clive says. "After that experience, I swore I would never work again for someone else."

29
CLIVE CUSSLER WASN'T GOING ANYWHERE

A few months after Clive was fired, Peter Lampack called with exciting news. Pyramid, a paperback publisher, had purchased *Catch a Teaser By The Fin* for $5,000. With a new title and a cover price of $1.25, *The Mediterranean Caper* was published in November 1973 and sold a respectable 32,000 copies. More good news followed when *Caper* was nominated for an Edgar Award by the Mystery Writers of America as one of the five best paperback original novels of 1973. Although he lost out to Will Perry's *The Death of an Informant*, the combination of his first published book and the nomination provided Clive with "a much-needed shot in the arm when the skies were gray."

Clive received another shot in the arm when Dodd Mead bought *Hermit Limited* for $5,000. When the publisher requested a photograph to be used on the book's dust jacket, Clive was not about to send them "a retouched ten-year-old photograph of myself, in my study wearing a smoking jacket."

Shortly after receiving the request, Clive and Barbara had dinner with Richard and his wife, Kate Lentz, who was a talented photographer. She was thrilled when asked to do the shoot and arrived at Clive's house on Saturday morning. Clive changed into his wetsuit, and they walked over to the golf course that backed up to the Cussler's house. Much to the astonishment of several nearby foursomes, Clive waded into one of the ponds located between the fairways and struck several poses while Kate shot a roll of film.

Now called *Iceberg*, the book was published in September 1975 and sold 3,200 copies. Clive's dedication reads, "This one is for Barbara, whose enduring patience somehow sees me through." On the dust jacket, Clive emerges from the water like a modern-day Poseidon. Readers never knew the photograph was staged in a four-foot deep water hazard in suburban Denver.

Clive's modest success provided a boost to his confidence, but it was not good enough for the bean counters at William Morris. Peter Lampack recalls, "It was right around the time when computers were beginning to be utilized, and our entire business was put on line." The computers determined 90 percent of the company revenue was being generated by 10 percent of their clients. Since computers were very large and very expensive, they were considered infallible and management decided to eliminate the bottom 50 percent of their client base. They were, after all, nothing more than freeloaders.

"My boss told me Clive Cussler wasn't going anywhere," Lampack says. "I was wasting my time and the company's money. It was time to dump him. I said, no way. Not only did I like Clive personally, I had a great deal of faith in his work and knew he'd catch on with the right book. I might have been a little green, but I had what I thought were good instincts." Fortunately for Clive, Lampack's track record persuaded management to back down and allow him to continue to represent Clive.

30
WHO THE HELL IS CLIVE CUSSLER?

Clive's *Titanic* manuscript arrived at Peter Lampack's office in late June 1974. After reading the novel, Peter Lampack agreed with Clive. *Titanic* was a great story and his best effort to date. Dodd Mead held the option on Clive's next book. Anticipating a quick sale, Lampack was taken completely by surprise when Margaret Norton, the editor who worked on *Iceberg* called to tell him *Titanic* had been rejected. Norton liked the book, but Dodd Mead's management felt the manuscript was overly long, making the book too expensive to print. Clive remembers the letdown after being informed of the publisher's decision. "Oh, the shame of it. Rejected by my own editor and publisher. It was me against the world, and once again, the world was winning."

Lampack did his best to take the sting out of the rebuff. "I told Clive, as I tell all my clients," he says, "my first thought is not the sale. It's more important to find the publisher that will ultimately do the best job." Now free to talk to other publishers, the agent submitted the manuscript to Putnam and Viking. He thought his best shot was Putnam since Clyde Taylor, the company's president, was a good friend. "Clyde," Lampack says, "had a really good sense for commercial books." Taylor liked *Titanic* but thought the plot was far too complicated. He would be willing to make an offer, but only if Clive would agree to simplify the story. Clive and Peter decided to "tuck the offer in their pocket." The agent would continue to shop the book, but it they got the same feedback, Lampack could always come back to Taylor and work out a deal.

Meanwhile, at Viking, the manuscript was read by Corliss "Cork" Smith. Viking has always tended to be a literary house, but Smith, who operated as a consultant and editor at large, was much more commercial in his orientation. His writers included first-rate names including Muriel Spark, Thomas Pynchon, Jimmy Breslin, Calvin Trillin, and Jeffrey Archer. When asked about his uncanny ability to pick winners, Smith explained, "I have a good nose for vanguard fiction. I handled all the sports books, and I have a golden touch with commercial crap."

After reading *Titanic*, Smith went to see Allen Williams, Viking's editor in chief. The book, he informed Williams, was a winner, and Viking would be crazy not to publish it. He even went so far as to suggest *Titanic* would probably become a bestseller. Viking immediately contacted Lampack, who recalls, "They made all the right noises, offering us a $7,500 advance, with minimal changes to the manuscript. I don't know if it was Allen Williams or Tom Guinzburg [Viking's president] who suggested changing the title to *Raise the Titanic!*, but we accepted the offer and the rest is history." Clive was elated, but he had no idea the sale to Viking was only a harbinger of much bigger things to come.

Graham Davis, a senior editor with Macmillan in London, happened to be in New York on business. He went to dinner with a friend who worked at Viking. When the friend told Davis about *Raise the Titanic!*, not only did the idea of raising the ill-fated liner grab Davis's interest, the subject appealed to his Britishness - the *Titanic* had sailed under the Union Jack. Davis read the manuscript on the flight back to London and immediately wanted to purchase the British paperback rights, but discovered Lampack had offered the rights to Nick Austin at Sphere, a small London imprint. Macmillan put in a higher bid, and Sphere countered. A bidding war broke out, and Sphere aced Macmillan, paying $22,000 for the rights, a healthy sum for a British paperback publisher in the 1970s.

News of the sale quickly spread through the New York publishing grapevine. Executives, editors, and agents were asking each other "Who the hell is Clive Cussler?"

Convinced this sudden interest in the mysterious Clive Cussler might actually lead to something, Clive set into motion a scenario he calls, "One of my craftier moves." First, he called Lampack and asked if it would be possible to buy back the rights to *The Mediterranean Caper*. "It was almost too easy," Clive says. "Peter contacted Pyramid. The book was out of print, and they signed over the rights without asking for a penny." Now setting his sights on *Iceberg*, Clive learned *Playboy* Publications had offered Dodd Mead $4,000 for the paperback rights. Lampack urged Clive to forget about the rights since the author's share would be $2,000. Clive not only told Lampack to turn *Playboy* down, he wanted him to call Johnathan Dodd, director of subsidiary rights at Dodd Mead, and offer him $5,000 for the exclusive rights to *Iceberg*. "Peter," Clive says, "went ballistic. He told me I was crazy. If you can get them for free, fine, but authors do not buy back their rights. He also pointed out I would be paying them $3,000 more than the $2,000 I would get from *Playboy*."

Clive told Lampack, in no uncertain terms, to offer Dodd $5,000. Two hours later, the agent called Clive: He had a deal.

There was, however, a problem. "Barbara and I had all of $400 in the bank," Clive says. "We might have tried to call our folks, but they would also think I was crazy." Barbara, now working at Memorex in downtown Denver, went to her credit union. They were willing to give her a loan, but not for the full $5,000. Clive was able to scrape together the balance by putting up the family's 1969 Mercury station wagon as collateral.

In his haste to cement the deal, Clive mailed the check before his deposits cleared and the check bounced. "I was devastated!" he says. "Momentum was building on *Raise the Titanic!,* and Jonathan Dodd could have used the bounced check as a reason to cancel the deal. But true gentleman that he was, Jonathan honored the deal when my check cleared."

31
QUIT YOUR JOB

While Clive was busy securing the rights to his earlier books, the buzz generated by *Raise the Titanic!* during the spring of 1975 convinced Lampack he could secure the best deal if he sold the U.S. paperback rights at auction.

Before the arrival of the auctions, hardcover houses would send manuscripts to paperback publishers they thought might be interested in the book. After all the bids had been received, the rights were awarded to the highest offer. Everything changed in the 1960s when mass market profits began to surpass those of hardcover editions, leading to lucrative auctions of paperback rights. Today, prospective buyers are notified of the auction dates well in advance and the agent (or publisher) will usually set a floor price "to get some money in the hat." As the auction heats up, directors of subsidiary rights stay up late, studying the profit-and-loss statements in an attempt to predict how many copies they have to sell before upping their bid. A misstep can end a career.

Held in June 1975, the auction for *Raise the Titanic!* attracted a premier lineup of paperback houses, including Bantam, Pocket Books, Avon, and Dell. For almost a week, Lampack fielded calls in his office as the bids came streaming in. On the morning of the final day of the auction, Clive and his family were in Colorado having breakfast (an unwritten publishing rule stipulates authors should not attend an auction). After the kids left for school, Barbara finished getting ready for work. "Just before she walked out the door," Clive says, "I told her, 'when the bidding gets to $250,000, you can quit your job.' I know people don't believe me, but I was truly being facetious."

After his customary morning walk, Clive sat down at his typewriter and attempted to concentrate on the work at hand, but his mind kept wandering - a group of strangers 2,000 miles away were involved in a guessing game that would have a major impact on the rest of his life. At ten o'clock, the phone rang. Lampack informed Clive that Bantam had prevailed with a winning bid of $840,000. Clive recalls little of the rest of their conversation, but he remembers calling Barbara. When she answered, he simply said, "Quit your job" and hung up. While Barbara walked into her boss's office and gave two weeks' notice, Clive tried to come to grips with what had just transpired.

Once the dust settled, Bantam's management was informed that *Raise the Titanic!* was not only the third in a series of Dirk Pitt adventures, Clive owned the rights to the other two books. Concerned the novels might not be up to the quality of *Raise the Titanic!*, the publisher paid Clive $40,000 for each book to keep them off the market until their merit could be ascertained. A curious editor located copies of *The Mediterranean Caper* and *Iceberg* and read them non-stop over a weekend. During Bantam's Monday morning editorial meeting, he suggested the publisher would be crazy not to publish both books. His advice proved to be prophetic: *The Mediterranean Caper* and *Iceberg* became bestsellers in their second incarnations.

Having invested a significant amount of money on an unknown author, a meeting was scheduled at Bantam's Manhattan offices to make sure he had ten fingers and toes. Clive and Barbara saw an opportunity for a mini-vacation, and Clive invited his parents, who had never been to New York, to join them. In addition to meeting his new publisher and editor, Clive and Peter Lampack would finally meet face-to-face. The two men had been working together for more than eight years but had always conducted their business by mail or phone. Clive had never told Lampack about the "Charles Winthrop" subterfuge because he was afraid the agent might drop him. With the success of *Raise the Titanic!*, he decided it would be safe to come clean.

Arriving in New York in July, Clive and Barbara met Peter and his wife, Diane, at the Sign of the Dove, a posh east side restaurant. Just before the waiter served dessert, Clive leaned over to Barbara and murmured, "The time has finally come." Beginning with Charles Winthrop's stationery, Clive recounted the entire scheme. After he finished, Lampack burst out in laughter. Regaining his composure, the agent exclaimed, "I always thought Charlie Winthrop was some guy I met when I was drunk at a cocktail party."

Clive arrived at Bantam's office with an entourage Lampack, accountant Vinnie Tepedino, and Eric Cussler. Clive had included his father not only because he thought Eric would find the negotiations interesting, he had an ulterior motive. "My father," Clive says, "always considered me to be something of a loser. That's probably not the best word, more like a 'mover.' In his mind, anybody who couldn't hold a job for at least five years was a 'mover.' I tried to explain, if you work in advertising you're lucky if you can keep a job for three years. The agency loses an account, you get sacked. Somebody doesn't like you, you get sacked. Another outfit buys the agency, you get sacked. It's just the way the business works. I don't think my father ever got it."

For the first half hour, Clive, Lampack, Tepedino, and Bantam's management discussed contracts, royalties, and book tours. During a lull in the proceedings, Eric, who had been following the proceedings with a great deal of interest, leaned toward Lampack. "May I ask what kind of money we're talking about here?" After looking at Clive, who smiled and nodded, the agent began to rattle off the numbers: $840,000 for the paperback rights, $40,000 each for the rights to Clive's first two books, and $100,000 from the Book-of-the-Month Club. "Eric," Lampack said, "Give or take, we are talking somewhere around a million dollars."

Clive glanced at his father. He had not seen that look on his face since Eric discovered a big, black Jewett touring car parked in the driveway. "I think my Dad," Clive says, "thought it was going to be, at the most, $50,000. He couldn't comprehend the numbers, especially since they were being paid to his 'mover' son."

Clive and Barbara were scheduled to return to Denver the next day, but Clive urged Eric and Amy to remain in New York - see the town, take in a show, eat at the best restaurants - he would take care of everything. His parents accepted his invitation and several weeks later, Tepedino received an itemized bill. Eric had carefully noted each and every expense incurred during their holiday, including several packs of chewing gum.

Amused, Tepedino showed Clive the bill. After a quick glance, Clive shrugged, "I guess Dad thinks I can afford it."

32
LOOKOUT MOUNTAIN

Under the headline, "*Titanic* Book Worth a Million," *The Denver Post* profiled Clive's sudden fame and fortune in July 1976. "Want to know how to make a million bucks?" the article asked. "Clive Cussler can tell you . . . '*Raise the Titanic!*' has already cleared nearly a million dollars and it hasn't even appeared on the bookstands yet." The article included a photograph of Clive holding the detailed scale model of the *Titanic* he built for reference.

In a letter to George Yeager, Clive included a copy of the article:

> As you guessed by the article, I'm now a world famous, renowned, successful, wealthy, revered, lionized, simonized novelist. None of this has gone to my head however. Henceforth, please address all correspondence to Your Authorship, Clive Cussler. No sense in spoiling my image. Can you believe it? All of a

sudden, just because my new book lucked out and hit the big time, people all over town are referring to me as Denver's leading author. The two-faced bastards are acting as if I'm a homegrown asshole. Hypocritically, they overlook the fact that I'm from California and pretend I popped from a cow's ass at Monfort Meat Packing . . . I can thank good old Mefford, Warren & Weir for my new status. If they had never fired me, I probably would have never written Raise the Titanic! and make a bundle.

Raise the Titanic! was published in hardcover by Viking in October 1976. To promote the book, Clive set out on his first book tour, appearing in cities throughout the United States. On December 5, 1976, the book appeared on *The New York Times* bestseller list. It would reach number two and remain on the list for twenty-six weeks. Author Catherine Coulter compiled a group of writer's reflections, including Clive's, on the moment they were notified their book had first appeared on the *Times* list. "The book was *Raise the Titanic!*," Clive recounted. "The clouds parted, the sun burst through, there came the sounds of harp music, trumpets, and a drum roll."

The sounds of celestial music quickly faded when Clive read a review in Harper's. "If good books were rewarded with flowers and bad books with skunks," Evan S. Connell groused, "on a scale of one to five, *Raise the Titanic!* would deserve four skunks . . . Buffeted by icy North Atlantic clichés, drenched with reeking balderdash, will we succeed in raising the *Titanic*? Never fear. The only question is whether Hollywood will buy it."

Unnerved by the review's vitriolic tone, Clive called Lampack and asked why the reviewer had been so hateful. Lampack told Clive to ignore the critics, explaining, "When your books start getting good literary reviews, we're in big trouble."

"It didn't take me long to realize Peter knew what he was talking about," Clive says. "Critics tend to apply literary criteria to genre writing in general, suspense adventure included. I started with suspense adventure, and I'm still at it. Literary writing just isn't me. Too often writers of Great Books gloss over the structure and story line, going instead into great depth on character development and descriptions of leaves on a tree, a stain on a character's tie, or the shape of a cloud. I have never had the desire to write mainstream fiction. I've found my niche, and I'm pretty good at it."

Asked if he considers himself to be commercial, Clive's answer is emphatic. "Yes, I'd be the last to deny it. If being commercial means writing for your audience, writing what appeals to them rather than the critics, then yes, I'm commercial."

When his first royalty check arrived, Clive splurged on a new refrigerator and a used Fiat. Eric Cussler had always preached to his son it was important not to live beyond your means. *Raise the Titanic!*'s unexpected success provided Clive with "a reward I could never have imagined, but I was going to wait and see what happened with my next book before I wrote a lot of big checks. For all I knew, it could just be a flash in the pan."

In the fall of 1977, Clive completed *Vixen 03*, the fifth Dirk Pitt adventure. The novel's prologue takes place in 1954. A C-97 Stratofreighter (code name "Vixen 03") takes off from Buckley Field in Colorado. Carrying a top-secret cargo from the Rocky Mountain Arsenal to Bikini Atoll in the Pacific, the airplane disappears without a trace. Thirty-four years later, Dirk Pitt is vacationing in the Rocky Mountains. When he discovers the remains of the ill-fated Stratofreighter at the bottom of Table Lake, Pitt finds himself up to his neck in a plot that involves a biological doomsday organism, African mercenaries, and a crazed ex-Royal navy officer who attempts to use the World War II battleship *Iowa* as a terrorist weapon against Washington, D.C.

The six-figure advance for *Vixen 03* convinced Clive his newfound success was not a fluke and the Cusslers moved up in the world - literally. Located a half hour drive west of Denver, Lookout Mountain is home to a mixed bag of attractions, including Buffalo Bill Cody's grave, Boettcher Mansion and nature preserve (the summer home of one of Colorado's early entrepreneurs), and the Mother Cabrini Shrine, dedicated to Saint Francis Xavier Cabrini, the first American citizen to be canonized by the Roman Catholic Church.

Charmed by the same natural beauty they fell in love with eight years earlier in Estes Park, Clive and Barbara purchased a home on Poco Calle Road. With only one other neighbor on the secluded street, the contemporary house included four bedrooms, four bathrooms, and a pool. The grounds sloped towards the east and provided a sweeping view of Denver. "The panorama at night," Clive recalls, "was spectacular. A tapestry of twinkling lights stretching across the entire horizon."

Dayna Cussler was with her parents when they first inspected the Lookout Mountain house. "It had two levels and a bridge with railings connecting the main entrance to the rest of the house," Dayna says. "There was a large room under the bridge where my father built his office. I thought the bridge was the coolest part of the house, but my parents were more impressed by the views and the built-in bookshelves that went from the bottom level up to the main level. We moved in during the summer of 1979."

Dirk describes the move to Lookout Mountain as culture shock. "My family was somewhat in awe of Clive's sudden success. It was exciting to move into such a luxurious home, almost like we had won the lottery. The most memorable thing was the joy the house brought to my mother. She was a modest woman and would have been happy to stay in Arvada, but she also appreciated the beauty of the house and its surroundings. Her happiness is what I recall most about living on Lookout Mountain."

The east wall of Clive's office was fitted with large windows and sliding glass doors, but he had his desk custom-built to face west, toward the bookshelves. Dirk believes there was a good reason for the desk's orientation. "Clive's a smart guy," Dirk says, laughing. "I'm sure he would have written fewer books if he spent his day's gazing at the scenery."

Teri, married, with two children, was now living in the Arvada house on 72nd Place. "We would spend our summers on Lookout Mountain," Teri says. "My kids practically lived in the pool. Dad would always manage to take a break from his writing and do cannonballs with them or see how far they could swim underwater, the same kind of things he did with us when we were kids. Dad has always been the best grandpa."

His client's transformation from a struggling unknown to a bestselling author convinced Peter Lampack, thirty-two and married, with one child, to make a career move. "Clive's success," he says, "made it feasible for me to leave William Morris and open my own agency. I had been thinking about it for a while - too many staff meetings and too much politicking by people who were threatened if you came in early and left late."

Lampack's father-in-law owned a clothing company located in mid-town Manhattan. In 1977, the agent moved into two empty offices - small, with no windows - but the price was right. "The low overhead," Lampack says, "allowed me time to get the wind behind my sails." Clive remembers having to navigate his way through a maze of clothing racks to get to his agent's office.

Two years later, Lampack moved his agency to a four-room office in the French Building, located at Fifth Avenue and 45th Street. In 2011, the agency relocated to the 53rd floor of New York's celebrated Empire State Building.

33
THE BOOK TOUR FROM HELL

Tom Guinzburg sold Viking Press to Penguin, a subsidiary of the London-based conglomerate, Pearson Longman, Ltd, in 1975. Irving Goodman, who headed Holt, Rinehart & Winston's trade books division, was installed as Viking's publisher, with Joe Friedman heading up sales. The management duo - Clive refers to them as "the hotshots" - moved the company from Madison Avenue to a renovated cast-iron building on West 23rd Street and instituted a drastic cost-cutting program. Guinzburg, who was promised he would remain as a consultant, was unceremoniously fired six months later while he was home sick in bed.

Vixen 03, with a 50,000 first printing, was released on October 1, 1978. "Ebenezer Scrooge spent money like a lottery winner compared to Goodman and Friedman," Clive says. "There was very little advertising for *Vixen 03*, and I was sent out on what can only be described as the book tour from hell."

In Chicago, Clive was scheduled to be interviewed on Bob Cromie's popular *Book Beat* television program. A good-natured fellow noted for his genuine love of books and authors, Cromie's show was broadcast on public television, from 1964 to 1980. After *Raise the Titanic!* was published, Clive had made his first appearance on *Book Beat*. "Bob did a great interview," Clive says. "I was really looking forward to talking with him about *Vixen 03*."

Clive and the Viking rep had only been in the studio for a few minutes when Cromie took Clive aside. "I'm very sorry to have to do this," he confessed, "but I can't have you on the show." Several months earlier, Cromie had contacted Viking and requested one of their authors for an interview. Not only did the publisher tell him no, they refused to give him an explanation. Cromie assured Clive it was nothing personal. He would love to have him on the show, but if Viking was going to treat him like that, he felt obligated to reciprocate. On their way out of the studio, Clive told the rep, "I get the feeling Viking doesn't want me anymore."

Clive's itinerary invariably scheduled him to fly at night, a strategy he believes was devised so he would eat for free on the airplane rather than billing Viking for meals in restaurants. Arriving in Cleveland well after midnight, Clive told the cab driver the name of his hotel. Peering at him in the rearview mirror, the cabby asked, "Mister, are you sure that's where you're going?" Arriving at the hotel, the night clerk gave him the same reception. "Are you sure you've got the right place?" His room, Clive recalls, "was an absolute horror. The television set had been ripped off the wall, and I used a coat hanger to wire the door shut.

New York was the last stop on the tour. Clive checked into the Gotham Hotel. "This was before millions were spent on renovations and the Gotham was transformed into the trendy Peninsula New York," Clive says. "The furniture was beat up, paint was peeling off the walls, and the plumbing in the bathroom was rusty and leaked."

Peter Lampack stopped by to see Clive. As his agent looked around the room, Clive could see he was horrified by his client's grim accommodations. After relating the tribulations of the book tour, Clive ushered Lampack into the bathroom where he was holding cockroach races in the bathtub. Clive chuckles, "I had to give the contestants a crumb of bread at each turn and thought Peter was going to lose his breakfast."

A few days after Clive flew back to Denver, Lampack was summoned to Viking's offices. Irving Goodman demanded to know why Clive had behaved so badly on the book tour. His client's transgressions included signing a book with an offensive comment, telling an anti-Semitic joke, and bad-mouthing Viking. Lampack was speechless. "I had been working with Clive for almost ten years, and he always behaved like a gentleman."

Lampack related Goodman's accusations to Clive, who immediately set him straight. After signing books for several hours at a Chicago bookstore, Clive was exhausted. A clerk asked him to sign her book. Slumped in a chair and out of ideas, he asked her for a suggestion. She cheerfully replied, "Write something wicked." Glad to oblige, Clive signed, "Stick it in your ear! Clive Cussler."

In San Francisco, Clive addressed a group of book dealers. He began his presentation by relating a conversation he had at a similar event in New York. "I was sitting next to a book dealer, Saul Greenberg, and asked him, 'Saul, should I talk about my book or something else?' Saul told me, 'Clive, I've read the book. For god's sake, talk about something else.'" A young man, characterized by Clive as "shaggy," stood up and started screaming, "You're anti-Semitic, you're an anti-Semite!" Clive and the audience were initially stunned, but the booksellers, including several who happened to be Jewish, ended up giving the heckler the bum's rush. As for the charge of bad mouthing his publisher, the Viking rep in Chicago had dutifully reported Clive's remark about "Viking not wanting me anymore."

The wretched book tour and Goodman's unfounded accusations convinced Clive and Lampack it was time to find a new publisher. There was, however, a major obstacle - Viking had the option for Clive's next book.

Determined to move on, Clive reached into his bag of tricks. When he was fired by the Denver agency, Clive had knocked out a farce skewering the mile high city's advertising follies he called, *I Went To Denver But It Was Closed*. "The story wasn't very good," he says, "but it was a great catharsis." Retrieving the forgotten manuscript, Clive gave it to Lampack, who sent it to Viking. The rejection was incredibly prompt. Now free to offer Clive's next book to another publisher, the agent contacted Bantam. It was fortuitous timing since the paperback house wanted to expand into the hardcover market, and Bantam jumped at the chance to sign up bestseller Clive Cussler.

34
I WANT TO DO A DEAL

After *Raise the Titanic!* was published, Peter Lampack contacted several production companies he thought might be interested in turning the book into a film. One of his prospects, Associated Communications Corporation (ACC), was headed by legendary British showman, Lord Lew Grade. Grade had not read the book but believed the subject had "been done to death" and passed.

A year later, after a business associate urged Grade to read *Raise the Titanic!*, he called Lampack. In an interview with *The New York Times*, Grade reiterated their conversation: "I said, 'I've read the *Titanic*. I want it.' Lampack said, 'I've got several offers.' I said 'I'm coming to New York Monday - you be at my hotel.' He came in the afternoon about four o'clock. I said, 'I want to do a deal, you won't leave this room until we do a deal. I don't want bidding. You are either in a position to do a deal, or else forget about it.' He said, 'I'll have to get back to Clive Cussler.' I said, 'Do it now, or I withdraw my offer.

Here's the telephone.' And he telephoned Cussler, and Cussler said, 'Okay, provided I have a walk-on part and one line.'"

ACC paid $450,000 for the rights, the most lucrative book-to-movie deal of 1978.

Raise the Titanic! would be the latest in a long line of films based in some way on the liner's demise. A silent ten-minute melodrama, *Saved from the Titanic*, was released only a month after the tragedy. The film starred Dorothy Gibson, an actress who survived the sinking. Gibson not only co-wrote the script, she appeared in the film in the same dress she allegedly wore on that fateful night. Following *Saved from the Titanic*, seventeen films - good, bad, and ugly - have recounted the tragic story. Unfortunately for Lew Grade and Clive Cussler, *Raise the Titanic* would fall into the latter category. Geoff Tibballs, author of *Business Blunders*, labeled the film, "Almost as big a disaster as the ship itself."

Lew Grade was in his early seventies when he turned from a successful small-screen career to feature films. Buoyed by success on *The Return of the Pink Panther*, *The Boys from Brazil* and *The Muppet Movie*, he was ready to take on *Raise the Titanic*. After meeting with Lampack, Grade heard rumors that Stanley Kramer (*High Noon, The Wild One, Guess Who's Coming to Dinner*) had been dropping hints he might be interested in producing a film based on Clive's book. To eliminate any chance of a costly bidding war Grade paid Kramer $400,000 and hired him as the film's producer and director.

In May 1978, Grade hosted his annual party at the Cannes Film Festival and announced he was going to make *Raise the Titanic*. Paul Newman, Steve McQueen, and Robert Redford were a few of the names bantered about to play Dirk Pitt, but they all turned the part down. Clive wanted James Garner, but Richard Jordan, an unfortunate choice, ended up with the role. Other members of the cast included Anne Archer, David Selby, Jason Robards, and Alec Guinness.

A year later in Cannes, Grade boasted, "Six million dollars has already been spent on model work" and promised filming would begin "next month in Malta." In fact, filming would not begin for six months, but the delay was the least of Grade's problems.

A large chunk of the $6 million spent on models went into a fifty-five-foot long, twelve-foot high *Titanic*. Weighing in at twelve tons, it was a fantastic rendering - accurate right down to the number and size of the rivets - but much bigger than it needed to be. To provide the effects they were seeking, the production team specified a water tank more than 250 feet wide and thirty-five feet deep. Constructed on the island of Malta, the tank took ten months to complete, held 9 million gallons of water and cost $3 million.

Cameraman Robert Steadman recalls, "The size of the tank caused real problems. One night, early in the game, I called the surface and asked for a reloaded camera. A diver was sent down with it, but after waiting for five minutes he didn't show up . . . He had gotten lost in this ten million gallon lake of ours . . . he was found, thoroughly disoriented by the blackness and lack of landmarks."

After only two weeks on the job, Stanley Kramer quit for "artistic reasons" and was replaced by Jerry Jameson (*Mod Squad, Six Million Dollar Man, Streets of San Francisco*). The script went through ten drafts and the final version strayed considerably from the book - even the exclamation point was dropped. An estimated $12 million was spent before one frame of film was shot. When Grade's right-hand man, Bernard Kingham, tried to convince his boss to abandon the project, he was ordered to "mind his own business."

While *Raise the Titanic* cruised toward another waterlogged disaster, Clive, back in Denver and busy with the next Dirk Pitt novel, received a call from his mother. Eric and Amy were now living in Laguna Woods Village, an upscale retirement community in California.

During an operation for a minor gastronomical problem, Eric had suffered a stroke. Clive immediately flew to California and spent several days at his father's bedside. Assured Eric was on the mend, Clive returned to Denver. Four days later, Amy, now frantic, called again. Eric's condition had worsened, and his doctors now labeled his condition as critical. Clive flew to Los Angeles and arrived at the hospital ten minutes before his father died. "I was holding him in my arms," Clive says, "when he left us." Eric Cussler died on December 28, 1979. He was interred at Pacific View Hospital Memorial Park, a cemetery high above the Pacific Ocean with sweeping views of Newport Harbor.

After Eric's death, Amy moved to Colorado and purchased a condo in Arvada. She enjoyed her new life, traveling, spending time with family and friends. After several minor strokes, Amy's health began to deteriorate in the late 1980s, and Clive arranged for her to live in a nursing home. Amy Adeline Cussler died on February 8, 1993, and was laid to rest next to her beloved husband.

Raise the Titanic opened in the U.S. during the summer of 1980. The film's premiere, complete with a parade and the mayor, was held in Boston. Clive, Barbara and Peter Lampack were riding in a limousine with director Jerry Jameson. Clive laughs, "There was a high school band in front of us. I knew we were in trouble when they began to play 'Turkey in the Straw.'" When the film ended, Lampack asked Clive how he liked it. "Somehow," Clive replied, "they managed to take what I thought was an exciting story and turn it into a boring movie."

Dark, dull, and disjointed, the film was shredded by the critics. Writing in *Screen International*, Marjorie Bilbow fumed, "water logged mass of unresolved subplots, insufficiently identified characters and a complexity of technical jargon." A reviewer in the *Guardian* groused, "The longer it goes on, the more one hopes that, if they ever do raise the *Titanic*, they'll heave the film overboard to replace it."

Composer John Berry escaped unscathed since everybody, including Clive, thought his score was the film's only saving grace. The film's dismal performance at the box office - *Raise the Titanic* lost almost $25 million - helped end Grade's involvement with major motion picture production. Clive, playing a reporter, appears briefly in one scene, but the single line he was promised ended up on the cutting room floor.

There was talk of moving the oversized model of the *Titanic* to Minnesota's Mall of America, but nothing came of it, and the miniature masterpiece was discarded in a desolate film studio yard on Malta, where it can be found today. The elements have taken a heavy toll, and like the real ship, the model is slowly turning into a rusty hulk.

35
IF YOU LET THEM PUBLISH THAT RAG, YOU'RE RUINED!

Moving from Viking to Bantam in 1979 threw Clive off his normal writing schedule, and it took him three years to finish his next book. The fifth Dirk Pitt adventure, *Night Probe!* was released in hardcover on August 3, 1981, followed a year later by the paperback edition. Appearing on *The New York Times* hardcover bestseller list for the first time on August 13, 1981, the book remained on the list for thirteen weeks.

Night Probe! provides a fascinating insight into Clive's creative process. The book's plot was hatched in May 1978, when Clive was reading *The Denver Post*. He happened upon an article detailing the grim fate of a Kansas Pacific Railroad freight train and its crew on a stormy night in the spring of 1878. Pulled by Engine #51, the train left Denver, headed for Kansas City, with a string of twenty-five freight cars and a caboose. Heavy rain had been falling for several days, and unknown to the crew in the engine's cab, the bridge across Kiowa Creek had been washed away. The locomotive and eighteen cars plunged into the raging water, killing the engineer, fireman, and brakeman. Despite an extensive search, the locomotive was never found.

"I knew nothing of the tragedy," Clive says. "At the time, I was not intrigued with launching a search for the elusive engine, but working its disappearance into a concept for an adventure starring my hero, Dirk Pitt." And so a long forgotten train wreck became one of the primary building blocks for a plot Clive and many of his fans consider one of his best.

The signature Cussler prologue is set in the spring of 1914. Great Britain is faced with an impending war and financial disaster. The prime minister, in league with King George V, has secretly agreed to sell Canada to the United States for $1 billion, with a $150 million down payment. Two copies of the treaty spelling out the details of the sale are lost in simultaneous accidents. The New York & Quebec Northern Railroad's *Manhattan Limited*, attempting to cross a downed bridge, plunges into the Hudson River; meanwhile, the liner *Empress of Ireland* sinks in the icy waters of the St. Lawrence River. When an enraged British Cabinet discovers the covert scheme, President Woodrow Wilson orders all records of the treaty destroyed.

Jumping ahead to 1989, an energy crisis threatens to ruin the United States economy. The world's oil reserves are running low and Canada, having invested heavily in hydro-electric power, is providing electricity to fifteen states in the northeast. America's future looks even bleaker when Dirk Pitt, testing an experimental NUMA research submarine, discovers a huge oil field located in Quebec's territorial waters. A navy officer working on her Ph.D. discovers a reference to the lost treaty in one of Wilson's letters and Pitt and NUMA are ordered by the president of the United States to search for the lost documents. Pitt is threatened by a formidable gathering of foes, including a former British secret agent, who may or may not be James Bond. Against all odds, Pitt recovers one of the original treaties, leading to the establishment of the United States of Canada.

In one of the novel's multiple plot twists, Pitt discovers the *Manhattan Limited* never plunged into the river. While the accident at the bridge was faked, a gang of robbers, after a cargo of gold, not the treaty, hijacked the train and secreted it in a quarry. The desperado's plans went awry when they blew up the entrance to the tunnel and the shock waves ruptured an underground fissure. Water filled the escape shaft and the thieves, passengers, and train crew died a slow death in the dank chamber.

The train-in-the-tunnel twist was inspired by *The Last Bandit*, a film Clive saw when he was a teenager. Starring William "Wild Bill" Elliott, Adrian Booth, Forrest Tucker, and Andy Devine, the horse opera follows the adventures of two brothers working on opposite sides of the law. The villainous brother comes up with a plan to waylay a train carrying $1 million in gold bullion and hide it in an abandoned tunnel. The high point for teenage Clive and his friends was probably the attractive Ms. Booth's bathtub scene, but almost thirty-five years later, the film provided Clive with a memorable story line.

Night Probe! was assigned to Alan Rinzler, a veteran editor whose author list included Jerzy Kozinski, Robert Ludlum, and Hunter Thompson. Rinzler recalls his association with Clive: "Passion, authenticity, discipline, self-confidence, modesty, decency, professionalism - Clive was an ideal author to work with. He was open to changes in the plot, line editing, deletions and additions, but he also had a very good idea of his own strengths and purpose."

Unfamiliar with Clive's earlier work, Rinzler asked him

how many of his books were in print. Clive explained *Night Probe!* was his fifth book, but Dirk Pitt actually made his first appearance in *The Sea Dweller*, a work that had never been published. The editor almost fell out of his seat. A bestselling author was casually telling him he had an unpublished manuscript gathering dust in a closet. Rinzler insisted Clive send him a copy of the manuscript. When Clive called Peter Lampack to tell him Rinzler was eager to read *The Sea Dweller*, Lampack's response was terse, "Not on your life. If you let them publish that rag, you're ruined."

Dismissing his agent's objections, Clive dug out *The Sea Dweller* and read several chapters. The plot was pretty good, but his writing had improved considerably in the past eighteen years. After spending three months on an extensive rewrite, Clive mailed the manuscript to Lampack. Although the agent still thought *The Sea Dweller* was weak, he sent it on to Rinzler, hoping it would quietly disappear.

On January 1, 1983, almost twenty years since Clive sat down to write the first book in his planned "little adventure series," Bantam published *The Sea Dweller* in paperback. Now called *Pacific Vortex!*, the dramatic double cover features a circular die-cut porthole opening to reveal a diver descending into the depths.

In the forward, Clive addressed his readers:

> Not that it really matters, but this is the first Dirk Pitt story.
>
> . . . Because this was his first adventure, and because it does not weave the intricate plots of his later exploits, I was reluctant to submit it for publishing. But at the urging of my friends and family, fans and readers, Pitt's introduction is now in your hands.
>
> May it be looked upon as a few hours of entertainment

and, perhaps, even a historic artifact of sorts.

Shortly before *Pacific Vortex!* was due to be released, Lampack called Clive and told him he was planning a vacation in Jamaica. He wanted to be far away from New York when the book bombed and Clive's reputation ended up in the toilet. A week later, a telegram arrived at Lampack's hotel. It read, "Screw you! *Pacific Vortex!* Just went number two on the *New York Times* paperback list."

"Screw you! *Pacific Vortex!* Just went number two on the *New York Times* paperback list."Once again, Clive, trusting his instincts, enjoyed the last laugh.

36
A PLATTER OF CHEESE: ONE KIND

Shortly after *Night Probe!* appeared on the *Times* bestseller list, Bantam's management organized an author's party. "The party started at five o'clock in the conference room," Clive recalls. "Bantam's employees had obviously been ordered to attend and it didn't take a genius to figure out they wanted to get the hell out of there and go home. The lavish spread consisted of a platter of cheese - one kind - and a platter of salami, no crackers, washed down with a gallon jug of Gallo Burgundy and Gallo Chablis. It was a very dreary event and should have alerted me to what was coming."

In the March 22, 1982, issue of *Time*, an article detailed the "Hard Times in Hardcover Country." Writers, editors, agents and publishers bemoaned ". . . a soft economy, cost increases and an uncertain audience." Among those quoted, Bantam's president, Louis Wolfe admonished, "At Bantam, we're paying more attention to what we pay up front and with good reason. We can't afford a lot of money for what might be a big book and then find out it isn't."

When Clive turned in his next novel, *Deep Six*, Bantam informed Peter Lampack the publisher would not only be offering less money than paid previously for *Night Probe!*, the royalty payment would remain the same. Clive and his agent were shocked. *Night Probe!* was not only Bantam's first hardcover bestseller, the book had stayed on the *Times* list for thirteen weeks.

Early in his career, Clive expected more from his publishers and editors. In more genteel times, editors were not only great teachers, they often took a personal interest in their writers. Maxwell Perkins advanced royalties, made private loans, and encouraged his writers in every way possible. Cork Smith - the same Cork Smith who predicted *Raise the Titanic!* could become a bestseller - shared both a working relationship and friendship with his authors. Bennett Cerf spent a great deal of his time at Random House playing nursemaid to Truman Capote.

Al Silverman, past president of the Book-of-the-Month Club and former editor at Viking/Penguin, regrets the changes that have turned publishing into a money game. "I determined," Silverman wrote, "that the golden age had to be the years from 1946, as the harrowing savagery of World War II was washing away, to the late 1970s and early 1980s, before the era of publishing ossification had fully set in . . . when the great old-line book people began to be replaced by bottom-line businessmen."

Clive quickly developed a realistic perspective of contemporary publishing. "A writer," he says, "is basically a manufacturer of a product. You have to be realistic and look at it that way. I put out the best product I can, and my agent sells it for as much money as we can get. Forget the wonderful old pal relationships like Max Perkins and F. Scott Fitzgerald. They don't exist anymore."

By late 1983, negotiations for *Deep Six* were at an impasse. Frustrated with Bantam's foot-dragging, Lampack put the book on the open market. A few days later his phone rang - it was Michael Korda, Simon & Schuster's editor in chief.

37
BECAUSE IT'S INCONVENIENT

It has been suggested Michael Korda may know more about what makes a bestselling book than anyone alive.

A bestselling author himself, Korda states, "Real editing is a profession, unlike publishing, which is merely a business... No one teaches it [editing], of course: You're born to it, the way a good surgeon is born with the right hands; it is something you either can or can't do."

Korda was instrumental in convincing Simon & Schuster to make an offer acknowledging Clive's bestseller status - $1 million for *Deep Six* - but Clive soon had reason to question his superstar editor's "right hands." When *Deep Six* was returned for revisions, Clive was appalled. "The editing was terrible, just terrible! I ended up writing 'stet' nullify a correction on all 600 pages and sent it off to Peter." Lampack not only agreed with Clive, he is convinced to this day Korda had absolutely nothing to do with the editing. "Michael was probably busy with another project," Lampack says. "An assistant probably farmed it out to some NYU graduate student."

Faced with a dreadful job of editing, ostensibly executed by a celebrity editor known for his monumental ego, Lampack was in no hurry to return the manuscript, but Korda forced the issue. In September 1993, he contacted Lampack, suggesting he, Lampack, and Clive meet for lunch in New York so he could review the revised manuscript. Despite the probability of an unpleasant showdown, Clive was delighted with the prospect of a trip to New York. After Dirk had graduated from Arizona State University in 1983 and earned an MBA from the University of California at Berkeley, he started working for the General Accounting Office in Washington, D.C. Following his meeting with Lampack and Korda, a short flight would have Clive and Barbara in the nation's capital in time for dinner with their son.

When Clive and Lampack arrived at The Four Seasons, the maître d' escorted them to Korda's back wall booth in the Grill Room. After ordering drinks, Clive handed Korda the manuscript. Without glancing at its contents, he deposited the envelope on an empty chair. Later, as they were getting ready to leave, Lampack could not resist asking Korda who had actually done the editing. Korda nonchalantly affirmed it was his work. "Peter and I looked at each other," Clive says. "This guy is supposed to be one of the world's sharpest editors, and he's sitting there taking credit for the worst job of editing either of us had ever seen."

After arriving at Washington's National Airport, a cab delivered Clive and Barbara to the Mayflower Hotel. Clive was paying the cab driver when the hotel manager stuck his head in the window. "If you're Clive Cussler, there is an urgent call for you at the front desk." Clive, concerned it could be a family emergency, was surprised to hear Korda's voice.

After leaving Clive and Lampack at the restaurant, Korda returning to his office. Flipping through the manuscript, he discovered the 600 pages marked "stet." Korda wanted Clive to return to New York - ASAP! Clive explained he and Barbara were spending a few days in Washington with their son. "Michael wasn't listening," Clive says. "Our discussion was getting pretty hot, and Michael finally demanded to know why I wouldn't jump on the next plane back to New York. After thinking for a moment, I replied, 'Because it's inconvenient.' The phone went dead."

When the story about the confrontation got around Simon & Schuster, Clive was known as "the guy who didn't give a damn." "Michael and I," Clive says, "enjoyed what could best be described as a 'distant' association." Asked to comment on his relationship with Clive, Korda stated succinctly, "He was extremely professional."

"Ultimately," Clive recalls, "Michael and I ended up compromising, and the final editing of *Deep Six* turned out to be no more problematic than my earlier books. We made very few changes, but I did take out one chapter he objected to."

Dirk Pitt's seventh adventure kicks off with Pitt and his NUMA team dispatched to find the source of a deadly poison killing everything in the waters off the coast of Alaska. When one of his crew is killed, Pitt vows revenge and the trail leads to Mim Bougainville, an elderly Korean shipping magnate who plans to kidnap the president of the United States and implant a mind-control chip in his brain. After thwarting the villain's plans with a rousing chase in a vintage paddle-wheel riverboat, Pitt dispatches the dragon-lady, sending her on a one-way ride down an elevator shaft.

Released in hardcover on May 21, 1984, *Deep Six* appeared on *The New York Times* bestseller list two weeks later, where it remained for fifteen weeks.

38
TOUCHED BY A CAR

D*eep Six* not only marked Clive's debut with Simon & Schuster, it was the first book in which he loaned his fictional hero a ride from his real-world car collection - a 1948 Talbot-Lego Coupe. On the back of the book's jacket, Clive stands next to the slinky machine. Since *Deep Six*, every Dirk Pitt adventure has featured Clive (and beginning with *Black Wind*, Dirk Cussler) photographed with the automobile Pitt borrows from Clive's world class collection.

All collections - stamps, art, porcelain birds, robots, snuff boxes, whatever - begin with one specimen. In 1974, Clive and Barbara were enjoying a Sunday drive in rural Colorado. Passing a farm, Barbara spotted a 1946 Ford club coupe, identical to the car she drove while attending UCLA, parked in the front yard with a "for sale" sign taped to the windshield.

After Clive had traded his Jaguar for a Nash Rambler, the obligations of a family and career limited his vehicles to utilitarian four-door sedans and station wagons, but the heart of a motor head still beat in Clive's chest. Realizing Barbara's interest in the Ford provided him with an unexpected opportunity to build another hot rod, Clive cranked a U-turn, offered the owner $400 and the club coupe was soon parked in front of 7731 West 72nd Place.

Unless it was snowing or raining, Clive and Dirk spent the majority of their spare time working on the Ford. "It wasn't a frame-off restoration," Dirk recalls. "More like a body-on cosmetic job. I crawled under the car and cleaned the frame and suspension, and helped rebuild the engine. My Dad was great about letting me learn on the job. I rebuilt the carb, set the timing, adjusted the brakes and replaced the wheel bearings - things I had never done before."

The majority of the father and son team's effort went into prepping the body for painting. "We primed the car with spray cans," Dirk admits, "but the final paint job and upholstery were farmed out to professional shops. It took about a year to get it done, and my father and I are still proud of the finished product. I learned to drive three-on-the-tree in that car, and the dual exhausts really sound good."

In 1976, following the success of *Raise the Titanic!,* Clive bought what he considers his first "collector car," a 1955 Rolls-Royce Silver Dawn. "The car was in excellent shape. I had never owned anything that classy, and it was a real experience to cruise around Colorado in the Rolls. Barbara always thought the car was special because 1955 was the year we got married."

A few months after he bought the Rolls, Clive and Barbara were in California visiting her parents in Huntington Beach. Reading the newspaper, Clive came across an ad for a collector automobile auction being held at Movie World in Buena Park. Andy Griffith and Susan St. James were listed as celebrity auctioneers. The museum (closed in the 1980s) featured an eclectic collection of movie memorabilia and "Cars of the Stars," including the original Batmobile and Munster Koach designed by George Barris.

Having never heard of a collector car auction, Clive was intrigued, and he and Barbara drove to Buena Park. Clive was content to watch the action until a bright red 1926 Hispano-Suiza rolled out on the stage. "That Hispano-Suiza took me back to when I was a kid," Clive says. "We had just moved to Alhambra. I was sitting on the curb in front of our house when this immense automobile swept past. In my neighborhood, everybody drove Fords, Plymouths, or Chevys. Not only did that amazing car seem to go on forever, there was no top over the front and a guy wearing a uniform and a hat was driving out in the open. Years later, I found out it was a town car."

"At some point in their life," Clive says, "just about everybody has been touched by a car. The town car I saw when I was a kid definitely touched me." When the bidding for the Hispano-Suiza reached $35,000, Clive, his judgment emboldened by several martinis, raised his hand. Not only did he win the vehicle with a final bid of $55,000, Clive also snared a 1921 Rolls-Royce Silver Ghost for $34,000.

After the auction ended, people were congratulating Clive on his winning bids. Little did they know he was on the verge of coming unglued. "I'm saying to myself, what the hell were you thinking, Clive? You just stuck your hand up and bought two old cars for $89,000! I was born during the Depression, a guy who always had to count pennies and had never written a check for more than $500. Then, a thunderbolt hit me: 'Clive, you can afford it!' I've always regarded the Movie World auction to be one of the pivotal points in my career - it helped me to both accept and enjoy my success."

Clive, who had not even bothered to register as a bidder, sought out Leo Gephart, the Phoenix vintage car dealer who had organized the event.

Recalling his first encounter with Clive in California, Gephart laughs. "He seemed like a nice guy, but it was obvious he was new to the car game. I had absolutely no idea who Clive Cussler was, so I sent my stepson to the bank to hammer his check. Once it cleared, I gave him the titles and he arranged to have the cars hauled back to Denver."

Clive's Arvada neighbor, Judy Morris, remembers the day the vehicles were delivered. "We didn't know what to think when those huge cars were rolled out of the truck. My husband and I always joked we wouldn't have bought our house if we knew Clive was going to open a used car business. The red car was parked in the driveway and once in a while I would see Teri and Dayna playing in the back seat."

In 1977, Clive was high bidder on a 1939 Rolls-Royce Wraith sedan at an auction in Tulsa, Oklahoma. The auction company made arrangements to ship the car to Denver, and a week later, Clive was surprised to hear Bob Esbenson's voice on the phone. When Clive was working for Mefford, Wolff & Weir, Esbenson, who owned an automobile restoration shop, provided the vintage cars Clive often used as props in his ads. After Clive was fired, the men lost contact. Esbenson had closed his restoration shop and now owned a restaurant, located a few miles from Clive's house. As a sideline, Esbenson was hauling collector cars for the auction houses and Clive's Rolls-Royce was sitting in the restaurant's parking lot, ready to be picked up.

Clive's collection was soon spilling out of his driveway. Anxious to maintain good relations with his neighbors and protect the cars from the weather, Clive rented a small warehouse and hired a young fellow to maintain the vehicles. "The kid was a genius," Clive says. "He could do anything, even made his own suits, but he had a serious problem with alcohol. I had to eventually let him go and replace him with Bob Esbenson, one of the best decisions I've ever made."

Clive and Esbenson were soon familiar faces on the vintage car auction circuit. "Bob, his wife, Moyne, and Barbara and I had a ball at the auctions," Clive says. "Bob worked as a pitman for Kruse and Barret-Jackson, which gave us a big advantage. He was wise to all the inside stuff - the real prices and reserves, the cars with mechanical problems or suspicious history and the owners with money problems or a messy divorce who had to sell their cars."

Clive laughs, "Don't get me wrong. Bob would never screw anybody he knew out of ten cents, but when he was working a deal, it was every man for himself. We always talked about writing a book about what really goes on behind the scenes at the car auctions, but the timing was never right. It would have been a real eye-opener for people who think the auctions are a genteel gathering of wealthy gentlemen and expensive automobiles."

By the spring of 1981, Clive's collection had outgrown his rented warehouse. When his search for a larger building came up empty, Clive purchased several lots in a small industrial park in Golden, Colorado and hired a contractor to build a 10,000 square-foot building. Two years later, a second 8,800 square-foot warehouse was erected next to the original structure.

39
IT'S A DUESY

One afternoon in August 1984, a young fellow hesitantly stepped into Clive's warehouse. Keith Lowden, a recent arrival from Ohio, was working as a fleet mechanic for a tree service company located in an industrial park adjacent to the warehouse. "These amazing cars were always coming in and out of that ordinary looking building," Lowden says. "My curiosity finally got the best of me, and I had to see what was going on in there."

Clive's collection had expanded to thirty-five vehicles and Lowden, who owned several collector cars of his own, was soon spending his lunch hours working with Esbenson in the warehouse. Two years later, Esbenson suggested Lowden quit his job and work full-time for him. "I had to think about it," Lowden says. "But in the end, the beauty of the collection won out."

On the evening of July 8, 1987, Clive and Barbara were

watching television when they received a phone call. "It was Moyne Esbenson," Clive remembers. "All she said was, 'Bob is dead.'" Clive found out later that Esbenson had complained earlier in the day of not feeling well and had suffered a heart attack. Esbenson's death at fifty-four was a devastating blow for Clive. "Bob was special. We were extremely close, and I've never met anybody like him, before or since." Clive delivered the eulogy at Esbenson's memorial service, an obligation he describes as, "the hardest thing I've ever had to do."

The day after Esbenson died, Lowden drove to the warehouse. "I sat down in a chair in the middle of the shop," he says. "I was really torn up. Clive and Bob had a close relationship, but I didn't know Clive that well. I was just the guy who worked on the cars and figured I'd be looking for a new job."

An hour later, Lowden was still sitting in the chair when the door opened. Clive walked in, grabbed a chair and sat down next to Lowden. "We talked for a while about Bob," Lowden says. "The auctions, the jokes, the cars, everything. Then Clive told me I was the guy he wanted to oversee the collection. He knew I was scared to death, but Clive convinced me I could do it. The way I look at it, the day Bob died, one chapter ended, and another began. I truly believe discovering Clive was my destiny."

Now attending the auctions with Clive, Lowden would often take along his wife, Coleen. "I like cars," Coleen says, "but nothing like Keith or Clive. They have always had their relationship, but Barbara was my special friend. Keith and I would stay in their home after they moved to Phoenix and she was so gracious - a great hostess and a fabulous cook. When we got bored at the auctions, the two of us would check out the vendor booths. Barbara would always offer to buy me things, but I always refused because I didn't want to ruin our friendship."

Dirk was at the Kruse auction when his father bought his first Duesenberg - a 1929 convertible sedan, with a winning bid of $472,000. Duesenberg Automobile & Motors Company's sales had dried up during the Depression, and production had ceased in 1937. Ranking among the world's most desired collectible cars, close to 600 of the approximately 1,200 Duesenbergs originally manufactured still exist. The phrase "It's a duesy" is still used to describe something important.

A master storyteller is naturally drawn to cars with a colorful history. "I don't usually look for cars in the classifieds," Clive says. "But one Sunday I came across an ad in the *Denver Post* for a 1948 Packard Custom convertible, a car I always liked. Although the guy on the phone said it hadn't run for twelve years, I decided the car was worth looking at. It was snowing, but I convinced Keith and his brother, Ron, to pick me up. They brought along a gallon of gas, several cans of starting fluid and a big battery. We were surprised to find the Packard in such great shape after sitting for twelve years, managed to get the car started and took it for a test drive."

When Clive questioned the car's owner how the vehicle ended up in his garage, he explained the Packard belonged to his deceased father who purchased the car in 1948, at a Denver dealership. He wanted a black car, but the dealership only had a yellow one in stock. As he was walking out the door, a salesman stopped him and led the way to the basement. There, covered by a large tarp, was a black 1948 Packard Custom convertible. When the salesman explained the car belonged to a notorious Denver prostitute who, unfortunately, was murdered in the car's back seat, the customer said he didn't care and drove the car home. "After hearing that story," Clive recalls, "I almost pulled a muscle reaching for my check book."

40
PARADISE VALLEY

During the four years Dirk attended Arizona State, Clive and Barbara would frequently fly to Phoenix and spend a week or two with their son. Captivated by the Valley of the Sun, they purchased a condominium in Scottsdale in 1984, the year after Dirk graduated. "It was originally intended as a retreat where we could occasionally escape from the Colorado winters," Clive says. "At first, Barbara and I would come down every couple of months. Soon, it was once a month. When we found ourselves spending every other week in Scottsdale, we decided it was time to think about buying a house."

In 1991, the Lookout Mountain house was sold. Clive and Barbara moved into a rambling Spanish-style hacienda in Paradise Valley, Arizona. Located east of Phoenix, the affluent town is home to twelve resorts, making it one of Arizona's most popular tourist destinations.

During the next four years, Clive added an office, guest house, serpentine swimming pool, and extensive landscaping, decorating the home with an eclectic collection of southwestern furniture, accessories, and art purchased in Mexico and local specialty shops and galleries.

Although they were delighted with Arizona, they missed the mountains and began a search for property on which they could build a second home. After looking at real estate in Wyoming and Montana, they checked out Telluride. Located in southwestern Colorado, the former silver mining camp is surrounded by the steep, forested peaks and cliffs of the San Juan Mountains. The combination of western history and rugged terrain have turned Telluride into an outdoor recreation mecca, attracting everybody from the rich and famous to vagabond ski bums.

A realtor drove Clive and Barbara out to see a piece of property. "It was the middle of winter," Clive says. "We had to trudge through three feet of snow, but it was worth it. The lot had a magnificent postcard view of the mountains, the perfect place to build a vacation home. We decided on the spot, this is it."

While Clive was creating his vision of southwest living in Paradise Valley, Barbara made it clear the Telluride house would be hers alone. Clive hired a local contractor to build the two-story log home. Clive laughs, "If Barbara saw me talking to the builder, she would want to know what we were talking about. I always told her we were discussing the plumbing, wiring or a structural problem." Teri describes the house as, "Colorado rustic. My mother wanted the house to be cozy, a place where our family could gather together, enjoy ourselves, and relax."

In spite of Barbara's vigilance, Clive managed to slip in one piece of Cussler creativity. After a visit to the studio of a local wood carver who fashions logs into bears, eagles, and other wildlife, Clive envisioned transforming a utilitarian support column in the living room into a totem pole. While Clive researched totem poles, the sculptor traveled to the Northwest, selected a suitable red spruce log, had it shipped to Colorado and set upon it with his chisels and rasps. Dayna remembers when the carving was installed. "It was 1993, the first Christmas our family spent at the house. Dad put out a bunch of cans filled with different color paints and an assortment of brushes. Everybody had the best time painting the totem pole."

41
THE REAL
CLIVE CUSSLER

Although he was producing a string of bestsellers - between 1984 and 1992, Simon & Schuster published five Dirk Pitt adventures: *Deep Six*, *Cyclops*, *Treasure*, *Dragon*, and *Sahara* - Clive was becoming disenchanted with his publisher. After turning in the manuscript for his next book, *Inca Gold*, Clive contacted Paul McCarthy, a senior editor at Pocket Books. McCarthy, whose responsibilities included publishing Clive's paperbacks, remembers the call. "Clive told me, 'Simon & Schuster is not publishing my books, they're simply printing them. I need a real editor to work on I*nca Gold*. How about you?'"

Initially thinking Clive might simply be blowing off steam, McCarthy soon realized he had a legitimate reason for being angry. "For the record," McCarthy says, "Michael Korda was Clive's editor. In all honesty, Korda was doing little, if any actual editing of Clive's manuscripts. S&S saw Clive as a bestselling, money-making machine. Millions of Clive's fans are out there, breathlessly waiting for the next Dirk Pitt novel. They will buy anything with Clive Cussler's name on the cover so it would be silly to spend time and energy on a sure thing. This has never been the way Clive operates. I ran Clive's idea past my boss, who thought it was an excellent idea."

Clive and McCarthy's relationship dated back to the days when McCarthy had worked at Doubleday Dell. "I sent Clive a manuscript and asked him for a quote. He immediately responded, and I know his blurb on the book's cover boosted sales significantly. Editing his hardcover books was a wonderful extenuation of both our friendship and professional relationship."

McCarthy continues, "Clive is the perfect author to work with. He doesn't let his ego get in the way of his writing. Even though his work never requires a great deal of editing, he demands the final manuscript has to be the best possible product. Clive and I both know his books were better after we got done with them."

Clive, in Denver, and McCarthy, in New York, began working on *Inca Gold* in the fall of 1993. "This was before the internet," McCarthy explains. "We talked on the phone and used snail mail." During one of their conversations, McCarthy asked Clive how long it had been since he visited New York. When Clive told him it had been some time, McCarthy was shocked. "Here's this guy," McCarthy says, "making S&S millions, and they won't even bring him to New York."

McCarthy arranged to have Clive and Barbara flown to New York and put them up at a five-star hotel. He personally escorted them on a whirlwind tour of the city, and he scheduled meetings with Simon & Schuster's sales, promotional, and production departments. "I wanted the employees to meet the real Clive Cussler," McCarthy says. "The man behind the name and photograph on the cover of all those bestsellers. It was also important to show Clive how much we appreciated him and what he meant to the company."

Published in May of 1994, *Inca Gold* spent fourteen weeks on the *Times* list, at one point reaching number two. After three months of negotiations, Peter Lampack and Simon & Schuster agreed to a record-breaking $14 million deal for Clive's next two books. HarperCollins, Clive's British publisher, offered $17.5 million, but Clive and his agent, discounting the value of the overseas rights, decided the difference between the bids would not warrant ending their relationship with Simon & Schuster.

42
THE HAND ROUTINE

Inca Gold features the same blending of fact and fiction that has made Clive's books so popular. While Pitt battles a gang of smugglers who deal in stolen antiquities, the plot references Pre-Columbian civilizations, ancient legends, Sir Francis Drake, Spanish galleons, Francisco Pizarro, Elizabeth I, and an uncharted underground river flowing beneath a Mexican desert.

Clive's fascination with historical artifacts began during the evenings he spent reading at the Alhambra library while his parents were grocery shopping. "Lafitte, Henry Morgan, Black Beard, and Captain Kid," Clive says. "I read everything I could get my hands on. Pirates, sailing ships, cryptic maps leading to buried treasure, you can't beat that! I dreamed of going to a desert island and trying to find a chest full of gold coins."

Clive's imagination was further energized during his excursions with Dick Klein in the Southern California deserts, and later, by the extensive research required when writing *Raise the Titanic!* Now, a bestselling author, Clive had the resources to turn his childhood fantasy into reality. "Threading the needle through investigation and study is my true love," Clive says. "I've often said that if my wife threw me out of the house, I'd take a cot and sleeping bag and move into the basement of a library. Nothing can match the intrigue and rapture of knowing you have pinpointed the location of the lost artifact and thus found the answer to a mystery thought unsolvable through the dust of centuries."

In 1977, Clive read *Diving for Treasure* by Peter Throckmorton, recognized as "the father of marine archeology." In his book, Throckmorton included a brief reference to English "wreck hunter" Sidney Wignall's claim he had discovered what was almost certainly the sunken remains of the USS *Bonhomme Richard*, a ship commanded by John Paul Jones during the Revolutionary War.

"When I heard Wignall was barnstorming around the United States trying to raise money to finance an expedition to search for the *Bonhomme Richard*," Clive says, "I had my British publishers track him down."

After several meetings, the two men hammered out an agreement. Wignall would share his data and organize the search, and Clive would provide the $60,000 needed to fund the expedition.

Clive soon discovered the wreck hunter's credentials might be reliable, but his organizational skills were abysmal. "Wignall chartered a decrepit World War II British minesweeper to serve as the expedition's survey craft," Clive recalls. "She was called the *Keltic Lord*, but certainly didn't look like one. The British crew were decent fellows, but operated in slow motion. No wreck had even been identified yet, but Wignall had two tons of diving equipment loaded aboard, including a decompression tank."

During August of 1978, the team gathered in Bridlington, a seaside resort on the North Sea located a few miles south of Flamborough Head. In addition to Clive's family - Barbara, Dirk, Dayna, Teri and her husband, Robert Toft - a trio of underwater search experts had been recruited for the expedition. Marty Klein owns Klein Associates, a leading company in the development and application of side scan sonar. Garry Kozak, an employee of Klein's, was responsible for the operation of the sonar. Retired U.S. Air Force test pilot, Walter Schob, who had helped recover Henry VIII's flagship, the *Mary Rose*, volunteered to dive on the wreck if they found the *Bonhomme Richard*.

Plagued by poor weather, assorted mishaps, and bad luck, the search quickly turned into a fiasco. Clive's frustration came to a head one morning when the dingy transporting the team members staying on shore came alongside the *Keltic Lord*. A crew member helped everybody aboard. Everybody, except Clive. "I was left ignored and forgotten on the leaky ferryboat in a rainstorm in a four-foot sea clutching a briefcase containing my research material, charts of the search area, assorted camera equipment, and a sack of cookies pressed on me by my wife."

After struggling over the railing, Clive arrived in the galley, soaking wet, only to discover all hands enjoying a hot cup of coffee. Adding to Clive's displeasure, no one gave him so much as a glance. "It was then I introduced my hand routine," Clive says, "a move that has proved beneficial over the years in dealing with mutinous boat crews and dive teams. Raising my right hand in the air, I told them no matter what happened, a typhoon, tidal wave, fire, we strike an iceberg, or we're torpedoed by the crew of a U-boat who forgot to surrender, you save this hand. One of the crew grabbed the bait. 'What's so special about your hand?' I looked him right in the eye and said, 'Because this is the hand that writes the checks.'

The point was made, and from then on, I received the proper respect due my wallet."

"That first expedition," Clive concedes, "was an unqualified disaster." Wignall's *Bonhomme Richard* turned out to be a freighter sunk by a German submarine during World War I, and when the bills were calculated, Clive's tab had ballooned to $80,000. A diver brought up a copper faucet salvaged from the freighter's sink, one of the few artifacts Clive displays in his office. "You don't find that many $80,000 bathroom faucets."

Tragically, six months later, the *Keltic Lord*, with all hands, vanished without a trace in the North Sea during a raging winter storm.

43
HUMBLE HERBERT I AIN'T

Bowed, but not beaten, Clive made the decision to return to England during the summer of 1979, and resume the search for the *Bonhomme Richard*. While making preparations for the expedition, he contacted attorney Wayne Gronquist. A longtime environmental activist and preservationist, Gronquist, whose office was in Austin, Texas, had met Clive during his first expedition to find the *Richard*. Concerned Wignall might have outstanding liabilities from previous searches, Gronquist suggested Clive create a new entity and incorporate his search activities as a nonprofit foundation.

"Wayne," Dirk Cussler says, "was the individual truly responsible for NUMA. He was an extremely nice, decent man of high integrity, with a great love of Texas history. Wayne's exuberant sense of optimism would at times wear on Clive, but he always tried to do the best job possible."

George Cofer, executive director of Austin's Hill Country Conservancy, recalls searching for lost cannons from the 1836 battle at the Alamo. "Wayne Cronquist and Clive Cussler were convinced they could find the Alamo cannons. When the San Antonio River was lowered for repairs, Wayne would organize a search, and we'd go out in the middle of the river, up to our knees in mud. We didn't find cannons, but we did find a few Saturday night specials."

The foundation's original trustees included Gronquist, who was named president; Peter Throckmorton; Dr. Don Walsh, a former naval officer who, along with Jacques Piccard, holds the record for the deepest dive in the bathyscaphe *Trieste* to 35,798 feet in the Marianas Trench; Admiral Bill Thompson, the navy's chief of information, 1971-75; and legendary educator and scientist, Dr. Harold "Doc" Edgerton, founder and president of the United States Navy Memorial Foundation.

When it came time to name the entity, the trustees, obviously taking into consideration who was footing the bill, suggested The Clive Cussler Foundation. "Humble Herbert I ain't," Clive says, "but my ego isn't quite that monstrous. I nixed the idea." Their second choice, the National Underwater & Marine Agency (NUMA), won out, and the fictional NUMA, first appearing in *Pacific Vortex*, became the real NUMA, an organization "dedicated to preserving American marine heritage by locating and identifying lost ships of historic significance before they are gone forever."

NUMA's primary mission is discovery, not salvage. After a wreck is discovered, NUMA relinquishes all claims, trusting federal, state, or local governments, corporations, universities or historical organizations to raise the wreck or retrieve important artifacts. Clive is extremely proud of the organization's record. "No member of NUMA has ever taken an artifact home from the historic wrecks. And items brought up from a wreck are turned over to the jurisdiction where it was found."

In one example, artifacts including fittings, apothecary vessels, clay pipes, cannon fuses, and a ship's bell were recovered from the wrecks of the Confederate raider *Florida* and the Union frigate *Cumberland*. NUMA entrusted them to the experts at the College of William and Mary for preservation, and the restored artifacts are now on display at the Hampton Roads Naval Museum in Norfolk, Virginia.

From the disappointing first expedition to locate the *Bonhomme Richard*, Clive had made contacts with many of the most respected individuals involved with underwater archeology. So he chose Eric Berryman, a marine historian, author, and former navy commander to organize the second expedition in 1979. The search flagship, *Arvor III*, was a major improvement over the ill-fated *Keltic Lord*. "She was a solid and comfortable boat," Clive says, "under the command of Scot Jimmy Flett, a finer man I've never met. Our crew included Peter Throckmorton and Bill Shea, a magnetometer expert who worked at Brandeis University for many years in the school's video department."

Although the second expedition managed to cover more than ten times the area at half the cost of the first effort, the *Bonhomme Richard* once again refused to be found.

44
HUNTING THE HUNLEY

After two unsuccessful expeditions in the North Sea, Clive decided NUMA should concentrate on a search closer to home. The riddle surrounding the Confederate submarine *H.L. Hunley* was a natural fit for Clive - a Civil War buff with an affinity for shipwrecks. "The more I read about the *Hunley*, the more I was hooked. Here was a mystery with a thousand clues but no conclusive leads."

During the Civil War, Union General Winfield Scott proposed a naval blockade surrounding the Confederate States to prevent them from receiving or shipping trade goods, supplies, and arms. The blockade was so effective - cotton exports were reduced by more than 95 percent - a wealthy southern businessman, Horace Lawson Hunley, financed the construction of a submarine. The "fish boat," fabricated from an iron boiler, was forty-feet long and forty-two inches in diameter. Fitted with two conning towers, dive planes and a pair of crude snorkels, the *H.L. Hunley* carried a crew of eight. The captain, standing with his head in the forward conning tower, steered and navigated. Seven men, sitting on a wooden bench, turned a crank connected to the submarine's propeller shaft.

Operating from a dock in Charleston Harbor, the boat proved more dangerous to its crews than the enemy - thirteen men died in training accidents, including the sub's patron, Horace Hunley. General P.G.T. Beauregard, commander of the Confederate forces at Charleston, considered duty aboard the sub so perilous he wanted it scrapped, but the South was desperate.

Under the command of Lieutenant George E. Dixon, the *H.L. Hunley* sailed into combat on February 17, 1864, and managed to embed a charge in the hull of the USS *Housatonic*, a 200-foot steam and sail-powered sloop with a crew of 155. Reversing direction, the charge was detonated, sinking the Union ship and killing five of her crew. Although there were reports that a pre-arranged lantern signal was displayed by the *Hunley*, the submarine vanished.

The search for the *Hunley* began even before the war ended and there were countless tales of sightings, often embellished with "Nine Skeletons at the Wheel." In the 1870s, showman P.T. Barnum offered $100,000 to anyone who could find the *Hunley*. As the years passed, the submarine was forgotten until the celebration of the centennial of the War Between the States. The chronicle of the *Hunley* and her brave crew was told in books, magazines, and on television. A group of students from a Charleston technical school presented the Charleston Museum with a full-size replica of the *Hunley*, based on the limited reference available at the time.

NUMA's first expedition to find the *Hunley* set sail during the summer of 1980. The crew included old hands: Doc Edgerton, Peter Throckmorton, Bill Shea, Dirk Cussler, Walt Schob,

Wayne Gronquist, and Admiral Bill Thompson. Also aboard: diver Dana Larson, archaeologist Dan Koski-Karell, psychic Karen Getsla, and an assortment of wives and girlfriends.

"Our first search for the *Hunley*," Clive says, "was in many ways as botched as the original search for the *Bonhomme Richard*. We were headquartered in a rundown motel, the search boat was a scow, and our crew was much too large. It turned into more of a vacation than a serious search, and I wasn't really surprised when we didn't find the *Hunley*. I've always affectionately recalled this expectation as the Great Trauma of '80."

A year later, Clive and NUMA were back in Charleston. "Walt Schob found a big, comfortable house on the beach at Isle of Palms," Clive says. "I chartered a dependable vessel owned by Harold Stauber, a guy who knew the waters around Charleston like his own living room." During the previous summer's follies, the team had managed to eliminate a two-mile long grid close to the shore. NUMA was now going to concentrate its search near the area where the *Housatonic* was attacked.

Joining the team for the first time were Ralph Wilbanks and Rodney Warren, two underwater archaeologists connected with the South Carolina Institute of Archaeology and Anthropology (SCIAA). Run by the University of South Carolina, the SCIAA regulates and issues the permits required for anyone looking to search for treasure or artifacts in South Carolina waters.

"Unlike the previous year," Clive says. "The equipment ticked away without missing a beat, the weather cooperated with smooth seas, and the only injuries were sunburn, seasickness, and hangovers. Although we did not find the *Hunley*, we discovered five Confederate blockade runners and three Union ironclads." During a post-search interview, Clive announced, "We don't know where the *Hunley* is, but we know where it ain't."

NUMA would not return to Charleston until 1994. "I can't really explain why," Clive says. "Perhaps I'd developed a mental block or just wasn't in the mood." During the ensuing thirteen years, NUMA roamed the world searching for wrecks in other waters. The party atmosphere and fun-loving throngs of the early expeditions were replaced with a tight-knit group of professionals and dedicated amateurs. Successful surveys included the discovery of the *Lexington*, a steamboat that burned and sank in Long Island Sound in 1840, with the loss of 151 lives, and the *Zavala*, one of the small fleet belonging to the Republic of Texas navy. Run aground at Galveston Bay in 1842, the remains of the *Zavala* were discovered buried twelve feet under a parking lot.

The *Leopoldville*, a Belgian liner converted into a troop transport during World War II, was torpedoed by a German U-boat on Christmas Eve 1944. More than 800 American GIs perished when the ship went down. NUMA found the Leopoldville in 160 feet of water off the port city of Cherbourg, France.

Not all of NUMA's searches involve shipwrecks. On April 3, 1933, the USS *Akron*, a 758-foot long rigid airship of the U.S. Navy plunged into the frigid waters of the Atlantic. Only three members of the seventy-six man crew survived. In 1986, NUMA located the "ship of the air's" galley stove and twisted beams in a 700-foot debris field twenty-seven miles off Beach Haven, New Jersey.

45
FISH BOAT FOUND

Still determined to discover the fate of the *Hunley* and her crew, NUMA returned to Charleston after a thirty-year hiatus. When Clive called the SCIAA to arrange for the necessary permits, he was put in touch with Mark Newell, an Englishman, who had spent ten years attempting to put together a non-profit organization to search for the *Hunley*. Motivated by the opportunity to tap into NUMA's research gathered during the past expeditions, as well as Clive's deep pockets, Newell suggested NUMA and SCIAA should form a joint venture. "Old softie that I am," Clive says. "I agreed. Not a wise move on my part as it turned out."

NUMA'S crew, aboard Ralph Wilbanks's boat, a twenty-five foot Parker named *Diversity*, would tow the detection gear, which Wes Hall was responsible for monitoring. When the NUMA crew detected a promising site, they would mark it with a buoy before moving on. Following behind in another boat, the SCIAA divers would go over the side and check it out.

The two boats left the dock on August 6, and it quickly became obvious they were headed for rough water. Newell had replaced Wilbanks at SCIAA, and there was no love lost between the two men. Newell thought Clive and Wilbanks had their own agenda and were not sharing everything they had compiled from their previous expeditions. With one exception, Newell's divers were amateurs who had no business poking around Charleston Harbor's dangerous waters. In addition to losing equipment, the SCIAA team had difficulty finding the buoys set by Wilbanks and Hall.

Prone to jumping to conclusions, Newell would proclaim every anomaly had the same dimensions and configuration as *Hunley*. Clive laughs, "One target he was particularly enamored of turned out to be an old steam engine." When Harry Pecorelli III, the only experienced diver on Newell's boat, ended up saving a divers' life, the SCIAA's dive-safety officer pulled the plug on the operation before somebody got killed. Newell, insisting they were close to discovering the sub, tried to convince Clive to extend the search, but the NUMA team wanted nothing more to do with him or SCIAA.

On the flight back to Arizona, Clive mulled over the events of the few weeks. His unfortunate decision to partner with SCIAA had turned another expedition into a fiasco. All he had to show for three years of frustration was a pile of charts documenting the fruitless hours combing the waters of Charleston Harbor and bills totaling $130,000.

Before he left Charleston, Clive persuaded Wilbanks and Hall to continue the search in their free time. "Ralph and Wes went out in rain or shine," Clive states. "They searched the grids I faxed them through the fall and winter of '94 and into the spring of '95. Those two guys wouldn't quit."

Sequestered in his Paradise Valley office, Clive might have been optimistic, but his team of sea-hunters - towing their electronic gear through miles of ocean with nothing to show - were becoming discouraged. Wilbanks remembers thinking, "The search for the *Hunley* was beginning to look like an expensive waste of time. Wes and I were starting to feel guilty about the bills we were sending Clive."

On May 3, 1995, Wilbanks and Hall were exploring some targets discovered the year before. Wilbanks was determined to investigate each target and find out once and for all if it was, or was not, the *Hunley*. Also on board was Harry Pecorelli, the man who saved the SCIAA diver. He had been enlisted as an extra hand to perform the actual probing of the seabed. Hard work, but Pecorelli was excited by the opportunity to spend the day with pros like Wilbanks and Hall.

When they reached a location known as Target 1, 1,000 feet from where the *Hunley* sank the *Housatonic*, Pecorelli went over the side in twenty-seven feet of water. Choosing a center point, he began to probe the sand, moving in a circle around the point. A few minutes later, he hit something, returned to the surface, grabbed the sand dredge and was soon back on the bottom, enveloped in a cloud of blinding silt. After clearing a three-foot wide hole, Pecorelli groped blindly in the opening and his hand brushed against something he described as "corroded but fairly smooth . . . in much too good a condition to have been down there a century." Back in the boat, Pecorelli told Wilbanks, "I don't know what it is, but it's not the *Hunley*."

Unwilling to move until he knew exactly what Pecorelli had uncovered, Wilbanks ordered Hall and Pecorelli to go down and take another look. As the duo began to extend the hole, a shape appeared in the murk. Hall thought "it looked like an iron pipe with a tree stump growing out of it." Blindly feeling his way around the projection, Hall came upon what he knew had to be a hinge. Kicking his way to the surface, Hall pulled the regulator out of his mouth and calmly announced, "It's the *Hunley*. That's it. That's all it can be."

Wilbanks joined Hall and Pecorelli on the bottom and, working furiously with the sand dredge, they exposed a section of a curved iron hull, covered with a thin layer of corrosion and listing forty-five degrees to starboard. In addition to the submarine's forward conning tower (Hall's "tree stump"), the *Hunley*'s breathing box (a primitive snorkel) and port side diving plane were also visible. They had seen enough. After carefully covering the wreck with sand, the three divers climbed back in the boat and Wilbanks hit the throttle. Wilbanks relationship with Clive and the ongoing search for the *Hunley* were well known around Charleston, and he did not want anybody figuring out what had just transpired.

After a celebratory steak dinner, Wilbanks called Clive, but nobody was home. The three men headed for the Charleston Museum. As they walked around the full-size facsimile of the *Hunley* displayed on the lawn, Wilbanks pointed at the hull. "That's wrong, that's wrong, and that's wrong. And we're the only people on earth who know it!"

When the phone rang in Paradise Valley, Clive remembers looking at the clock and thinking, "Who the hell is calling at six o'clock in the morning?"

It was Wilbanks. "I guess I'm going to send you my final bill."

Baffled why Wilbanks would call at the crack of dawn to quit, Clive, still half-asleep inquired, "Are you giving up?"

"No," Wilbanks declared, "we found it."

Clive recalls, "wandering around in a fog for three days before the significance of our achievement truly sank in."

To provide unequivocal documentation of their discovery, Wilbanks, Hall, and Pecorelli returned three days later and filmed the submarine's most distinguishing features with a video camera. Before he returned to the surface, Wilbanks shoved a watertight plastic box through a hole in the *Hunley*'s forward conning tower. In addition to their business cards, the box contained a laminated note Hall wrote on a piece of NUMA stationery: "Today, May 3, 1995, one-hundred thirty-one years and seventy-five days after your sinking. Veni, Vidi, Vici! Dude. Yours respectively, Clive Cussler, Chairman, National Underwater & Marine Agency."

Before they left, the men once again cloaked the hull with a mantle of sand.

46
CUSSLER GAVE GOOD QUOTE

Shipwrecks, unless they happen to contain chests filled with Spanish doubloons, seldom cause much of a stir. The *Hunley* was different. A hallowed Confederate relic, the little submarine was a tomb holding the remains of eight brave sons of the South who paid the highest price in an attempt to turn the tide of the Civil War. "Almost immediately," Clive recalls, "the vultures came to roost like gargoyles brooding over a derelict cathedral."

Since the *Hunley* was built in Mobile, the state of Alabama wanted it. South Carolina claimed ownership because the Hunley sailed into battle from the state's shore and was sunk in Charleston Harbor. The Federal Government got involved because all abandoned Confederate property falls under the jurisdiction of the General Services Administration. Adding to the mix, several descendants of sailors who were aboard the *Housatonic* when the *Hunley* sent her to the bottom filed claims for ownership of the submarine.

Things really heated up when SCIAA not only demanded NUMA turn over the wreck's coordinates, they suggested a buoy should be placed on the site, ostensibly to dissuade vandals. Clive told them to forget about it. "I wasn't going to share anything with those incompetent clowns," he growls. "A buoy was no different than a big neon sign proclaiming, THIEVES, COME ONE, COME ALL."

Clive was aware of the rumors that collectors of Civil War artifacts had offered $50,000 for the *Hunley*'s hatch cover and $100,000 for its propeller. When he refused to tell them the location of the *Hunley*, Clive was, "accused of desecrating the grave of Confederate war heroes, raping the wreck, ransoming the sovereign state of South Carolina, and scheming to carry off the *Hunley* and set it in my front yard. I didn't spend fifteen years looking for it only to have it broken up by amateurs. The *Hunley* was going to stay lost until we were reasonably assured the submarine would be recovered and preserved in a proper and scientific manner."

When Mark Newell learned of the discovery, he was incensed. Not only had NUMA found the *Hunley*, they did it without him. He would later claim his "competent research was preempted by a glory-hunting millionaire." Newell quit SCIAA, and a month after the sub was discovered, a group of his supporters announced a Cussler book burning would be held in Augusta, Georgia. When the fire department put the kibosh on the roast, Clive was disappointed. "I might have shown up to strike the first match. You can't buy publicity like that."

A press conference to officially announce the discovery of the *Hunley* was held on May 11, 1995. Standing in front of the replica of the submarine on the Charleston Museum's front yard, Clive played the underwater videotape of the wreck and answered reporters' questions about the prolonged search for the submarine and its discovery. Brian Hicks, a reporter for the *Post* and *Courier*, recalls, "The assembled media ate it up. Cussler knew what they wanted to hear and told great stories. In reporters' parlance, Cussler gave good quote."

After the press conference ended, one of the onlookers congratulated Clive on his find and then went on to remind him, and anybody else who would listen, that he had actually discovered the *Hunley*.

Edward Lee Spence grew up on Sullivan's Island, a small town located at the mouth of Charleston Harbor. By the time he was twenty-three, Spence claimed he had dived on more than fifty shipwrecks along the South Carolina coast. In 1970, a local newspaper reported he was planning to lead an expedition to find the *Hunley*. A few months later, Spence and a few friends were fishing a few miles outside of Charleston Harbor. When a trap snagged on the bottom, Spence volunteered to dive down to free it and discovered the trap was hung up on something made of iron. He would later describe, "running his fingers along its raised rivets." Back in the boat, Spence, convinced he had found the *Hunley*, lined up a channel buoy with the Sullivan Island lighthouse and drew a large X on a map.

For the next thirty years, Spence wrote letters to every agency he could think of, including the state of South Carolina, the U.S. Navy and the General Services Administration, recounting his discovery of the *Hunley*. In newspaper articles, television appearances, and lectures at Civil War conferences, Spence advertised himself as "The Man Who Found The *Hunley*." When nobody was willing to give him the official recognition he thought he deserved, Spence filed an admiralty suit in federal court in Charleston, claiming he was the sole owner of the *Hunley* under the law of salvage and the law of finds. Although the judge refused to hear the case, Spence left the courthouse claiming victory.

Over time, Spence's attempt to persuade the world he discovered the submarine became increasingly strident. In addition to writing several books, numerous magazine articles, and rambling dissertations on the internet, Spence graciously donated his "rights" to the *Hunley* to the state of South Carolina in 1995. After NUMA's discovery, Spence called Clive "a liar" saying, "Cussler uses his alleged shipwreck discoveries as a way to garner free publicity for himself and his novels." In 2001, Clive ran out of patience and filed a suit to prevent Spence from further attacks on his reputation. Spence filed a countersuit, claiming he had suffered damages anywhere from $100,000 to $309 million, but a judge ruled against him. A year later, Clive ended his lawsuit. "Being one who is by nature not litigious, I am pleased with this step toward ending the long unnecessary conflict with Mr. Lee Spence. Thought I commend Mr. Spence's perseverance, it has been proven time and again that he did not locate the H.L. *Hunley*."

Commenting on the outcome, Clive's attorney, Ric Tapp, stated, "The court has now barred Mr. Spence's claim, and the public, the *Hunley* Commission, and the National Park Service have expressly credited NUMA with the discovery of the *H.L. Hunley*."

Six months after the *Hunley* was located, a deal was worked out that satisfied everybody involved. The U.S. government would retain the title to the *Hunley*, but the submarine would have a permanent home in Charleston. The *Hunley* Commission, an agency set up by the state of South Carolina, would have the final say on how the restored craft would be displayed. Satisfied his find was finally in good hands, Clive provided the submarine's coordinates to the Naval Historical Center on November 9, 1995.

Five years later, the little sub was lifted off the bottom, secured to a barge, and towed past boatloads of cheering spectators to the Warren Lash Conservation Center.

Dirk Cussler believes, "The *Hunley* really is Clive's most important legacy. I would like to think that people will be standing before the remains of the *Hunley* centuries from now, and that at least a few of them will give a small nod to the guys who found her."

47
THE BOOK NOBODY WANTED

During the summer of 1995, shortly after Wilbanks, Hall, and Pecorelli found the *Hunley*, Clive became convinced a non-fiction book, detailing NUMA's search for shipwrecks, including the *Hunley*, would appeal not only to his existing fans but an entirely new audience intrigued by the world of underwater archeology.

Clive also knew, despite his success with the Dirk Pitt series, the book would be a tough sell. He had spent the last thirty years writing bestselling fiction, and his publisher would be extremely reluctant to let him venture into unknown territory.

His first job was to convince Peter Lampack since it would be the agent's job to sell the idea to Simon & Schuster. Clive explained he would select a group of NUMA's preeminent discoveries and tell two related stories - the history and events surrounding the ship's demise, followed by an account of the search and ultimate discovery. Although Lampack had reservations about Clive shifting gears, he thought the idea had enough merit to run it by Paul McCarthy.

"I thought it was a natural," McCarthy says. "The book would be a real-life extension of Dirk Pitt, guaranteed to attract the same audience." McCarthy shopped the idea around Simon & Schuster but ran into a brick wall. "Management didn't want to take the risk," he says. "They were concerned if the book didn't do well, it would drag down Clive's future books. To be fair, it had happened before when authors went from fiction to non-fiction, or the other way around, but I knew Clive could pull it off."

Unwilling to let a potential winner die on the corporate vine, McCarthy kept pushing, and Simon & Schuster reluctantly gave in, offering an extr)emely modest - for Clive - $50,000 advance: $35,000 earmarked for research and $15,000 for the author.

When he signed the contract, Clive was working on *Shockwave*, the thirteenth Dirk Pitt adventure. Since the Pitt book had to take precedence, Clive selected Craig Dirgo to assist him with the non-fiction book, the first time Clive collaborated with a co-writer.

The son of an Air Force officer, Craig Dirgo grew up on air bases in England and the United States. While he was attending high school in Colorado, Dirgo met Bob Esbenson's son, and Esbenson hired the boys to help maintain Clive's car collection. In 1986, Clive invited Dirgo along on NUMA's unsuccessful hunt for the Alamo's cannons in San Antonio. Three years later, he was selected as NUMA's special projects director and produced the short-lived NUMA NEWS.

Dirgo had always wanted to try his hand at writing and Clive's offer to co-author the book was a godsend. *The Sea Hunters* was published on October 7, 1996. The nine chapters, divided into two sections, are each devoted to a particular ship (or group of interrelated vessels) including the Republic of Texas Navy Ship *Zavala*, the troop transport *Leopoldville* and the *Hunley*. The first section, based on historical records, presents a fictional account documenting the events leading to the disaster that sent the doomed ship to the bottom. The second section describes NUMA's dogged, stirring, often humorous and sometimes futile search for the wreck.

In addition to the shipwrecks, one chapter documents the search for the *Lost Locomotive of Kiowa Creek*. This was the disaster that inspired *Deep Six*. Although the Kansas and Pacific Railroad attempted to recover Engine #15 almost immediately after the wreck, the search team only found the tender. It was assumed the locomotive was swept downstream and buried in quicksand. Clive and his NUMA cohorts launched an intensive search for the engine in 1989. Despite the efforts of an army of volunteers armed with shovels, metal detectors, and ground-penetrating radar, they came up empty-handed.

The mystery was solved when Clive was contacted by an employee of the Union Pacific Railroad (the Kansas Pacific was consolidated with the Union Pacific in 1880) who had access to the company's archives. The Kansas Pacific salvage crew actually found the locomotive shortly after the disaster. Lifted out of the mud in the middle of the night, the locomotive was towed to the railroad's shops in Kansas City. In the meantime, the railroad filed an insurance claim for $20,000 for the "lost" engine. Rebuilt, with a few cosmetic changes and a new number, the engine was back on the rails hauling freight. Instead of a long-lost steam engine, Clive discovered a 111-year-old insurance fraud.

Clive's belief in the book was confirmed when *The Sea Hunters* appeared on *The New York Times* hardcover non-fiction list on October 13, 1996. The paperback edition, published a year later, captured the number one spot on the *Times* paperback list on August 17, 1997, the first of Clive's books to reach that exalted position.

The book's success was also a personal coup for Paul McCarthy. "I knew the minute Peter Lampack told me what Clive had in mind that it was a solid concept," McCarthy states. "The book was no one's priority in-house but mine, but I wasn't about to give up." He continues, laughing, "In the end, Simon & Schuster's lack of faith worked to Clive's advantage. Since they were sure it was going to bomb, the advance was modest, but they agreed to pay substantially higher royalties. The deal ended up costing S&S a lot of money they wouldn't have had to spend if they had simply listened to Clive in the first place."

Clive refers to *The Sea Hunters* as, "the book nobody wanted." He is convinced it would have never been published without McCarthy's confidence and determination. "Paul believed in the book when everybody was telling him I was crazy to go off on a tangent that was certain to fail. He fought for the book, and we ended up with a winner."

On May 10, 1997, Clive, resplendent in a purple velvet robe and matching tam, stood on a podium in the shadow of New York City's Throgs Neck Bridge. He was there to address the graduating class of the State University of New York Maritime College. In lieu of a Ph.D. dissertation, the school was awarding Clive with an Honorary Doctor of Letters Degree for *The Sea Hunters*, the first time in the school's 123-year history the honorary degree was awarded.

Teri Cussler vividly recalls the event. "It was a wonderful weekend. My father and mother were originally the only ones who were going to attend the graduation, but Mom wanted to surprise him. So Dirk, Dayna, and I flew to New York. Dad looked like Mark Twain in his robe, and I was so proud of him. When he saw us in the crowd, he was caught off guard and choked up for a moment."

Clive began his address: "Admiral Brown, distinguished faculty and guests, it is indeed a rare privilege to be here today. I know that some of you out there are disappointed I don't look like Dirk Pitt. I used to. When Dirk and I started out together, we were both thirty-five, now he's pushing forty and I'm sixty-five. It just ain't fair." He went on to assure the graduates, "You are to be envied because you're going to create and work over, on and under the sea . . . It is said that if the ocean be the lifeblood of this small planet, then every breaking wave is its heartbeat. Fortunate indeed are those who are drawn to its water."

48
LET'S BREAK NEW GROUND

If Clive's sidestep into non-fiction with *The Seahunters* added a new dimension to his persona, his next undertaking would be the first step in the creation of a literary phenomenon.

Taking note of the success of Tom Clancy's co-written *Op-Center* series, Simon & Schuster approached Clive and asked him if he would be interested in a co-written Dirk Pitt spinoff series featuring a new cast of characters and Cussler's signature non-stop action. *The NUMA Files* would follow the adventures of NUMA's Special Assignments Division, a group of highly trained professionals who operate outside the realm of government oversight. Although the team would be new, some of the characters from the Pitt novels would occasionally make an appearance.

In a letter to Peter Lampack dated 8-95, Clive addressed the original premise as proposed by the publisher:

The NUMA Files concept sounds good to me. But it will need some fine tuning before it flies in my mind. The danger with plots involving a deep sea exploration vessel puts it too close to the trite and banal Sea Quest show. The idea here is to be creative, to take paths no series of books or programs have traveled before. That's why Dirk Pitt is what he is. The NUMA gang does not follow the common story lines of other authors. For better or worse, we at least stand in a class by ourselves.

I like the team aspect, especially changing the specialists who cooperate with them in each tale. As to the characters. Let's get real. Here we come on like we're casting a grade B movie. A navy seal, who is a jack-of-all trades, and the team leader. Ho hum. Better is an ex-ship's engineering officer, who became a designer and builder of deep sea vehicles.

A female Marine captain, with special underwater engineering training, and cross-trained as a pilot of every flying machine ever produced. In her late twenties no less. Naturally, she would look like Sharon Stone. Gag, retch, puke. Not believable. This character has to be a man. Also, keep the military out of the team. The natural personnel can enter via the various plot lines, along with intelligent female character, scientists, government officials, business executives, etc.

The brilliant oceanographer from Woods Hole? Here is an opportunity to be original. I suggest a husband and wife team or a couple who live together, particularly if they had a little spark and warmth between them. Here you get two for the price of one, a man, along with a woman who is bright and feminine... Let's break new ground, let's be fresh and original. I personally detest anything mundane.

Let's break new ground, let's be fresh and original. I personally detest anything mundane. Clive replaced the navy seal with Kurt Austin, the son of a wealthy marine engineer. A professional diver, Austin worked for the CIA before being recruited by NUMA. The foxy Marine aviatrix was scrapped in favor of Joe Zavala. Born in Santa Fe, Zavala graduated from the New York Maritime College. A gifted mechanic and accomplished pilot, Zavala boxed professionally to pay his way through school.

Paul and Gamay Trout met when they were attending the Scripps Institute of Oceanography. An expert diver, Gamay has a doctorate in marine biology. Paul Trout, fascinated by the mysteries of the sea since he was a child, earned his Ph.D. in ocean science.

With his characters fleshed out, Clive now needed a co-writer.

In late 1997, Paul Kemprecos was surprised when he answered the phone and heard Clive Cussler's voice. Kemprecos smiles when he recalls their conversation. "Clive explained the *NUMA Files*, a spinoff of the Dirk Pitt novels was in the works, and would I be interested in co-writing the series. I would do all the work, and he would get all the money. Hey, how could I pass up an offer like that?"

Kemprecos grew up in Brockton, Massachusetts. After graduating from Boston University's School of Journalism, he spent twenty-five years as a reporter and managing editor for two local newspapers on Cape Cod. When a reporter covering the search for a pirate ship lost during a storm in 1717 unexpectedly quit, Kemprecos took over the story. "The *Whydah* was reportedly carrying a fortune in gold when it was driven onto the shoals near Wellfleet," Kemprecos says. "During the early 1980s, three salvage outfits were going head-to-head and the competition got pretty hot at times. I thought it would make a good non-fiction book, but nobody was interested."

Although his only previous attempts at fiction were several Christmas stories for the newspaper, Kemprecos decided to use the salvage theme as a vehicle for a detective novel. His hero, private eye Aristotle "Soc" Socarides is an ex-cop, fisherman, and accomplished diver. "I used the last name of a high school English teacher," Kemprecos explains, "who passed me despite my aversion to homework." More philosophical than hard-boiled, Soc lives in a boathouse on Cape Cod with a cat named Kojak.

Kemprecos sent several chapters to an agent who sold a two-book contract to Bantam Doubleday Dell in 1986. Elated over the sale, but concerned about finding time to write, his problem was solved when the newspaper let him go. After Kemprecos turned in his first manuscript, his editor sent it to Clive who provided a favorable blurb used on the book's jacket. *Cool Blue Tomb* was published in 1991, and a year later, won the Private Eye Writers of America's Shamus Award for best first P.I. paperback novel.

Kemprecos personally sent Clive a copy of his second novel, *Neptune's Eye*. "Clive called," Kemprecos says, "and told me he usually doesn't do two blurbs - 'one to a customer.' Nobody was more surprised than I was when he wrote, 'There can be no better mystery writer in America than Paul Kemprecos.'"

When *Inca Gold* was published in June 1994, Kemprecos, who had never met Clive in person, learned he was going to be signing books at a Boston bookstore. After an eighty-mile drive and standing in line with more than 200 Cussler fans, Kemprecos finally arrived at the table where Clive was sitting, pen in hand, waiting for the next customer.

When Clive asked him what he would like inscribed, Kemprecos immediately responded, "To Paul Kemprecos, who taught me everything I know about writing." Caught off guard, Clive looked up, grinned, and wrote, "To Paul

Kemprecos, who taught me everything I know about writing and then some!"

"After he signed my book," Kemprecos says. "Clive stood up, shook my hand and told me, 'If you came all the way from Cape Cod just for me, you made my day.'"

Although four more "Soc" books were published during the next six years, Kemprecos was ready to call it quits. "My books lingered in mid-list hell," he says. "The victims of low press runs and even lower promotional budgets. After finishing *Bluefin Blues* in 1997, I told my wife, Christy, I don't think I'm going to write any more books. I was drained both creatively and financially, and considering a job that might be more lucrative - like working in a 7-11."

Kemprecos's convenience store career was put on hold after Clive called and offered him the co-writing job on *The NUMA Files*. Thrilled by the opportunity to work with Clive, Kemprecos also had serious reservations. "It was one thing to write Cape Cod regional private eye mysteries," he says. "I wasn't sure I could make the jump to a globetrotting adventure series with the expectations of a bestselling author."

Hearing nothing from Clive for several months, Kemprecos called and asked him what was going on with *The NUMA Files*. "Clive told me," Kemprecos says, "there had been some legal hold-ups because, as he put it, 'the lawyers have to justify their existence.' I'm convinced it was dragged out because Clive was making sure from the get-go he maintained tight control of the spinoffs. Tom Clancy was signing contracts for writers to simply use his name and Clive wasn't going to go that way. I told him my finances were getting pretty tight, and he said he would try to hurry things along."

A week later, Kemprecos opened his mailbox and found a letter with a check for $10,000 drawn on Clive's personal account. When Kemprecos called to thank him, Clive told him there was no reason to wait for a contract, and they should begin working on story lines. A week later, Clive sent Kemprecos another $10,000.

During their early phone discussions, Clive outlined the cast of characters. "The inclusion of the married couple, Paul and Gamay Trout," Kemprecos says, "is a typical stroke of Cussler genius. Married people talk differently, and it was fun to play around with their relationship." Clive suggested a possible plot - Atlantis is discovered at the South Pole. Kemprecos spent several weeks dutifully researching Atlantis and the South Pole, only to have Clive call and tell him he had decided to use the Atlantis legend in his next Dirk Pitt book (*Atlantis Found*, published in 1999). "I told him," Kemprecos says, "If I knew you better I'd say you were a bastard."

The lost continent was replaced with a plot revolving around Pre-Columbian contact between the old and new worlds. Kemprecos, who had considered using the sinking of the *Andrea Doria* in one of his "Soc" books, suggested the disaster might provide an exciting prologue if the Italian liner was sunk on purpose. Clive liked the idea, suggesting there might be something aboard the ship that the villains are determined to keep from getting to America.

"We went back and forth," Kemprecos says, "and came up with a priceless ancient carving that went down with the ship. Clive added another wonderful Cussler touch, stashing the carving in an armored car in the *Andrea Doria*'s hold."

After researching Pre-Columbian civilization, Kemprecos went to work, completed the first 100 pages and sent them to Clive. "He told me it was terrible," Kemprecos says, "couldn't believe it was written by the same guy who wrote the 'Soc' books. I knew I couldn't match Clive Cussler, but I was determined to write the best adventure novel Paul Kemprecos was capable of. I confessed I didn't like it either and told him I could use some guidance."

Clive suggested Kemprecos fly out to Phoenix. The two men sat down in Clive's office, and Clive was soon regaling Kemprecos with a story. "I'm sitting there," Kemprecos says, "worried sick about how I'm going to write this book, and he's off on a story. Then, somehow he got me telling a story, and another, and another. I began to see the light. Clive has always told me I'm a better writer than he is - which is flattering - but he is a consummate storyteller and has an amazing instinct for what people are interested in reading. I went home and finished the book during December of 1998."

Serpent, A Novel from the NUMA Files was published as a paperback by Pocket Books on June 5, 1999. One reviewer wrote, "I'm not even a full chapter into the book and I'm drawn." Another reported, "Cussler has taken on a co-author, which may account for a fresh poetic reach and smoothness to many of the pages here."

Die-hards were put off by what they perceived as an unnecessary deviation from Dirk Pitt. "Sorry Clive," one critic grumbled, "I like my usual hero better." A number of Clive's readers, convinced *The NUMA Files* signaled Dirk Pitt's retirement, contacted his publisher with their concerns. "One irate fan," Kemprecos recalls, "sent an email to Simon & Schuster telling them he wanted Dirk Pitt to kill Kurt Austin in the next book."

When they were totaled up, the yeas overwhelmingly outnumbered the nays and *Serpent* made its first appearance on *The New York Times* paperback bestseller list on June 20, 1999.

49
THE CUSSLER THING

"I always felt like an orphan at Simon & Schuster," Clive says "We didn't live far from Michael Korda's house in Santa Fe, but he never bothered to invite me over. His special pets, like Mary Higgins Clark and Jackie Collins, were always there."

In 1992, Simon & Schuster invited a group of their top selling authors, including Clive, to attend the American Booksellers Association trade show in Los Angeles. "Larry McMurtry had a no-holds jazzy party in Beverly Hills," Clive says. "Mary Higgins Clark was treated to champagne and caviar in Hollywood. Me? My party was at some joint called the Fire House in downtown Los Angeles. I spent the evening eating meatloaf with a bunch of bored bookstore clerks."

Downsizing, Simon & Schuster eliminated more than seventy jobs in January of 1999, including Paul McCarthy's. "I would never have left Clive," McCarthy says, "but I had no choice.

My assistant became Clive's editor, another splendid example of S&S's corporate indifference regarding what was best for Clive and his product."

Losing his trusted editor and ally, was a major blow, but the growing tension between Clive and Simon & Schuster was ratcheted up a couple notches when he turned in the manuscript for *Atlantis Found*, the fifteenth Dirk Pitt novel. After several unsuccessful attempts to set up a meeting to discuss money, Peter Lampack realized he was getting jerked around and let it be known the book was on the table. He would be willing to talk with anybody interested in making a serious offer.

Lampack was contacted by Phyliss Grann at Putnam. *New York Magazine* cited Grann as, "The undisputed queen of New York's book business." Tom Clancy's assessment of Grann - "good wife, good mother, good boss, and a dear friend." An article in *Book* magazine included Grann in a list of "Ten People Who Decide What America Reads."

Born in London, Grann attended Barnard College. After graduating, she was hired as Nelson Doubleday's secretary. In 1970, Grann joined Simon & Schuster, ultimately heading up the publisher's mass-market imprint. Six years later, Grann was hired as Putnam's editor in chief and proceeded to transform the stagnant company into a thriving $100 million operation. Richard Snyder, Simon & Schuster's former CEO, explained Grann's innovative approach to publishing. "In those days, they used to spread their authors out. Say, he'll come out every three years. Phyliss was really the first to prove that an author was like a brand - you could come out every year."

Clive was astonished when Grann flew out to see him in Phoenix. "She sat right there," he says, pointing to a chair in his office. "I told Phyliss I've been in the business for thirty years and she was the first executive from a New York publishing house to come out to Arizona to visit. She couldn't believe it."

After Grann returned to New York, she contacted Peter Lampack and offered him the same advance for *Atlantis Found* that Simon & Schuster had paid for Clive's last Dirk Pitt book, *Flood Tide*, published two years earlier. Clive and Lampack were tempted, but there was a major drawback to jumping ship: Simon & Schuster controlled Clive's backlist. After discussing their options, they were inclined to stay put, but with the offer from Grann on the table, Clive instructed Lampack to put the screws to Simon & Schuster.

Lampack finally got through to Jack Romanos, Simon & Schuster's president, but Romanos brusquely informed the agent he was having a house built in Savannah and would be overseeing the construction for a least a week. When Romanos was back in his office, he would call Lampack and they would schedule a meeting to discuss, as he put it, "the Cussler thing." When Lampack called Clive to relate his conversation with Romanos, Clive remembers thinking, "I wasn't hearing right and asked him to run it by me again." When Lampack got to "the Cussler thing," Clive abruptly cut him off. "Peter, call Phyliss Grann."

"Peter, call Phyliss Grann."On the front page of the March 15, 1999, issue of *Publishers Weekly*, an article announced, "Pitt makes a move." It went on to explain: "Bestselling thriller novelist Clive Cussler who only recently signed for a new series at Pocket Books, will publish his next two novels about his hero Dirk Pitt with Penguin Putnam, in a deal personally worked out with president Phyllis Grann. Cussler's agent, Peter Lampack . . . said, [Grann] had presented 'an extremely aggressive marketing plan' to the author, traveling out personally to discuss it with him at his Arizona home, 'and it was that, rather than the very considerable financial offer, that decided us.'"

Two months after the article appeared in *Publishers Weekly*, a cab dropped Clive off at G.P. Putnam's Sons' offices in lower Manhattan. Neil Nyren, Putnam's senior VP/publisher and editor in chief, recalls his first encounter with Clive. "He had left Simon & Schuster and we were in the process of signing him up. Phyliss Grann was still here and she selected me to be his editor." (Grann left Putnam two years after Clive arrived and served as executive editor at KnopfDoubleday until her retirement in 2011). Nyren, who joined Putnam in 1984, had previously worked at Random House, Arbor House, and Athenaeum. In addition to Clive, Nyren's inventory of powerhouse authors includes Tom Clancy, Jack Higgins, Dave Barry, W.E.B. Griffin, Mike Lupica, Frederick Forsyth, and Daniel Silva. During one memorable week, Putnam had a total of eight books on the *Times* hardcover fiction and non-fiction lists - four were edited by Nyren.

"I would never presume Clive had an agenda," Nyren says, "but shortly after we met, he related the story about Michael Korda's heavy-handed editing on one of his books. Clive wrote 'stet' on every page and sent it back to Korda. During the more than thirteen years we've worked together I've made sure Clive's books are published exactly as he wants them published."

Clive was scheduled to be in New York for three days and Michael Barson, Putnam's co-director of publicity, was given the task of finding him a place to stay. Putnam's travel agent suggested "The W," a recently opened luxury hotel in Union Square. "A limo would pick Clive up every day," Barson says. "None of us had been in the hotel until the last day when I picked him to go to lunch with a group of Putnam executives. I walked into the lobby, and it was filled with twenty-seven-year-old Euro-trash and neo-beatniks. Clive comes down and says, 'Well, Michael, as you see, I'm the only one in this building who is under thirty.'"

During lunch, somebody asked Clive how he liked the hotel. "He explained his room was in a funny corner of the building," Barson says. "There wasn't room for a big bed and he couldn't really stretch out. All eyes turned to me. I've been torturing their new bestselling author for three days. When I asked Clive why he didn't say something, I remember his answer, 'Oh, I didn't want to make any trouble.'"

50
JUST CALL ME DAD

*A*tlantis Found, the fifteenth Dirk Pitt adventure arrived in bookstores early in December 1999. "At that time we didn't always go on tour with authors," Michael Barson explains. "Putnam had a huge list, but management decided Clive's first book with Putnam was so important I should go with him."

After two days in New York and New Jersey, the duo flew to California. Three days later, they were in Colorado. "I was amazed," Barson recalls, "how many fans Clive has in Colorado." After three days in Colorado Springs and Denver, they headed for Texas and hit stores in San Antonio and Dallas. The tour, ten days in all, ended in Albuquerque.

Barson's boss, Marilyn Ducksworth, wanted to make Clive's first Putnam tour special. Having learned his drink of choice was tequila, she arranged with a New York liquor store to FedEx a different brand to each hotel along the way. "It was a grand gesture," Barson says, "but Clive was only able to take a sip because we were moving fast and getting up early. Those heavy bottles of tequila began to accumulate and guess who got to lug them from airport to airport? Clive insisted I pick out a bottle when we hit our last stop, but at that point, I never wanted to see a bottle of liquor again. That trip with Clive was one of the most enjoyable tours I have been on since joining Putnam in 1994. Seeing the way his fans greeted him at each stop really made an impression on me. It was a special launch for a very special guy."

Based on the plot Clive "borrowed back" from Paul Kemprecos, *Atlantis Found*'s prologue introduces two seemingly unrelated events – a comet slamming into North America in 7120 BCE and a nineteenth-century whaling ship discovering a 1770s merchant ship entombed in the Antarctic ice.

On hundred and fifty years later, Dirk Pitt becomes involved with the discovery of a previously unknown ancient civilization and the Fourth Empire, a gang of genetically engineered neo-Nazis planning to destabilize the ocean's current by fracturing the Ross Ice Shelf from the Antarctic mainland. After the world is ravaged by earthquakes and tidal waves, the would-be world conquerors, safe on a fleet of four super ships, will be free to create their tyrannical vision of a new world order.

Pitt and Giordino head for the South Pole but find themselves stranded with no transportation to reach the Fourth Empire's base before they unleash their nefarious scheme. With the future of the civilized world in the balance, they encounter an elderly mining engineer heading up a team that has recovered the *Snow Cruiser*, a vehicle abandoned during Admiral Byrd's third Antarctic expedition. Pitt realizes the old-timer, who tells him, "Just call me Dad," may hold the key to saving the world.

The *Snow Cruiser* is an example of Clive's knack for reaching back into history and extracting little-known technology.

Not only do these elements add interest to his novels, they also enlighten his readers. Built by the Pullman Company in 1939, the *Antarctic Snow Cruiser* (also known as *Penguin I*) was envisioned as a more efficient way to travel on the ice than conventional snow tractors. Fifty-five feet long, sixteen feet high and weighing 750,000 pounds, the vehicle carried a crew of five in accommodations resembling a modern motor home. Electricity, generated by a pair of diesel engines, powered four motors driving ten-foot diameter tires.

The *Snow Cruiser* arrived in Little America, Antarctica, in January 1940. Smooth, with no tread, the vehicle's tires provided almost no traction, and the transmission proved inadequate to the demands of the frozen landscape. Ultimately covered with timber, the *Snow Cruiser* was used as a stationary headquarters for scientists until the outbreak of World War II, when it was abandoned. In 1958, the *Snow Cruiser* was discovered buried in the snow, but later expeditions found no trace of the vehicle. Although there was speculation the Soviet Union might have hauled it off, the Antarctic ice shelf is constantly breaking off, and the *Snow Cruiser* undoubtedly rests on the bottom of the Southern Ocean.

In Cussler's story, Dad, the old miner, has his technicians cut grooves into the smooth tires with chainsaws and beef up the transmission. Pitt and Giordino convince Dad to loan them the vehicle, and they arrive in time to dole out harsh justice to the sons and daughters of the Fourth Empire.

WWWWWDad is Clive's fictional alter ego. Mimicking Alfred Hitchcock's film cameos, the appearances of an old fellow with gray hair, a gray beard, and blue-green eyes have been a familiar component in a Dirk Pitt novel since Clive first introduced himself as a character in *Dragon*. During a classic car show at a Virginia racetrack, Clive drives a 1926 Hispano-Suiza while racing Pitt, behind the wheel of a 1932 Stutz town car (Clive owns examples of both cars). As expected, Pitt manages to beat his creator by half a car length.

Clive maintains writing himself into *Dragon* was a joke, and he was certain Simon & Schuster would eliminate it. "Michael Korda," Paul McCarthy says, "probably gave the manuscript a cursory glance, if he read it at all, and Clive's deus ex machina made it into the book." The usually perceptive Pitt never recognizes the helpful gray-haired stranger, whose disguises have included a mining engineer, fisherman, yachtsman, prospector, and bartender/cook.

After *Dragon* was published, Simon & Schuster received more than 300 letters prompted by Clive turning up in his own book. "My favorite," one fan avowed, "is where the author writes himself into the story to get himself out of a corner he's written himself into. Makes me smile." Another agreed, "I always enjoy Clive Cussler's novels . . . I couldn't keep a straight face when Clive wrote himself into the novel to race Dirk Pitt." Predictably, a few readers were annoyed. One griped, "He's far too into himself for my tastes, writing himself into your own novels. Come on!"

Atlantis Found was an instant bestseller, racking up sales of 600,000 copies in six months.

A year later, on August 1, 2000, *Blue Gold*, the second collaboration between Clive and Paul Kemprecos was published as a paperback. Often referred to as *NUMA Files 2*, Kurt Austin and his team find themselves facing a tyrannical eco-extortionist plotting to control the world's fresh water supply. Clive's readers, convinced the appearance of Kemprecos and Kurt Austin was not a conspiracy devised to send Dirk Pitt into early retirement, headed for their bookstores and *Blue Gold* added another title to Clive's list of bestsellers.

A year later, Dirk Pitt returned to action in *Valhalla Rising*. The multi-layered plot - Vikings exploring North America, metallic monsters threatening shipping in the Caribbean

Sea during the 1880s, Captain Nemo, a modern Red Baron, cruise ship disasters, and murderous oil magnates and cartels - inspired one reviewer to declare: "*Valhalla Rising* is Clive Cussler's most audacious novel yet."

In the last few pages, Clive adds an unexpected twist when a set of twins show up at Pitt's door. The usually unflappable Pitt is staggered to discover Dirk Jr. and Summer are the result of his tryst with Summer Moran, daughter of the evil Delphi who menaced Pitt in *Pacific Vortex!* Pitt assumed Summer was killed in the collapse of Delphi's underwater city, but she managed to survive. Horribly disfigured, and not wanting Pitt's pity, Summer never contacted him, only revealing the identity of their father to her children shortly before her death.

After an emotional outpouring of embraces and tears, Pitt, Sr. takes Dirk, Jr. and Summer on a tour of his collection of classic automobiles and aircraft. Spotting a 1929 Duesenberg, Dirk Jr. tells his father how much he loves antique automobiles.

Now, Pitt was really touched by his newly found offspring. "Ever drive a Duesenberg?"

"Oh, no, never."

Pitt put his arm around his son and said proudly, "You will, my boy. You will."

51
THE INVISIBLE TYCOON

Attendees at the 2001 Cannes Film Festival were stunned when Howard Baldwin announced his production company, Crusader Entertainment, had acquired the motion picture rights to the action-adventure books of Clive Cussler. Clive's experience with Lew Grade and *Raise the Titanic!* had left such a bad taste in his mouth, he had turned down a succession of extremely lucrative offers to turn his books into films. Dick Klein remembers a conversation with Clive where he insisted, "They screwed up *Titanic* so bad I don't want anything more to do with those Hollywood phonies."

Clive's about-face was set in motion by a phone call Peter Lampack received from Baldwin a year before his announcement at Cannes. "Howard told me," Lampack says. "Philip Anschutz was putting his toes into the entertainment field and wanted to meet with Clive and myself."

In 2001, *Forbes* estimated Philip Anschutz's worth at more than $7 billion. Refusing interviews and maintaining a low-key lifestyle, "the invisible tycoon" made his fortune in oil, railroads, telecom, professional sports, and the entertainment industry.

When, during June 2000, Clive and Lampack were ushered into a conference room on the twenty-fourth floor of Anschutz's office tower in downtown Denver, they felt like Custer at the Little Big Horn. In addition to Anschutz and Baldwin, six of Anschutz's attorneys were seated around the table. After a few pleasantries, Anschutz got down to business, suggesting the $30 million Lampack was asking for the film rights to three Dirk Pitt books was excessive. When it became apparent the agent was not going to yield, Anschutz suggested Clive accompany him and Baldwin on a tour of his extensive collection of Western art, housed across the street in another Anschutz building. "As soon as they left," Lampack says, "it became apparent taking Cussler out of the room was simply a ploy. They wanted me alone."

The negotiations began to sour when William Immerman - an ex-Los Angeles district attorney turned entertainment lawyer - tried to modify the conditions Clive and Lampack had stipulated in their original conversations with Baldwin. "I explained," Lampack says, "probably for the thousandth time. We were not going to enter into any deal without those absolute approvals. Clive had vowed never to allow Hollywood to film his books after the *Raise the Titanic!* disaster. If there was any chance of making another picture, he wanted to exercise some control over the production."

When Clive, Anschutz, and Baldwin returned from the tour, Lampack was packing up his briefcase. "This negotiation," he declared, "is over!" Clive remembers looking at Baldwin, "I thought he was going to have a stroke." Anschutz suggested everybody calm down and keep talking. After several hours of intense wrangling, a compromise was struck: Crusader would buy the rights for *Sahara* and another unnamed Pitt book for $10 million each. In return, Clive would get "total and absolute discretion" over the first picture and consulting approval rights over subsequent films.

When the meeting ended, Clive and Anschutz shook hands. "Anschutz," Lampack recalled, "made a reference to the fact that he intended this series to be as successful, if not more so, than the James Bond series. Baldwin appeared extremely relieved."

Baldwin's interest in bringing the Dirk Pitt books to the big screen was sparked by Lowell Weicker, the one-time senator and governor of Connecticut. Weicker, a hockey fan and avid scuba diver, was introduced to the Baldwins when they had owned the Hartford Whalers. He already knew Clive from a week spent in the Hydrolab together back in 1980.

When Weicker was informed the Baldwins were headed for Hollywood, he told them, "you'd better do this movie [*Sahara*]." Ranking among the most popular of the Dirk Pitt novels, *Sahara*'s plot kicks off a week before the South surrenders. President Lincoln is captured by Confederate forces and spirited aboard the CSS *Texas*. Loaded with government files and Southern gold, the ironclad manages to break through the Union blockade but disappears in a dense fog. Shifting the action to 1931, aviatrix Kitty Mannock vanishes while flying over the Sahara Desert.

Sixty-five years later, Dirk Pitt, searching the Nile for the remains of a pharaoh's barge, rescues Dr. Eva Rojas, a scientist investigating a disease turning the natives into crazed savages. Pitt and NUMA are soon engaged in a battle with Yves Massarde, a ruthless French industrialist, assisted by a corrupt warlord, operating a bogus nuclear waste facility. In a race to save the world's oceans, Pitt figures out the connection between the fate of the Confederate ironclad and Kitty Mannock's final flight, outwits Massarde and his henchmen, and learns that Abraham Lincoln is not buried in Springfield, Illinois.

On August 29, 2001, a headline in *Newsday* announced: "Clive Cussler in Control/Bestselling Author Lands $30 Million Deal." Columnist Liz Smith reported, ". . . some say it's the most successful book-to-movie deal in Hollywood history . . . In this amazing contract with Crusader Entertainment, the author has final approval of scripts, casting and directors. *Sahara* begins shooting in the fall in Tunisia or Morocco. The lead has not been cast, but the wonderful William Macy is to play Admiral Sandecker."

Speaking to the press, Baldwin gushed, "We have forged a unique relationship with Clive, and are committed to maintaining the strength and integrity of his original vision and the amazing adventures he's created. We intend to make these movies true to his books - action adventures that will appeal to everyone in the family."

Clive's enthusiasm matched Baldwin's. "Over the years, I've been fortunate enough to have been approached by many companies looking to translate my books into movies. It's a testament to the people at Crusader and their business philosophy that we will be working together on *Sahara* and other films. They are true collaborators and have the best interests of my readers and myself in mind, which is no small feat."

52
SHE WALKS WITH THE ANGELS

While *Sahara*'s production forged ahead and his books continued to hit the bestseller lists, Clive was facing a personal crisis.

During the weekend Clive received his honorary degree from the Maritime College in 1997, Barbara had informed her family she had been diagnosed with breast cancer. "We were shattered," Teri says. "When I asked Mom why she hadn't said anything earlier, she said she didn't want to ruin Clive's wonderful moment."

At the time, Dirk recalls thinking, "My mother was the last person you would think had cancer. She was a borderline health nut, always ate well, took lots of vitamins and liked to exercise. She apparently smoked for a while in her twenties, but like Bill Clinton, always claimed she never inhaled." In the fall of 1997, Barbara underwent a double mastectomy and reconstructive surgery at the Mayo Clinic in Scottsdale. After a successful recovery, she resumed her normal activities and Dirk, along with the rest of his family, "assumed that would be the end of it."

During a routine physical in 2001, Barbara's doctor discovered several suspicious spots on her lungs. When tests suggested it might be serious, her doctors scheduled her for surgery. "My mother's illness took us completely by surprise," Dirk says. "The entire family was there when the surgeon came out to the waiting room. He told us they had removed a small section on one of her lungs and some cancerous tissue in her lymph nodes. This didn't mean anything to me, but I've often thought of the grim look on his face. He must have known then that my mother's long-term prospects were not good. Barbara sailed through chemo - quietly, without complaint - and life for our family was soon back to normal."

Teri, now separated from her husband, was living in Denver with her son and daughter and working as a teacher's assistant for the Arvada school system. Dayna moved to California when she was twenty-two and worked in Hollywood as a costume assistant. An accomplished dancer, actress, and musician (she plays the drums), Dayna was now selling real estate, performing in a local theater, and freelancing as a wardrobe consultant. Single, she shares her life with, "a wonderful boyfriend and an equally wonderful Weimaraner hound named Otto."

After working in Washington for two years, Dirk earned an MBA at Berkeley. In 1987, he moved to Phoenix and was hired by Motorola as a financial analyst for the Iridium program.

Iridium turned out to be an expensive disaster for Motorola, but a boon for Dirk. In 1998, Kerry Kennedy was hired as a program planner. A native of Los Alamos, New Mexico, Kerry graduated with an MBA from the College of Santa Fe. "We met during a training class," Dirk recalls. "I hit on her during a company ski club trip. For reasons I don't understand, Kerry overlooked the fact that she was a much better skier than I am."

Dirk and Kerry were married on March 16, 2002, in Scottsdale. "Clive and Barbara," Dirk says, "let us use their backyard for the reception. My mother looked beautiful and happy. After we came home from our honeymoon, I learned the doctors had found some spots on her brain shortly before the wedding. The summer and fall of 2002 would turn out to be the final fight in my mother's losing battle."

Barbara received radiation treatments and chemotherapy, but by the first week in December, her condition had worsened, and Teri and Dayna flew to Telluride to see her. "Dad had to do a mini book tour back east," Teri says, "I remember Mom looking so frail."

On Christmas Eve, the family gathered at Dirk's house. "My mother's physical condition was distressing," Dirk recalls. "She had lost a lot of weight and had trouble walking." Dayna remembers a conversation with her father while they were decorating the tree. "He told me they had called hospice for Barbara. Mom was lying on the couch, but she was not actually there. I have always been the goofy comedian of the family and that night I only managed to get one little smile out of Mom."

Assisted by Bertha Garcia, a caregiver provided by hospice, Teri and Dayna were now providing around the clock care for their mother. "We didn't even have a kitchen," Teri says. "Dad was having the kitchen remodeled and was adding an addition to the house. Everything was blocked off with tarps, and Dayna and I ended up heating prepared food in a microwave. I know Dad was doing the remodeling for Mom because he thought if the house was fixed up she wouldn't dare die. It was his way to hope for the best."

"The hospice people did a great service," Dirk ways, "but they were a bit liberal with the painkillers. We bullied them to ease back on the meds, and Mom was more lucid." He laughs, "Kerry and I needed a new dining room table. Barbara had offered to purchase one for a wedding present, but it was put on the back burner when she got sick. While I was visiting her one afternoon, she tried to climb out of bed, with a slew of IVs sticking in her arms, and take me furniture shopping. Mom was always thinking of someone else."

By mid-January, it was obvious Barbara's time was short. "The last three days," Dayna says, "were the hardest. They put her on a respirator and Teri was painting Mom's nails when she stopped breathing. I ran to get Clive, and we all fell into each other's arms. Mom had an inner, quiet beauty that she never lost, even at the end."

Dirk recalls a bright moment in those melancholy days. "Kerry was a few months pregnant and had an ultrasound scheduled for January 20th. I know Barbara was fighting hard to see her new grandchild. We brought the video over to my parent's house and my mother, alert as ever, was joking about baby names. The next morning, she left us."

Barbara Claire Cussler died on January 21, 2003, and was laid to rest in Dallas Park, a cemetery situated in Ridgway, a small town near Telluride. Surrounded by the mountain beauty she loved, Barbara's grave is marked by a pink marble stone, engraved with an inscription composed by Clive: ENDEARED TO EVERYONE SHE TOUCHED. SHE WALKS WITH THE ANGELS. The stone is also engraved with Clive's epithet: IT WAS A GREAT PARTY WHILE IT LASTED. I TRUST IT WILL CONTINUE ELSEWHERE.

Five months later, a few days shy of what would have been Barbara's seventieth birthday, Kerry and Dirk welcomed Lauren Barbara Cussler into the world. "We both marvel," Dirk says, "how much she looks like Barbara."

53
THE SON ALSO RISES

During the months following Barbara's death, Dirk recalls, "It was obvious my father was grieving deeply over my mother's death. We lived a few blocks away, and Kerry and I would have him over for dinner or haul him off to see a movie. The only time Clive appeared relatively happy was when he was holed up in his office. If my father has anything you could call therapy, it's work."

Clive's office, best described as a "man cave," is located in a separate building adjacent to the main house. Entered through an oversized set of carved doors he brought back from Mexico, the two-story sanctuary is home to Clive's imposing custom-made desk, an extensive library, assorted memorabilia, and a collection of museum-quality models and paintings commemorating many of the shipwrecks discovered by NUMA.

If taking refuge in his office was Clive's way of coping with Barbara's death, there was more than enough work to keep him occupied. In addition to the final editing of the next Dirk Pitt book, *Trojan Odyssey*, a second spinoff series was in the works.

In *Flood Tide*, published in 1997, Clive had introduced the *Oregon*, a decrepit tramp freighter whose crew helped Pitt out of a tight spot. The *Oregon*'s rusty hull, peeling paint, and decks littered with broken machinery are camouflage for a high-tech super-ship bristling with an awesome assortment of weapons, an interior combining the headquarters of a fortune 500 company with a NASA control center, and a futuristic propulsion system providing performance matching anything on the high seas.

Operating under the auspices of a mysterious organization known as "The Corporation," the *Oregon* is commanded by swashbuckler Juan Cabrillo. Assisted by his highly-trained soldier of fortune crew, Cabrillo is hired by powerful Western interests to engage and defeat the forces of evil - for a price.

Encouraged by the success of the *NUMA Files*, Putnam suggested the *Oregon Files*, a series centered on the exploits of Cabrillo and the *Oregon*. Clive agreed and selected Craig Dirgo to co-write the series. In addition to his collaboration on *The Sea Hunters*, Dirgo had co-written *Clive Cussler and Dirk Pitt Revealed*. Released in 1998, the book is a potpourri of all things having to do with Clive and his books, including a fictional "reunion" Clive spends with Dirk Pitt and his supporting players at Pitt's Washington hanger.

During December 2002, the sequel to "the book nobody wanted" was published. *The Sea Hunters II*, co-written with Dirgo, picks up where *The Sea Hunters* left off. Clive once again takes readers along on NUMA's search for the wrecks of the Mississippi steamboat *New Orleans*, the legendary "ghost" ship *Mary Celeste*, and the RMS *Carpathia*, the ship that came to the rescue of the *Titanic*'s survivors, among others. *The Sea Hunters II* was another bestseller, arriving on the *Times* list on December 22, 2002.

In addition to his working relationship with Clive, Dirgo was involved with Dirk Cussler on a writing project. After the Iridium debacle, Dirk was ready for a new career. "Growing up with a father who is a writer, you wonder if the genes have been passed along. Rather than jumping back into the corporate world, it was time to test my family's genetics." Dirk and Craig teamed up to write a series they called *Through the Eyes of History*. The first volume would highlight the pioneers of aviation: Glenn Curtiss, the Wright Brothers, Charles Lindbergh, etc. After completing several chapters, they sent them to Peter Lampack. The agent's lack of enthusiasm, coupled with the fact Dirgo was scheduled to begin work on the *Oregon Files*, put the kibosh on the project.

On a spring afternoon in 2003, Clive and Dirk were eating lunch in a Paradise Valley bistro. After listening to his son relate the frustrations of his search for a new profession, Clive suggested, "Why don't you take a shot at Dirk Pitt?" Dirk might have been caught off guard, but the idea of enlisting his son as a co-author had been percolating in Clive's mind for some time. "I was starting to feel burned out," he acknowledges. "After nineteen Dirk Pitt books, it was getting progressively harder to come up with something fresh. I have always enjoyed the research, but the actual writing is hard work. While I was writing *Trojan Odyssey*, it hit me - what at one time had been simply a chore had turned into something approaching drudgery."

While Clive wrestled with Dirk Pitt's future, his loyal readers were picking up hints Clive might be changing course. A concerned fan shared his fears on the internet. "When Kemprecos and Dirgo arrived I wondered if Clive was getting ready to retire. Also, when he introduced Dirk, Jr. and his sister, it suggested the Pitt books were being tailored for a new generation." Another reader worried, "From the tone of this book [*Valhalla Rising*] I wonder if someone else other than Clive will end up writing a series of Dirk, Jr. and Summer Pitt novels."

Dirk Pitt's maturing convinced Wayne Valero that Clive might be ready to pass the torch. "As Dirk Pitt began to age," Valero wrote, "his character naturally evolved more. He now had a wife (Pitt married long-time girlfriend Congresswoman Loren Smith at the end of *Trojan Odyssey*) and a family he never knew, notably Dirk Jr. and Summer. To some extent, the elder Pitt was beginning to suffer the aches and pains that accompany age."

One reader praised Clive's realistic approach. "Unlike James Bond, who will forever remain young, Clive has treated us fans to one simple reality: we all grow older, and so has Pitt." Another preferred fantasy. "As a man of a certain age facing the realities of getting older, I want to escape with a character who has heroic adventures, harrowing scrapes and dalliances with beautiful women, not somebody coping with the problems of an expanding waistline and reduced libido."

After the significance of his father's proposal had sunk in, Dirk concedes to a few pangs of guilt. "Let's be honest," he says. "I'm Clive Cussler's son, a relationship that has provided me with a huge advantage. Choosing me to continue the Dirk Pitt franchise is somewhat unfair when you consider the number of talented writers struggling to get published." Clive dismisses any insinuation that choosing his son as a co-writer was an act of nepotism. "During the year Dirk was going to school and later, when he was living in Washington and Phoenix, he wrote Barbara and myself wonderful letters. Those letters, along with his extensive business writing, convinced me he deserved a shot at Pitt."

It was going to take more than Dirk's letters to convince Peter

Lampack the collaboration was going to work. "I admit," Lampack says. "I had my doubts when Clive suggested Dirk could step in and co-write the Pitt books. He's a proud father and Dirk's a good kid, but there was a lot riding on what Clive was proposing." Although it would ultimately be up to Dirk to demonstrate he could write bestselling fiction, Lampack believed the success of the NUMA Files and Oregon Files would work to Dirk's advantage.

"The success of the spinoffs," Lampack says, "can be attributed to Clive's high level of quality control and his willingness to coach his co-writers until they get their bearings. I was confident Clive's readers would give Dirk a chance, but I also knew Clive would never accept anything beneath his standards, even from his son."

At Putnam, Neil Nyren also had reservations about Dirk's lack of experience, but he was confident Clive would not allow anybody, including Dirk, to put out a substandard product under his name. "Clive is very conscious of his brand," Nyren explains. "I've seen it before with his other co-writers. He's not shy about sending a manuscript back and saying this isn't good enough. If Clive is satisfied, I know I will be satisfied."

Well aware of the ramifications if the father/son collaboration failed to produce a "real" Dirk Pitt adventure, Dirk took home a draft of *Trojan Odyssey*. Although he had been reading his father's books since he was twelve, reading a Dirk Pitt novel is one thing, writing a Dirk Pitt novel is a horse of a different color. Analyzing the manuscript, Dirk strived to unlock the secret to his father's characters, pacing, and style - the critical ingredients that keep Dirk Pitt's fans coming back for more.

After dissecting the draft for several weeks, Dirk sat down with his father and they fashioned a plot wrapped around a Japanese submarine aircraft carrier sunk near the end of World War II. Resting on the bottom off the coast of northern

Washington State, the rusted sub's hull contains an intact cargo of genetically engineered smallpox virus. A fanatical South Korean industrialist, determined to reunite the two Koreas at any cost, plans to salvage the deadly biochemical weapon and unleash it on the United States. Most of the action is carried by Pitt Jr. and his sister, but in the end, Pitt senior saves the day. A missile containing the virus and aimed at Los Angeles is ready to be launched from a modified offshore oil rig. Jumping into his trusty submersible, Pitt batters the legs of the rig and the launch is foiled.

Dirk retired to a local library, and writing in longhand on a legal pad, he began his first draft. Several weeks later, he walked into Clive's office and handed him the prologue.

"When Clive called," Lampack says, "I knew he was excited. Not only had Dirk picked up on his father's style, there was little rewriting to do other than suggesting Dirk consolidate this or that - this is too long, that is too short. I was still a little skeptical, but Clive sent it on to me and I couldn't believe how good it was. I'm sure Putnam had their reservations, but they took me at my word the book would be up to par and bought it sight unseen."

On the last Tuesday in November 2004, *Black Wind* was launched at the Poisoned Pen bookstore in Scottsdale. Founded in 1989, by ex-librarian Barbara Peters, the Poisoned Pen has launched Clive's books for more than twenty years. In an age when booksellers, large and small, are disappearing at an alarming rate, the Poisoned Pen, combining clever marketing, a carefully selected inventory, and an ongoing schedule of author events not only manages to survive but prospers.

"Miles of shelves filled with books are a thing of the past," Peters explains. "Bringing authors to their audiences is the future. As the digital age progresses, people will want more human interaction between authors and their fans. Our relationship with Clive, Dirk, and Clive's other co-authors has developed into a family affair. There is always a huge crowd and the signings go on for hours. Peters smiles, "We keep Clive's personal tequila bottle on hand to help him through the evening."

Although *Black Wind*'s signing was not scheduled to begin until six o'clock, fans arrived early, and the line soon stretched down the block (the final count was more than 1,200, the largest crowd recorded at a Poisoned Pen Cussler book signing). "I don't recall feeling nervous," Dirk says, "I had attended enough of my father's signings to know what to expect. It was exciting to be part of the signings process, and it went on for at least two and a half hours. A number of my friends who worked with me at Motorola showed up, and that was fun. What impressed me the most is how genuinely nice everybody was, welcoming me aboard and treating me with the same respect they showed Clive."

Reviews for *Black Wind* were mixed, with the majority of the complaints prompted by Pitt Jr. and his sister taking center stage and Clive's enlisting his son as a co-writer. Once again, the majority voted with their credit cards, and *Black Wind* first appeared on the *Times* list December 19, 2004, at number four, remaining on the list for eight weeks.

54
A SQUEAKY WHEEL

Golden Buddha, the first book in the *Oregon Files* series, co-written by Craig Dirgo, was released as a paperback on October 7, 2003. Riding on the strength of Clive's name, *Golden Buddha* landed on the *Times* bestseller list, but the reviews were lukewarm, especially from readers who were put off by the book's interminable cast of characters. A list of thirty-four players, along with their job description, is included at the front of *Golden Buddha*. Wayne Valero notes, "Even this list is incomplete. Keith Lowden, the real-life curator for Cussler's automotive collection who appears as a character by the same name, in Chapter 44, is not included."

Publishers Weekly reported, "Readers will burn up the pages following the blazing action and daring exploits of these men and women and their amazing machines," but went on to add, "the list of characters, both good and evil, is long and sometimes confusing." Reviews ranged from apathetic to brutal: "Did Cussler even see the book before Dirgo went to the publisher? This is not Cussler"; "You can tell which part he [Clive] wrote versus Dirgo - Cussler's flows beautifully while Dirgo's is choppy and often contains odd words. The worst was 'containerized ship' - as far as I know - they're more commonly known as 'container ships'"; "I suspect that the *Golden Buddha* will be my last Cussler novel!"

A year later, *Sacred Stone*, the second book in the *Oregon Files* was published. The number of characters had ballooned to fifty-four and the reviews, with few exceptions, were even more acrimonious: "Boring, confusing and slapdash"; "The whole thing reads like a *Mission Impossible* TV episode but nowhere near as good or exciting"; "Boring as watching paint dry"; These books will never satisfy a Cussler Fan"; "This one stinks!"

While Clive was overseeing his co-writers and ever expanding publishing empire, his children were dealing with more mundane matters. "After Mom died," Dayna says, "we realized how much she did to take care of Dad's affairs. He is not the kind of guy who likes to worry about bills or deal with accountants and attorneys. My mother kept track of an extremely complicated business in her quiet, tactful way."

A few months after Barbara's death, Clive discovered a truck parked in front of his house and somebody standing on the lawn. When Clive inquired what he was doing, the intruder replied, "I'm turning off the water. Whoever lives here hasn't paid the bill." After glancing at the work order, he peered at Clive. "Cussler. Are you the guy who writes the books?" Sensing a possible reprieve, Clive flashed his signature grin, "Yes, that's me." The workman was willing to leave the water on if Clive drove straightaway to the water department and took care of his delinquent bill. After standing in line, Clive dutifully wrote a check to the Scottsdale Water Department.

To avoid further disruptions, Teri, Dayna, and Dirk divvied

up their father's business responsibilities - Dirk would supervise the actual publishing business, royalties, contracts, etc. Public relations was assigned to Dayna, while Teri would pay the bills and oversee the houses in Phoenix and Telluride. "I made sure," Teri says, "the lights were on and Dad could run the dishwasher and take a shower."

Preliminary work on the next book in the *Oregon Files* series was scheduled to begin in the spring of 2004, but the process ground to a half when Craig Dirgo announced he wanted to terminate his relationship with Clive and concentrate on his own series. Dirgo's departure provided Clive with the opportunity to enlist a co-writer who has elevated the *Oregon Files* to a new level of originality and popularity.

Jack Du Brul grew up in Colchester, Vermont, a small town near Burlington. "You probably think I'm making this up," he says. "*Raise the Titanic!* was one of the first books I read. When a new Pitt adventure came out, I'd spend the day reading it from cover to cover." Inspired by Clive, Du Brul tried his hand at a thriller during his senior year in prep school. Unhappy with his first effort, he gave it another try while attending George Washington University and submitted the manuscript to several agents. "They all turned me down," Du Brul says, "but one was nice enough to tell me I had some talent and should keep trying." After he graduated, Du Brul worked as a bartender in Florida, but, rather than carousing with his co-workers, he would write until three or four in the morning. "I made a vow to myself," Du Brul says, "If I wasn't published by the time I turned thirty, it was time to get a real job."

Moving back to Vermont in 1997, Du Brul went to work for his father, a real estate developer. He laughs, "I was the best-educated carpenter in Vermont." With time about to run out on his self-imposed deadline, Du Brul finished *Vulcan's Aide*. His protagonist, geologist and ex-CIA commando Dr. Philip Mercer, saves the world from a rampaging volcano created by the explosion of an atomic bomb. Like Clive, Du Brul is obviously gifted with an exceptional memory since the novel's plot was inspired by his fourth-grade teacher's description of a Mexican volcano's eruption in 1943.

"My Uncle Jack," Du Brul says, "is a real reader - 120, 130 books a year - so I gave him *Vulcan's Aide*. He liked the book and sent it on to Todd Murphy, a book and magazine distributor." Murphy passed it on to Bob Diforio, a literary agent with offices in Weston, Connecticut. After hearing nothing for a month, Du Brul was getting antsy and asked Murphy to call Diflorio. When Murphy informed Du Brul the agent did not like the book, Du Brul urged him to call Diforio one more time. "I wanted to find out," Du Brul says, "exactly what he didn't like so I could fix it the next time."

After talking with Diforio for a few minutes, Murphy realized the agent was not talking about *Vulcan's Aide*. The manuscript had been sent to the agent without a cover letter because Du Brul's uncle did not want the fact that the book was written by his nephew to color his opinion. After tracking down the real manuscript, Diforio promptly signed Du Brul to a contract. A month later, the book, retitled *Vulcan's Forge*, was sold to Forge Books and arrived in bookstores during January 1999.

"My father has a favorite saying," Du Brul says. "The squeaky wheel gets greased. When I was growing up, he used to drive me nuts with that line, but if I didn't ask Todd to call Bob, I might still be pounding nails."

Du Brul finished *Charon's Landing*, his second Mercer adventure, in 2000. Hoping for a blurb from Clive, he contacted Paul McCarthy at Simon & Schuster. As luck would have it, McCarthy had not only read *Vulcan's Forge*, he liked the book. A short time later, Du Brul received a note from Clive:

> Have read Charon's Landing. You're a helluva writer. You certainly turn a phrase better than I do. Your

attention to detail and your research boggles the mind. The technology you come up with is on par if not superior to Clancy. I consider it a privilege to have your work compared favorably with mine in your reviews. You're coming along at a good time and I'm honored to give a quote for Charon's Landing: "Jack Du Brul has to be the finest adventure writer on the scene today." You've got the gift, Jack . . . your big bestseller is just around the corner.

Readers agreed with Clive, and the strong sales of *Charon's Landing* allowed Du Brul to hang up his nail gun and pursue a full-time writing career.

In early summer, 2004, Du Brul was working on *Havoc*, the seventh novel in the Mercer series. One afternoon, he and his wife Debbie walked in the door just as the answering machine clicked off. After playing the message, Du Brul returned Clive's call. Hoping stories about Clive's sense of humor were correct, Du Brul explained he screened his calls, and Clive didn't make the cut. "Without missing a beat," Du Brul says. "he came back with, 'I get that a lot.' After we chatted about the Explorers Club for a few minutes - I was thinking about joining - Clive casually asked me if I would be interested in co-authoring the *Oregon Files*. I couldn't say yes fast enough!"

Peter Lampack suggested Du Brul submit an outline and two sample chapters. A month and a half later, the assignment arrived at Lampack's office, and everybody involved agreed Jack Du Brul was the man for the job. Clive suggested Du Brul fly to Phoenix so they could get to know each other and discuss possible story lines. "I stayed with Clive for two days," Du Brul recalls. "I didn't know what to expect, but he turned out to be a down-to-earth guy who is extremely easy to talk to. We're both history buffs, and the two of us spent the second night bullshitting - while we polished off a bottle of tequila."

Kick starting the *Oregon Files*, Du Brul not only cut back dramatically on the long list of characters that irritated readers of the Dirgo books, he dreamed up Juan Cabrill's remarkable "combat" leg. "Cabrillo lost his left leg," Du Brul says, "during an attack by a Chinese destroyer in the Pitt novel, *Flood Tide*. Dirgo never went anywhere with the disability, and I thought it could provide an interesting twist." Cabrillo's ultramodern titanium prosthetic leg is fitted with "tools of the trade" - wire garrote, hand cannon, knife, etc. - often helping him escape from tight situations.

Dark Watch, Clive and Du Brul's first collaboration, was published by Berkley Books on November 1, 2005. Three weeks later, the book landed on *The New York Times* paperback bestseller list. Critics of the earlier *Oregon Files* books made an abrupt one-eighty: "When two great authors come together and write a book, you know it is going to be great . . . a breathtaking novel that you can't put down"; "Jack Du Brul and Clive Cussler team up to breathe life into what appeared to be a dead-end series"; "To be perfectly honest, I could not make it through the first two *Oregon Files* books. There were too many characters and not enough plot. *Dark Watch* is a whole new ballgame."

The overwhelming verdict was in - Jack Du Brul had passed muster.

55
SAND STORM

Immediately after Clive and Crusader joined forces to turn *Sahara* into a film, the big question was - who was going to play Dirk Pitt? "Since Errol Flynn was dead," Clive says. "my first choice was Hugh Jackman, but he was signed to do *X-Men 2* and a Broadway play." Other names kicked around included Tom Cruise, Christian Bale, Owen Wilson, Heath Ledger, and Christian Slater.

The Baldwins liked Bale, but Sherry Lansing, Paramount's CEO, disagreed, declaring, "He will ruin the franchise." Lansing's preference was Matthew McConaughey, described by film critic Richard Corliss as, "A 'ladies' man,' a species of which McConaughey may be the last, best example." *Sahara*'s director, Rob Bowman, who had directed Bale and McConaughey in the post-apocalyptic action thriller, *Reign of Fire*, preferred Bale, but he turned the role down.

McConaughey, realizing the role of Dirk Pitt could lead to

a once-in-a-lifetime multi-film franchise, had been after Clive for more than seven years. "I was in Telluride," Clive says. "There was a knock on the door. It was Matthew McConaughey and his agent. He really pushed for the role. Went up the Niger River on his own to check out the territory and came to see me a couple more times in Phoenix. Not a bad guy, but a little affected. I didn't necessarily want him, but we kept him on tap. It got stupid. How about this guy? No! This guy? No! That guy? No!"

When it appeared the process was on the verge of becoming hopelessly bogged down, McConaughey, who Harold Baldwin suggested, "would crawl on his hands and knees to do this part," was hired to play Dirk Pitt.

The first script was written by Thomas Dean Donnelly and Joshua Oppenheimer, the team that worked on another Baldwin film, *A Sound of Thunder*. Suggesting only minimal corrections, Clive approved their treatment and would later acknowledge, "They came closest to the book." For reasons unknown, the producers were unhappy with the script and hired David S. Ward (*The Sting* and *The Milagro Beanfield War*) to overhaul the screenplay. Ward, whose opinion of Clive was, "insistent but not overbearing," was surprised to discover how much control the novelist wielded. "As the screenwriter, you usually have the final say. This situation was completely reversed. You were basically the hired gun."

"I approved David's script in an eye blink," Clive says. "David even came up with some stuff I wish I'd put in the book." Crusader, after paying Ward $600,000, rejected his script. On April 24, 2001, Clive received a note from Karen Baldwin. "We are thrilled to tell you that Paramount wants to put their No. 1 'polish' writer on the project. This is really exciting." Adding the polish was Jim Hart, whose credits included *Bram Stoker's Dracula* and *Hook*. "Jim is a good writer," Clive says, "but he threw in all these psychedelic scenes with whales and dolphins jumping into the sunset."

Fearing another *Raise the Titanic* was in the making, Clive attempted to save Hart's script, replacing the frisky sea creatures with new material and rewriting segments lifted from earlier drafts. He sent it to Lansing who, in September, assured Clive, "You've done a wonderful job with your polish. I think we have a real winner. Paramount LOVES the script we submitted."

Hart, working with Clive's overhaul, continued to massage the script. In early February 2002, Baldwin told Hart his latest efforts were "close to being perfect. Please know how much we appreciate everything you have done." A few weeks later, Hart was fired. "I want you [to] know that the biggest problem is the fact that Clive is insisting on another writer. I wanted to be honest with you. It is an ego thing with him. Everyone thinks you did an excellent job for us."

After Baldwin fired Hart, she called Clive. "Karen fed me this absurd story that we all thought Hart's draft was mediocre. I never told them anything of the sort. She also said Jim turned in two more scripts and I turned them down. I never saw either of them."

Josh Friedman (*The Black Dahlia* and *War of the Worlds*) was the next writer to climb on the *Sahara* merry go round. For a fee somewhere around $500,000, Friedman promised to deliver a new script by Memorial Day 2002. "This guy was supposed to be a prodigy of Spielberg," Clive says. "He not only cut several important scenes, his writing was terrible." Clive returned Friedman's script with a note scribbled on the cover page: "This dialogue is so trite it defies comment. This Josh Friedman should have his keyboard shoved up his anal canal."

Ron Bowman and Paramount were anxious to begin shooting and wanted to go with Friedman's screenplay. Bowman was unaware of Clive's creative control. "We asked the Baldwins," he said, "but they would never tell us. When the director issued an ultimatum, "Either I make this movie the way I think it needs to be or goodbye," Clive refused to sign off on Friedman's script, and it was goodbye for Bowman.

Bowman's replacement was Breck Eisner, the son of then Disney Studios' CEO, Michael Eisner. The younger Eisner had directed a series of award-winning commercials and mini-series for television but had never been involved with a big-budget feature film. "I went along with him," Clive says, "because I wanted somebody creative. When he told me he watched *Lawrence of Arabia* ten times, I thought, that's the kind of desert scenes I want. Michael Eisner called me twice to lobby for his son. He probably thought *Sahara* was going to be Breck's big break, but in the end, he didn't have it."

In a futile attempt to bring the story back closer to his book, Clive told Karen Baldwin he was going to take another shot at the script. "Clive," she informed her husband, "is now hell-bent on doing this next version himself. This is a monster and we have a problem. As we all know, Clive simply doesn't know what he is doing." The producers not only rejected Clive's latest effort, they also canned Friedman. "She [Karen] said that I was forcing her to choose between me and Clive," Friedman stated, "and in that case she would choose Clive every time." Reversing course, the Baldwin's rehired the original team of Connelly and Oppenheimer, offering them $250,000 to take another stab at the script. The idea was to cobble together Friedman's draft with Clive's latest version, but it went nowhere when Clive would have nothing to do with anything involved with Friedman's draft.

On February 4, 2003, Paramount's vice chairman, John Goldwyn, and production chief Karen Rosenfelt, met with two more writers, Douglas Cook and David Weisberg (*The Rock* and *Double Jeopardy*). "We had the understanding that this was a process in trouble," Weisberg said. "People's asses were on the line." After listening politely to their proposed ideas for a new script, Clive told them, "That's very nice, but that's not my book." Cook and Weisberg produced a screenplay, but it was rejected. "We did the work," Weisberg quipped, "they paid the dough ($550,000), then said, 'See you later.'"

While the producers battled over scripts, *Daily Variety* reported, "Steve Zahn is in negotiations to portray Al Giordino, the wisecracking sidekick to McConaughey's Dirk Pitt character." Two months later, Penelope Cruz was signed to play the role of Eva Rojas, the UN scientist Pitt rescues who helps him discover the source of the disease driving the North Africans into madness.

With a cast, but no script, the Baldwins hired writer number eight, John Richards (*Nurse Betty*). Richards also eliminated several scenes Clive considered essential, and he rejected his script. Richards tried three more times, but Clive, fed up with a process that was verging on absurdity, severed his relations with the Baldwins. "You have stroked me for the last time," he wrote. "And one more thing. I absolutely refuse to go to any more restaurants and sit with all those Tinsel town phonies."

When Philip Anschutz was informed Clive had dissociated himself from *Sahara,* he realized the franchise "destined to surpass James Bond" was in big trouble. He called Clive and asked him to meet him at the Scottsdale Airport. "Anschutz arrived in his big private jet and we went into a conference room," Clive explains, "He told me everybody involved with *Sahara* would like me to come back and give them some input. I said, 'Why do you want my input now? You never wanted it before.' He treated me like I was a piece of furniture, but I politely told him I would think about it. Phil climbed into his jet and flew off to London."

Clive called Lampack. "Peter wanted to know what Anschutz

had offered. I told him, they offered nothing, other than wanting me to show up on the set in Morocco and help promote the movie.""Screw them," Lampack said, "We're going to sue!"

"Screw them," Lampack said, "We're going to sue!"

56
BOMBS AWAY

In early January 2004, Dayna Cussler, dressed in the flying attire of a 1930s aviatrix, climbed a shaky ladder on a sound stage at Shepperton Studios in England. Reaching the top, she crawled into the mockup of a vintage airplane cockpit perched on top of a multi-axis hydraulic system. Dayna was performing the role of Kitty Mannock, the pilot who perishes after crashing in the prologue to *Sahara*.

Once Dayna was settled in the cockpit, the camera would roll while the hydraulics bounced her around to simulate an airplane in trouble. The final shot was a close up of the crash. After Dayna yelled, "Oh, my God!," the special effects team shattered the sugar glass windshield and hurled two large funnels filled with sand in her face. "The first time," Dayna says, "the sand hit me square in the eyes and had to be washed out. Thankfully, everything worked on the second take and we wrapped."

While Dayna was having sand thrown in her face, the entertainment community was stunned when they read the front page of the *Hollywood Reporter*:

> Author Cussler Sues Over Unauthorized Script . . . Bestselling author Clive Cussler sued producers Crusader Entertainment and its parent company on Thursday for allegedly altering a screenplay that Cussler had approved of one of his books. Cussler, the famed American action/adventure author who has sold more than 125 million books worldwide, wants more than $10 million in damages and an end to his relationship with Crusader, a Beverly Hills based film company owned by Denver billionaire Philip Anschutz. "Crusader materially altered the approved screenplay without Cussler's written consent, denied Cussler's express screenplay approval rights under the agreement and has begun to film a screenplay which it knows was explicitly disapproved by Cussler," according to the complaint filed in Los Angeles Superior Court by attorney Bert Fields.

"Anschutz thought I was some bush-league writer from Arizona who was going to fold up and disappear," Clive says. "Fortunately, Peter knew Bert Fields. Bert had already crossed swords with Anschutz and agreed to take the case because he thought it would be a shoo-in - Crusader had breached the contract, I wanted the rights to my second book back, it was that simple." Appearing on the television show, *Celebrity Justice*, Fields was resolute. "We intend to take the matter to trial and fully litigate it. I want to get these people in front of a jury."

Shortly after Fields announced Clive was going after Crusader, Anschutz fired back. His countersuit accused Clive of blackmailing Crusader by withholding consent over the script, inflating the numbers of Pitt books sold, slandering the movie before it opened, making derogatory remarks about blacks and Jews, and attempting to organize a fan campaign to coerce Crusader into letting him write the screenplay.

While the case wound its way through the legal system - it would be three years before Cussler v. Crusader Entertainment ended up in court - the cameras were rolling in Morocco. Bedeviled by blinding sand storms, flash floods, fierce winds, 120-degree temperatures and unscrupulous bureaucrats demanding bribes, principal photography for *Sahara* wrapped in January 2005.

A month later, Matthew McConaughey served as the Grand Marshall at the Daytona 500. After watching Jeff Gordon take the checkered flag, the actor climbed into his pickup truck - towing an Airstream trailer that had been turned into a rolling billboard - and set out on a six-week publicity tour to promote *Sahara*. According to McConaughey, the campaign was dreamed up by one of the film's executive producers. Stopping at major cities, tiny hamlets, military bases, parking lots, and trailer parks, the actor covered more than 8,600 miles. Along the way, he handed out 3,000 hats and 4,000 T-shirts.

Talking to reporters along the route, McConaughey declared, "Is it my obligation to go on the road to sell the film? No. But it's a win/win - usually." Asked about Clive's well-publicized aversion to the film, the actor tried to put on a happy face. "Please, baby [Clive]. Just come see this," he pleaded. "See what we did ... This should be a great limelight time for him 'cause this is not *Raise the Titanic*. We went off and worked hard ... I had a lot of great conversations with Clive, and then there were none."

I had a lot of great conversations with Clive, and then there were none." The producers also tried to put a positive spin on the situation. A few days before the film's release, Howard Baldwin announced, "Cussler is a terrific guy. He had somewhat of a distrust of Hollywood . . . But we developed a positive relationship and then thanks to forming our partnership with Phil Anschutz we were able to get the whole deal done."

Sahara's premier was held on April 6, 2005, at Grauman's Chinese Theatre. McConaughey made his grand entrance from his Airstream, parked in front of the theater. Breck Eisner considered having Penelope Cruz ride a camel past the photographers, but was afraid she might fall off. Instead, the actress, radiant in a backless pastel green gown, led the animal down the sand-colored carpet on a halter.

Dayna was the only member of the Cussler family invited to the premier. When Eisner was informed Dayna had sent in an RSVP, he called her the morning of the event to explain the plane crash scene had been cut from the film. "It wasn't that much of a surprise," Dayna says. "I've worked enough in the film industry to know this happens all the time. However, I found it rather peculiar he decided to break the news on the morning of the premier."

Dayna invited a friend to accompany her to the event. While they were driving down Hollywood Boulevard, Dayna began to have second thoughts. "I was curious to see how the movie came out," she says, "but I decided, because of the lawsuit, it was probably not in my Dad's best interests to show up." Spotting a young couple near the theater, she asked if they would like to see a movie. Dayna laughs, "They happened to be tourists and couldn't wait to tell their friends they were going to walk down the carpet at a Hollywood premier."

Sahara's closing credits list James V. Hart, Thomas Dean Donnelly, Joshua Oppenheimer, and John C. Richards as screenplay writers (they neglected to mention the additional six) based on Clive Cussler's novel. One week after it opened, *Sahara* was the number one rated film and went on to ultimately earn $122 million in gross box-office sales, a respectable performance until the film's production costs - $160 million (twice the original budget) - and $81 million spent on distribution are figured into the equation. After all the numbers were computed, *Sahara* lost $84 million, placing the film (as of 2016) the top ten list of all-time box office bombs behind *Cutthroat Island, The Alamo,* and *The Adventures of Pluto Nash.*

The critics were unkind. Writing in the *New York Observer*, Rex Reed declared, "Despite the vast beauty of location settings in Morocco and Spain, the vast lack of chemistry between the two stars is appalling." The *Washington Post's* Stephen Hunter stated, "a mediocrity wrapped inside a venality, toasted in a nice, fresh cliché." The Toronto Star's Peter Howel was equally unimpressed. "Unlike *Raiders of the Lost Ark*, which this movie wants so desperately to be, there's nothing here to engage the brain along with the eyeballs." Claudia Puig, *USA Today's* film critic stated, "A testosterone-drenched escapade that misses because it lacks the tension to make it a thrill ride." Roger Ebert was a tad kinder, "*Sahara* is essentially a laundry line for absurd but entertaining action sequences." Rotten Tomatoes gave the film an anemic 39 percent rating.

Moviegoers struggled to give *Sahara* a break. "I am sure Mr. Cussler feels like they threw out his baby with the bath water, but please enjoy the movie as a movie." "For the first shot as a real attempt at a Cussler book - not bad at all." "Matthew McConaughey, graduate of the Keanu Reeves school of acting is a dumbed down version of the book Dirk Pitt but he still has his moments."

Clive's readers, disappointed the movie had little resemblance to the book, were not as forgiving. "Sorry folks. Sorry Clive. *Sahara* was pretty sorry. I gave it 2 out of 5." "Steve is just not a 'swarthy' Italian, with a body 'like a fireplug.'" "I left the movie knowing that to enjoy a Clive Cussler story you must read the book." "McConaughey comes across as a shallow, slow-talking former frat-boy, or maybe ex-football jock who never lost his taste for weekend keggers." Speaking for the majority, one unhappy fan suggested, "Clive, have you considered producing a Dirk Pitt movie yourself and writing the script the way it should be done?"

57
I'LL PAINT THEM ANY COLOR I WANT

In May 2005, a routine physical exam indicated Clive was suffering from heart fibrillations. "I had been feeling a little out of sorts," he says. "Nothing serious, just tired. My doctor told me not to worry because the situation could be controlled with pills." A few days later, the phone rang, and the caller informed Clive he was scheduled for heart surgery on Thursday.

"I was completely taken by surprise," Clive recalls. "It's Monday, and this guy is talking about heart surgery on Thursday? I asked, 'Who the hell are you and what are you talking about?'" Dr. Michael Caskey, a cardiothoracic surgeon, had reviewed the results of Clive's angiogram and determined his arteries were so clogged that he required immediate quintuple bypass surgery. Clive dutifully reported to the hospital on Thursday, and the operation was a complete success. After spending four days in the hospital and recuperating for a few weeks, Clive was back at work, "With more energy than I had in quite a while."

Clive would need that energy. During the next three years, Putnam published *Treasure of Kahn*, the second Dirk Pitt novel co-written with Dirk Cussler; two books in the *Oregon Files* series, *Dark Watch* and *Skeleton Coast*, co-written with Jack Du Brul; one book in the *NUMA Files* series, *The Navigator*, co-written with Paul Kemprecos; and he officiated at the grand opening of the Clive Cussler Museum.

Friends, car clubs, and the occasional journalist were always welcome to tour Clive's car collection, but for the majority of the time, the cars resided in hushed seclusion.

"The idea for a museum," Teri Cussler says, "first came up when Dirk, Dayna, and myself were tossing around ideas for the collection's future. We all agreed something had to be done because it was sad. All of those beautiful cars were just sitting in the warehouse, and very few people had the opportunity to see them."

When the decision was made to create a museum, Teri, who lives in Denver, was elected to explore what would be required to make it happen. "I was a little scared at the thought of running a real business," Teri says, "but the museum has turned out to be an exciting and rewarding challenge."

Named the museum's director, Teri set up an office in an unused room at the warehouse and The Clive Cussler Museum welcomed its first visitors on June 13, 2005. Assisted by her daughter Amie and son Jason, Teri is delighted with the museum's growing popularity. "The numbers have gone up every year since we opened," she says. "Our visitors seem to be evenly divided between people who like cars and Clive's fans who want to see the Dirk Pitt cars."

Teri's enthusiasm is echoed by Keith Lowden. Thirty-five years after he stepped in as curator - with his brother, Ron Posey, and Wade Klein - Lowden is still looking after Clive's collection. "Turning the collection into a museum has meant more work, but it's worth it to see people's reactions." Lowden will often accompany a group of visitors and provide them with a history of the automobiles and their connection with Clive. "Keith," Teri says, "is a walking encyclopedia when it comes to anything about cars, especially the collection's history."

The Cussler Museum's 120 vehicles (at last tally) constitute one of the world's finest vintage car collections owned by one individual. With a few exceptions, the vehicles fall into three categories: foreign classics, town cars, and American luxury cars of the 1950s. The late Gordon Apker, a noted Seattle collector, concours judge, and Duesenberg authority, described Clive's collection as unique. "Clive has always been interested in the entire world of classic cars, and the collection reflects his diverse interests. This is especially true of the town cars, a group of very rare and important cars."

Teri admits feeling lukewarm about her father's cars when she was growing up. Her association with the museum has not only provided her with a new appreciation for the collection, she has several favorites - "the 1948 Talbot, the 1939 Mercedes Benz 540K, and the 1958 Buick Limited. I also have a personal connection with the 1925 Minerva town car."

Named for the Roman goddess of wisdom, Minervas were manufactured in Belgium between 1902 and 1938. Advertised as "The Car of Kings and Queens," the marquee's customers included royalty, movie stars, and captains of industry.

When Teri was planning her wedding, she asked Clive if it would be possible to use the Minerva. The event was scheduled for September 10, 1977, at the Bear Tooth Lodge in Evergreen, a mountain town located fifteen miles west of Denver. Clive explained it would be impossible to drive the vintage vehicle up I-70's steep grades. Teri was disappointed but understood her father's decision.

On the day of the ceremony, Teri and Barbara left early to

drive to Evergreen and oversee the preparations. When they were approaching Genesee, the women spotted a truck plugging along in the slow lane with smoke pouring out of the back. Clive was driving, and the Minerva was secured to the back of the truck. He had planned on getting to the lodge before everybody else, but the Minerva weighed so much, he was having a hard time negotiating the hills.

"When everybody arrived for the ceremony," Teri says, "Dad played chauffeur and Bob and I rode in the back seat for our grand entrance. The surprise my father planned might have been lost, but it was a wonderful gesture. I still cry when I think about it."

Clive's collection has received worldwide acclaim, though some purists disapprove of his preference for colorful paint jobs. The candy-colored vehicles include a mauve 1936 Avions Voisin (a tribute to Tom Swift's electric runabout?), an opulent 1932 Stutz town car dressed in vibrant aqua, a 1931 Marmon in ravishing lavender, and an extremely smart two-tone burgundy and buff L-29 Cord. Leo Gebhart is conflicted. "Some of Clive's cars are painted a little too bright for me, but you can still tell what they are, and for me, that's the point."

Clive recalls several animated arguments he had with the late Otis Chandler — *Los Angeles Times*'s publisher and well-known automobile collector. "Otis thought my paint jobs were much too garish," Clive says. "After going back and forth, I would always end the argument by telling him I didn't care what he or anybody else thinks. They are my cars, and I'll paint them any color I want."

58
VIN FIZ

Clive's decision to write a children's book originated with the bedtime stories he told his children. "After we were tucked under the covers," Dayna says. "Dad would tell us wonderful adventures about a set of twins named Winkie and Binkie whose favorite modes of transportation were a blimp and a submarine. The stories were so much fun because we never knew what he was going to come up with next."

Although he had been writing bestsellers for thirty years, Clive quickly discovered his new audience - children between six and ten - would require a new language. "It took me several months to figure out the writing style," Clive says. "I had to reconsider the elements I was comfortable with - sentence structure, vocabulary, dialogue, and plot. After I finished *The Adventures of Vin Fiz*, I asked three librarians who specialize in children's literature to read the manuscript and give me their thoughts. They were extremely helpful in pointing out words or ideas children in that age group might not understand."

Clive's inspiration for *The Adventures of Vin Fiz* was the first successful U.S. transcontinental flight. Inspired by a $50,000 prize, Calbraith "Cal" Rogers left Brooklyn on September 17, 1911. Flying a Wright biplane, Rogers, sponsored by the Armour Company to promote the company's new grape soft drink, Vin Fiz, arrived in California eighty-four days later. Although he missed the prize deadline by nineteen days - Rogers crashed sixteen times - the intrepid aviator was welcomed by a cheering crowd of 20,000. The airplane is on display today at the National Air and Space Museum in Washington, D.C. As for Vin Fiz soda, it was described as "tasting like a cross between river water and horse slop" and had a very short shelf life.

The Adventures of Vin Fiz begins on a California herb farm owned by the parents of ten-year-old twins Lacey and Casey Nicefolk. Mr. Sucoh Sucop ("hocus-pocus" spelled backward) arrives one day and offers to work for room and board. After a few months, Mr. Sucop moves on, but before he leaves, presents the twins with a magical mat that can transform a toy into the real thing. After trying the mat out on a tractor - it works - Casey turns his Wright Flyer model airplane into a full-sized aircraft the twins christen *Vin Fiz*. Accompanied by their faithful basset hound Floppy, the twins set out on a cross-country adventure. Along the way they discover the airplane is endowed with magic tricks that help them foil gold robbers, stop a runaway train, and rescue two girls about to plummet over Niagara Falls. Clive also includes a brief history of Cal Rogers and the cross-country flight of the real *Vin Fiz*.

The Adventures of Vin Fiz was published on February 21, 2006. Although several reviewers were put off by the "overly cute names" and "subtle ethnic and gender stereotyping," Kidsreads.com praised the book as, "A fun and imaginative high flying adventure . . . For an extra bonus, Cussler slips in some interesting trivia, like how a steam engine works, so readers may even learn something along the way."

In May 2010, the twins appeared again with the publication of *The Adventures of Hotsy Totsy*. Casey Nicefolk uses the magic mat to turn a model boat into a full-sized powerboat named *Hotsy Totsy*. The original *Hotsy Totsy* was a championship hydroplane that raced during the 1930s. Entering a race on the Sacramento River, the twins manage to outwit a gang of bank robbers, and aided by their faithful dog, Floopy, cross the finish line first.

59
PLEASE PASS THE SALT

In November 2005, Clive attended a charity ball at a Scottsdale hotel. Janet Horvath, a Phoenix art consultant, was supervising the event's silent auction. "At some point, a man walked in the door," Janet says. "I told my friend I would like to meet that guy. Later that evening, the ball's chairman pointed to the man I had seen earlier. 'That's Clive Cussler, the author. Would you like to meet him?' I told her to forget about that. He's famous, probably has a huge ego and wants a couple of twenty-five-year-olds."

There was no denying Clive was famous, but as far as his having a huge ego and lusting after young women, Janet could not have been further off the mark. After Barbara's death, Clive recalls feeling, "Kind of at sea. Barbara had always been there, and I realized how much I missed her. Now, I was all alone. I went out with several women. They were nice, and we had fun, but nobody I felt compatible with. Going on a date - getting dressed up and meeting a stranger who expected a famous author to be witty and charming - was actually kind of a chore. I'd go to a friend's house for dinner and inevitably be introduced to a woman they were trying to set me up with. If I was going to meet somebody I wanted to get to know and spend time with, the answer was a dating service."

Coincidentally, Janet, "tired of the bar scene and meeting people I didn't have anything in common with," signed up with the same dating service. In late July 2006, the matchmaker called Janet. She wanted to introduce her to a very successful author. "Perhaps," she asked, "you've heard of Clive Cussler?" Janet almost dropped the phone. "It had been a year since I first saw him at the charity ball," she says. "I repeated my reservations, but she finally wore me down, and I agreed to go to dinner with him."

"The service called," Clive says, "and gave me the pitch on Janet - attractive blonde, college graduate, had her own business." Two weeks later, Clive called Janet. "We ended up talking for forty-five minutes," Janet recalls. "He asked me if I would like to attend an event at the Hermosa Inn. The hotel has an artist-in-residence program, and Clive was the artist." Since the hotel was sending a car, Clive suggested Janet should drive to his house, and they would go together. "I parked the car," Janet says, "took a deep breath and knocked on the door. Clive appeared and said, 'My, you're very pretty.' It caught me off guard. The way he said it didn't come off like a line."

They had only been at the party for a few minutes when the hostess rushed over, put her arm in Clive's and told Janet, "Hope you don't mind, dear, I'm only going to borrow him for a moment." Two hours later, Clive reappeared, and the couple sat down to dinner at a table for twelve. "Everybody was firing questions at Clive," Janet says. "Except for 'please pass the salt' or 'do you take cream in your coffee,' Clive and I never said a word to each other."

On the return trip to Clive's house, he asked Janet if she had a nice time. "I told him it was interesting, but the reason I went out with him was to meet the real Clive Cussler. I wanted to spend time talking about him, his family, and his work. We got to Clive's and said good-bye. On the way home, I was thinking, that didn't go very well." A week later, Janet was surprised when Clive called, invited her out to dinner and promised he would answer any and all questions. "The restaurant," Janet says, "was so noisy we spent the evening looking at each other, but when we got back to his house the two of us ended up having a wonderful conversation until three in the morning. This time I left thinking, here is a guy who not only has both feet on the ground, he enjoys a wonderful relationship with his family."

Janet Horvath grew up in Fairfield, Connecticut. After graduating from Newton College of Sacred Heart (the school merged with Boston College in 1974), she worked in New York for several years before enrolling at the University of Bridgeport. After earning a teaching degree, Janet taught photography and art in the Fairfield school system. By 1998, she had one daughter, Whitney, and was divorced.

After her daughter started school, Janet went to work for her father who owned a plastic injection molding company in Bridgeport, Connecticut. "I had worked for him during the summer while I was going to school," Janet says, "and knew how to break down a die, rebuild it, shim up the stock - whatever had to be done." After her father died in 2000, Janet and her brother, Tom, relocated the company to Arizona. "Bridgeport was going steadily downhill," Janet explains. "Tom and I thought the move would not only make the company more profitable, we had both spent time in Arizona and fell in love with the desert. Not long after we moved to Phoenix, the writing was on the wall - the plastic industry was moving off-shore and we sold the company. I opened a consulting business, working with art galleries and interior decorators."

"A week after our second date," Janet says, "Clive sent me flowers. The card was signed, 'From your swashbuckler.' When I called to thank him, I asked him how he knew it was my birthday. He said he didn't, but suggested we go out and celebrate. It did not take me long to realize I was in over my head. Clive was not just a guy I wanted to go to dinner with, and I had to think long and hard if I wanted to get serious. I finally decided I did."

While Clive and Janet's relationship blossomed, Clive was exploring a new genre. "I always wanted to write a western," he says. "But not a conventional horse opera with gunslingers, rustlers and a whore with a golden heart." Originally called *Wild Illusions*, the novel's setting in the western U.S in the early 1900s would allow Clive to combine classic western motifs with recently developed technology - automobiles, motorcycles, semi-automatic weapons, telephones, etc. During an interview, Clive was asked about his latest project. "The book isn't going to be anywhere near a bestseller, but it will be a lot of fun."

A phone call from Bert Fields would relegate Clive's western to the back burner. Cussler v. Crusader Entertainment was finally headed for court.

60
HARDBALL

Janet and Clive flew to Los Angeles in July of 2006, only to discover the trial had been rescheduled for August - the first of four delays. "It was frustrating," Janet says. "We would fly to California, find out the trial had been postponed, turn around and fly back to Phoenix. The strain begins to wear on you. Finally, in November, the judge assured us the trial would start in January. Clive and I ended up living in the Omni Hotel until mid-May."

Jury selection began on Monday, January 29, 2007, in Judge John P. Shook's cramped courtroom in downtown Los Angeles Superior Court. Five days later, with eight women and four men seated in the jury box, the opposing attorneys presented their opening arguments. Bert Fields, assisted by Elisabeth Moriarty and Caroline Heindel Burgos, was raring to go. "It's drama," Fields says, "and you get a chance to be a director, a producer and an actor. And you have a captive audience." Warming up to the jury, he exhorted, "For weeks, you are going to hear personal stuff about Mr. Cussler. You'll hear them claim that he was difficult and cantankerous and grumpy and even rude. Hold your ears."

Fields described his client as a successful, bestselling author who, having been extremely disappointed by the film adaptation of *Raise the Titanic!*, was determined to have some degree of control over the script and casting of *Sahara*. Nobody, the attorney suggested, held a gun to Philip Anschutz's head when he agreed to what many in Hollywood considered unprecedented approval rights. In fact, it was the Baldwins and Anschutz who sought out Clive in the first place. When Crusader ignored Clive's suggestions, Fields asserted, "They tore the heart out of the story. The story died, lost all this money because they gutted it."

Anschutz was represented by Alan Rader, Marvin Putnam, William Charron, and Jessica Stebbins from the firm of O'Melveny & Myers. Listed as the world's twenty-ninth largest law firm, O'Melveny & Myers employs more than 900 lawyers in fourteen offices worldwide. First up was Rader, who told the jury Clive had intentionally torpedoed what should have been a blockbuster by capriciously rejecting scripts, publicly bad-mouthing the film, and inflating the number of books he had sold. The numbers were a major source of contention since Anschutz insisted it was Clive's highly publicized 100 million sales that convinced him to agree to the $10 million-a-book deal.

The opportunity to gawk at Hollywood stars, a steamy off-screen romance (Cruz and McConaughey), a bestselling author, a publicity-shy billionaire, and accusations of behind the scenes double-dealing and squandered millions turned the trial into a media circus. Photographers camped out in front of the courthouse and *Los Angeles Times* reporter Glenn F. Bunting provided the paper's readers with a day-by-day, blow-by-blow account, as did Janet Shprintz in *Variety*.

The internet was inundated with blogs discussing the case and anybody who had anything to do with publishing or Hollywood - real or imagined - was more than happy to share his or her opinions.

Peter Lampack was the first witness to take the stand. The agent described the meeting in June 2000, at Anschutz's Denver office tower. After Clive had agreed to drop the price from $30 million to $10 million, he testified, both Anschutz and Howard Baldwin had agreed Clive would get "total and absolute discretion" over *Sahara*'s script and cast, and a consulting role on subsequent films. Rader grilled Lampack on Clive's sales numbers. Instead of the 100 million Dirk Pitt novels Cussler, Lampack, and Putnam claimed had been sold, the figure, Rader insisted, was closer to 42 million. This glaring disparity not only "perpetrated a massive fraud" to secure an "unprecedented contractual agreement," it meant Clive's audience was much smaller than he asserted and the major reason *Sahara* bombed at the box-office.

An hour after Lampack completed his sixth day of testimony, Anschutz's lawyers filed a lawsuit against the agent, alleging Lampack intentionally inflated his client's book sales. Fields was outraged. "It is a typical Anschutz bullying tactic to try to intimidate a witness on the other side by suing him personally. It is disgusting and despicable."

On February 16, the jury, attorneys from both sides, the judge and his staff, escorted by a company of sheriff's deputies, boarded a bus in front of the court building. Their destination was a screening room at Paramount Pictures studio lot where they watched a private screening of *Sahara*. The field trip was Rader's idea. "It is important for the jury to decide whether audiences enjoyed the movie or not. The only way to do that is to see it in a real movie theater with a real projection system." Fields argued the viewing would not only put "too much emphasis" on the movie, "It's prejudicial and pandering to the jury." A wag suggested the jury was being "subjected to something that tilted toward the cruel and unusual." The *Los Angeles Times* reported, "Sadly, no popcorn will be served."

On February 21, it was Karen Baldwin's turn to testify. Called as a hostile witness by Fields, she was shown several memos, including one in which she declared $10 million was a bargain for the rights to a Clive Cussler novel. When Fields asked her to reiterate Crusader's tortured odyssey to produce a suitable script, Baldwin admitted Paramount's production chief Karen Rosenfelt deliberately misled Clive by telling him the studio "loved" his screenplay when, in fact, nobody liked it. In a 2003 e-mail introduced into evidence, Baldwin informed Clive, "Paramount is a studio notorious for distortion of the truth whenever necessary in order to avoid conflict or cast themselves in a good light."

When Anschutz's lawyers criticized Fields for attempting to "sully" Baldwin's reputation in an effort to shift the jurors' attention away from the facts of the case, Fields responded, "The real disruption to the movie was the breathtaking duplicity of Karen Baldwin telling one person one thing and another person another thing. I can't help if she has no credibility."

As the trial progressed, dozens of witnesses were called to testify. Among them were two experts who provided very different opinions of Clive's talent. Robert McKee, actor, professor, and creative writing instructor best known for his bombastic, profanity-laced Story Seminars, was brought in to testify for Anschutz's side. Asked to critique Clive's screenplay, McKee responded, "I mean, I cannot overstate how terrible the writing is. It is flawed in every way writing can be flawed." When he was informed *Sahara*, the book, was a commercial success, McKee scoffed, "Bad writing often makes a lot of money." During Fields's cross-examination, McKee described *The Da Vinci Code* as, "flawed," and characterized *Citizen Kane* as, "Heartless," "emotionally empty," and "cold."

Testifying on Clive's behalf, Lew Hunter, chairman emeritus and professor of screenwriting at the UCLA Department of Film and Television, stated changes made to the screenplay, including the elimination of a scene where a hero kills a villain, were a major mistake. "We're a justice-driven audience," he explained. "We want to see the bad guys gone." Hunter was also critical of the film's "juvenile humor" and "superficial" romantic scenes he classified as "Marina del Rey-like," not at all typical of Clive's writing.

On April 15, the attorneys from both sides were called into Judge Shook's office. They were shocked when he told them he might declare a mistrial.

61
THE $100 MILLION QUESTION

Judge Shook's threat of a mistrial was provoked by a special report appearing in the business section of the *Los Angeles Times*. Written by Glenn Bunting, the headline asked, "How do a bestselling novel, an Academy Award-winning screenwriter, a pair of Hollywood hotties and a No. 1 opening at the box office add up to $78 million of red ink?" Based on leaked confidential documents entered into evidence, Bunting provided an item by item enumeration of *Sahara*'s $160 million budget, exposing the mind-boggling money nonchalantly thrown around by Hollywood executives.

"The concern that I have," Judge Shook said, "is that the jury is going to be deciding this case on something other than the evidence that was presented during the trial." Marvin Putnam was outraged. "I'm floored that these documents could have been provided by someone, despite the fact that there is a clear agreement within the litigation ensuring that they are confidential." Before he declared a mistrial, Shook decided he would think about it. "I hate to do it," he said. "Both sides have spent so much money."

"Movie budgets," Glenn Bunting reported, "are one of the last remaining secrets in the entertainment business, typically known to only high-level executives, senior producers, and accountants." Among the items in the purloined ledger - McConaughey was paid $8 million for the twenty-four-week shoot. He also received an additional $833,923 in "star perks," including $179,262 for entourage travel, $114,000 for his assistant, and $72,800 for his hair colorist. Penelope Cruz earned $1.6 million. Her hairstylist took home a check for $135,550. Steve Zahn's $2.2 million salary was augmented with perks totaling $264,153, including two fitness trainers, first-class round-trip airfare to Morocco, business-class airfare for his wife, two children, and nanny, and coach tickets for his personal assistant. Ten screenwriters shared $3.8 million, and a total of $237,386 was doled out for "gratuities" and "local bribes." Dayna Cussler's deleted forty-six-second crash scene cost $2 million and a list of "incidentals" included $1.4 million for catered meals, $105,556 for bottled water, and $16,744 for prop skeletons.

Judge Shook decided that the *Los Angeles Times* airing of Hollywood's dirty laundry was not an adequate reason to declare a mistrial and the proceedings ground on. Thirteen weeks after the trial began, Clive was finally called to testify. Fields was able to persuade the judge to throw out testimony about Clive's alleged use of racial and anti-Semitic slurs and any reference to a cartoon Clive drew depicting Howard Baldwin planting a kiss on Sherry Lansing's derriere.

The unflattering cartoon was rendered on a copy of a 2002 news release announcing Paramount had signed a three-year deal to distribute Crusader's films. Clive had sent it to Lampack who inadvertently allowed it to fall into the hands of Anschutz's lawyers.

As he had done earlier with Lampack, Putnam clobbered Clive on his sales numbers. Anschutz had paid a litigation consulting firm, Freeman & Mills, $200,000 to examine Clive's royalty statements and sales reports from three publishing houses. Their "forensic" report suggested the 100-million number was actually half of that. When Putnam asked Clive if he pulled the 100-million figure out of thin air, Clive replied, "Pretty much." Clive also admitted Lampack had warned him in the late 1990s against mentioning the number of books he had sold since the actual amount was not known. Instead, he should talk about the number of books "in print."

Instead, he should talk about the number of books "in print." There is a big difference between books printed and books sold. Not only do publishers often hype the numbers to create interest, stores can return unsold copies to the publisher and receive full credit. When books were shipped to thousands of small stores, nobody knew how many copies were sold except the publisher and the author - and sometimes not even the author.

In 2001, Nielsen BookScan was launched, a service that tracks and reports information gathered from approximately 70 percent of the U.S. book market. Although BookScan has added a new level of accuracy, the actual number a book sells still depends on how much information publishers are willing to share. Commenting on Clive's sales numbers, Albert Greco, professor of marketing, communications, and media management at Fordham University stated, "If Anschutz was willing to pay Freeman & Mills Inc. $200,000 to investigate Clive's sales numbers, he probably should have done it before agreeing to spend $10 million for the rights to *Sahara*. If you don't do your due diligence, this is what you end up with - a lawsuit."

"When it came time for me to testify, Burt and his girls really screwed up," Clive says. "They didn't prime me. Just wanted me to play the kindly old grandpa and not come off like a curmudgeon. 'Say yes, no, or you don't remember.'" Clive insisted neither he nor Lampack had mentioned the 100-million number during their original meeting with Anschutz in Denver. Putnam's habit of constantly asking the same questions over and over exasperated Clive to the point where, at one point, he buried his head in his hands. "I did all right the first four days," Clive says, "but the last day, they kept harping on the numbers and slaughtered me. There's a photograph taken after I finished testifying and I look like I've just been mugged."

During the trial, Clive's family was a steadfast presence in the courtroom. Dayna, living in Los Angeles, attended three or four times a week. "The LA County Courthouse is old and dirty," Dayna says. "I couldn't help but feel for the poor jury who gave up three months of their life, especially with some of the nonsense that went on. I almost got kicked out of the courtroom for laughing when they put Karen Baldwin on the stand. When Clive's lawyer asked her if it was her signature on a contract, which it obviously was, all she could say was, 'I'm not sure.'"

Dayna's decision not to attend *Sahara*'s premier proved to be a wise move. During her deposition by Anschutz's lawyers, they asked her what she thought of the movie. When Dayna told them she had never seen it, they insisted she had received the tickets and somebody was sitting in those seats. "When I explained the tickets were given to a couple of tourists," Dayna says, "Those lawyers didn't know what to say."

Janet spent almost every day in the courtroom. "The experience," she says, "was extremely tedious - I must have finished a million crossword puzzles - and often turned ugly. Anschutz's lawyers were trying to make Clive out as a confused old man and a liar. We were all worried about the toll it was taking on him." Marvin Putnam took everybody by surprise when he unexpectedly rested his case after the lunch break on Clive's fifth day of testimony. "This case," Putnam announced to the press, "doesn't have to go a minute longer. I don't think there is a soul in that courtroom that believes what Cussler was saying."

On May 1, Fields presented his closing arguments. First, he countered Putnam's portrayal of his client. "They have tried to smear Clive with all kinds of side issues that don't go to the main point - the breach of contract." He then went on to ask, "Of course, we have the $64-billion question, 'Where is Philip Anschutz?'" By resting his case, Fields reminded the jury, Putnam ensured Anschutz would not have to testify. "Cussler," Fields said, "took his lumps. You really got to know him. He sat there and took it. Yes, he has a bad memory. Yes, sometimes he struggles for words. I think you will conclude he is not an evil man . . . Mr. Anschutz failed to take the heat off. [Yet] it is Mr. Anschutz that wants you to enrich him at Mr. Cussler's expense."

The next day, it was Putnam's turn. He asserted Clive received "the largest payday ever" based on the misleading claim he sold 100-million copies of his books. It was the numbers, and only the numbers, that led to the film's failure at the box office. "*Sahara*," Putnam exclaimed, was a "big beautiful popcorn movie . . . Everybody got paid except Crusader." As far as Anschutz's failure to appear, Putnam explained, "He had no reason to be here because he wasn't sued . . . It's an easy shot to make him sound like a cigar-chomping Daddy Warbucks in his luxury penthouse, but he didn't do anything except say, 'I'll give you the money because you sold 100 million books.'"

Dirk, who was in the courtroom for the closing arguments, contrasts the two attorneys. "Marvin Putnam was showy and theatrical, playing for an emotional response from the jury. It was extremely difficult to sit there and listen to the baseless attacks on my father. Putnam tried to paint the entire process as a planned effort by Clive and Peter to never honor the deal and pocket the money."

"Bert Fields," Dirk continues, "was calm and rational in his delivery and argued his points in a thoughtful manner, but I don't think I was alone in wishing he would have defended Clive's integrity more in the closing. We were all anxious, not only because Clive was visibly worn down, he could have been hit with a huge adverse judgment."

On May 15, 2007, following eight days of deliberation, the jury returned their verdicts. Clive had breached his contract and must pay Crusader Entertainment (now Bristol Bay Productions) $5 million. Clive also fraudulently misrepresented the number of books he sold, but no actual harm had been done, and Anschutz was not awarded the $115 million in punitive damages he was seeking.

Crusader, the jury found, owed Clive for the second book and he was awarded $8.5 million. Both sides claimed victory. Putnam declared the verdict was "a complete victory . . . It was a complete finding of liability, just not a finding of damages." Fields saw it differently. "We feel like Cussler is the clear winner. We're $3.5 million ahead, and Clive got his book rights back." The jury foreman, Anthony Villa, told reporters the complex contract between Clive and Crusader played a major part in the jury's deliberations. "The contract was a nightmare," Villa said. "There were problems on both sides and both parties were at fault. We didn't stick to one side." He added the jury never considered awarding the huge damages each side sought.

Outside the courtroom, Clive, hugged Janet. "I'm relieved that it's over," he said, smiling. "Now we can go home. If I knew the trial was going to turn into a personal attack, I would have passed, but it wasn't over the money. I just wanted my book back." When a reporter asked him if Dirk Pitt would return to the big screen, Clive declared, "There won't be another Clive Cussler film, at least not during my lifetime."

62
CHATTED WITH CLIVE

After three months in California, Clive was finally back in his office. In addition to the final editing of his western, he was putting together another list for a new co-writer. Gamay and Paul Trout's introduction in the *Numa Files* had been so well received, Clive had proposed a new series featuring a professional husband and wife team who travel around the world searching for treasure.

In early spring, 2007, Putnam gave the green light for *The Fargo Adventures*. Tom Golden, an executive editor at Putnam, contacted Grant Blackwood, who had written three thrillers published by Berkeley Books and was high on Clive's list. "Tom asked me," Blackwood recalls. "How would you feel about throwing your hat in the ring for a chance to work with Clive Cussler? I doubt if it was more than a nanosecond before I said yes."

A year earlier, Blackwood attended the first ThrillerFest in

Phoenix (the annual event has since moved to New York). Founded by David Morrell (*First Blood*) and Gayle Lynds (*Masquerade*), the three-day ThrillerFest attracts anybody interested in the genre – authors, agents, publishers, and fans.

Clive was on hand to accept the first ThrillerFest award for lifetime achievement. Before the emcee introduced Clive, she asked anybody in the audience who had been inspired or helped by him to stand. "I looked around the room," Blackwood recalls. "There wasn't anybody sitting down, including me. To influence a community by being great at what you do, that's fine. To influence a community because of how you treat people, that's a whole different thing."

"After Tom called and told me I had the job," Blackwood says, "I was walking on air." Clive provided Blackwood with the background for his fictional couple - Sam and Remy Fargo - how they lived, worked, and thought. Clive also suggested Blackwood should watch *The Thin Man,* a classic film inspired by Dashiell Hammett's novel of the same name, published in 1934. In the book, Hammett replaced his usual hard-boiled private detectives with Nick and Nora Charles, an urbane couple who solve murders while exchanging witty banter and consuming vast amounts of alcohol. Hammett's novel inspired six films starring William Powell and Myrna Loy. Nick and Nora's sophistication, irreverence, and sex appeal were extremely popular and became the prototype for a radio show and a host of contemporary television series featuring crime-fighting couples.

"Clive explained," Blackwood says, "Nick and Nora Charles's relationship and urbane style was the kind of dynamic he had in mind for our heroes. I rented the DVD that night, and when I sent Clive the first third of the book, he said I hit it right on the head."

Grant Blackwood grew up in Texas, California, and

Minnesota. After graduating from high school, he attended a community college before joining the navy. Trained as an Operations Specialist and Pilot Rescue Swimmer, he spent three years aboard a guided missile frigate. "I was discharged on May 23, 1987. Walking off the ship with my sea bag over my shoulder I thought, 'What now?' I knew it was time to go back to school, but I had read Clive's books since I was a teenager. It was a long shot, but I would try to write my own story that would pin someone in their seat."

During the next eleven years, Blackwood earned an associate's degree, majored in history at the University of Missouri in St. Louis, labored at a string of mundane jobs, and wrote his first thriller, *End of Enemies*. The novel's hero, Briggs Tanner, takes on an assortment of evildoers including a renegade Japanese industrialist and Arab terrorists. "My agent, Christie Cardenas, sold the book to Berkley on May 23, 1999, exactly twelve years after I walked down that gangplank."

Seeking a cover blurb, Blackwood, asked his editor, Tom Colgan, if they dared ask Clive. Colgan sent the manuscript to Putnam and Clive graciously responded. "Pure fun, pure adventure. The action and intrigue keep accelerating." Blackwood wrote Clive a thank you note, and a few weeks later, he says, "I was astonished when he called to thank me for my thank you note. We chatted for fifteen minutes and I remember calling him Mr. Cussler. I wrote on my calendar, 'Chatted with Clive.'"

Blackwood wrote two more Briggs Tanner novels but soon discovered getting published, even with good reviews, was only half the fight. "Your books are published, and you think, okay, I've made it. But the sad truth is you've come up against a bigger wall - selling enough books to pay your bills." Blackwood turned to ghostwriting. "I liked the work, but you serve a lot of masters and have to accept the fact your name won't be on the cover. Everybody involved with the book has an opinion. Clients can be difficult, and it's imperative not only to find a middle ground, but to do it in a diplomatic way. You come up with a plot, write the book, they give you a flat fee, and you walk away. After I signed on with Clive, I was fortunate to be able to quit ghostwriting and concentrate all my energy on the *Fargo Adventures*."

While Blackwood focused on Sam and Remi Fargo, Clive finished the western he had started before the trial. Now called *The Chase*, the book Clive dismissed as, "fun . . . but nothing like a bestseller," was published by Putnam on November 6, 2007. Two weeks later, Clive was proved wrong when *The Chase* appeared on *The New York Times* hardcover bestseller list, ranked a very respectable number three.

Instead of Clive's familiar historical prologue, the story opens in 1950, when a rusted steam locomotive is salvaged from a Montana lake, and then shifts to the past. The relic is soon tied to events that took place in 1906, when a bank robber, known as the Butcher Bandit, was terrorizing the western U.S. After brutally murdering any witnesses, he manages to escape without a trace. Issac Bell, a handsome, charismatic, well-educated detective, is hired to solve the case. The epic Cussler climax features a rip-roaring race between two fire-breathing steam locomotives.

The Chase's unexpected strong sales convinced Clive and Putnam there was a market for a series following the adventures of Issac Bell and the Van Dorn detective agency. Needing yet another co-writer, Clive was about to make one of his time-honored lists when Barbara Peters came to the rescue.

63
A SLOSH OF JOSHUA SLOCUM

When Barbara Peters was informed Clive was looking for a co-writer for a western series, she suggested he should consider Justin Scott. Peters originally met Scott in 1996, at a conference in Phoenix hosted by the Poisoned Pen. Some authors were invited to speak about their favorite mystery writer, and Scott gave a presentation on Robert Louis Stevenson that Peters called "brilliant." Two years later, Peters edited the collected works of the authors in the book, *AZ Murder Goes . . . Classic*.

Growing up on Long Island, Justin Scott was surrounded by writers. His father, Alexander Leslie Scott, wrote 250 Western novels and reams of poetry under a variety of pen names. Scott's mother, Lily K. Scott, was also a prolific author, writing novels, romances, and short stories for magazines and pulps. After graduating from Harper College with a master's degree in American history, Scott drove trucks, built beach houses, tended bar, and edited an electronics engineering journal. "I started to write seriously in 1973," Scott says. "That first year I produced four novels. The first was not literate, the second, barely, but it managed to attract a literary agent, Henry Morrison, who sold the third. When I handed him the fourth, Henry explained one hardcover novel a year was considered a stately pace."

Unwilling to bide his time, Scott came up with a pen name, and Morrison went shopping for a new publisher. What originally seemed like a good idea turned into a can of worms when Justin Scott's *Many Happy Returns*, and "J.S. Blazer's," *Deal Me Out*, were both nominated as Best First Mystery Novel by the Mystery Writers of America. "I had to call the Mystery Writers and explain I was Justin Scott and J.S. Blazer," Scott says, laughing. "That proved a lot easier than coming clean with two publishers."

After writing two more mysteries under his own name, and another by J. S. Blazer, Scott decided to shift gears and take a crack at thrillers. Between 1978 and 1994, Justin Scott wrote eight novels, including his biggest hit, *The Shipkiller*. The plot follows a sailor's quest to avenge the death of his wife after the *Leviathan*, a million-ton supertanker runs down their sailboat. Reviewing *The Shipkiller* in *Time* magazine, Michael Demarest wrote, "As heady as Francis Chichester's narrative, with a draught of Melville and a slosh of Joshua Slocum."

In addition to his thrillers, Scott was also busy with a mystery series centered around Ben Abbott, a small-town Connecticut real estate agent who alternates between selling center-staircase Cape Cods and freelance sleuthing. After four Ben Abbott books - the series was twice nominated for the Edgar Allen Poe Award - Scott wanted to write a sequel to *The Shipkiller*. Concerned publishers would be hesitant to buy a thriller since Scott was now considered a mystery writer, so Morrison suggested another pen name. When Scott pointed out the book was a sequel and the main characters, although ten years older, were the same, Morrison assured him, "Don't worry, everyone you ever met in publishing has been fired."

"Suddenly," Scott says, "I was also 'Paul Garrison,' an international businessman based in Hong Kong whose seagoing grandfather wandered the South Seas in the last of the square-rigged trading vessels." Morrison sold *Fire and Ice* to HarperCollins and the book was published in March 1999. Although the reviews were glowing, one astute reader questioned the author's originality. "As an avid sailor, I appreciate the accuracy of Garrison's portrayal, but he obviously read and enjoyed Justin Scott's *The Shipkiller*."

Everything was fine until Hollywood showed an interest in *Fire and Ice*. Scott and Morrison, remembering their earlier problems with J. S. Blazer, went to see a copyright lawyer. "We registered Paul Garrison as a 'real' person," Scott says. "The Library of Congress needed a birthday, and the lawyer asked me how old I wanted to be." Scott laughs, "Shamelessly, Paul Garrison bounded down that narrow staircase ten years younger than Justin Scott was when he plodded up them."

Scott produced four more sea tales under Paul Garrison's name, but the pen-name game occasionally caused problems. Editors who asked to meet Garrison were politely informed the author's high-power business dealings in the Orient made it impossible for him to fly to New York, much less go out on book tours. While Scott was writing Paul Garrison's thrillers, the Ben Abbott mysteries had been moved to the back burner. "Small talk among old acquaintances," Scott says, "began to touch upon the question of my death. Those I occasionally bumped into at a party would suddenly exclaim their glass was empty and flee to the bar, afraid to ask where my career had gone."

When the elusive Paul Garrison was invited to attend an important book event at London's Barbican Performing Arts

Centre, Scott initially declined. "Too many people in British publishing knew me," he says. "My cover would be blown. But after some thought, I decided it was too important to miss, and contacted the event's organizers. I told them I would be having lunch with the writer Justin Scott and his fiancée. Could they come too? They said, 'Why not?'"

Scott prevailed upon an old friend, John Mincarelli, to play the part of Paul Garrison. The trio, Scott and Amber Edwards (she and Scott are now married), along with "Paul Garrison," spent the night hobnobbing with England's publishing elite. Mincarelli, a professor of fashion merchandising at New York's Fashion Institute is, according to Scott, "strikingly handsome. He was dressed like a million bucks and my British editor fell completely in love with him - not me."

In 2006, Scott revealed the truth about Paul Garrison's real name in an article in *The Boston Globe*. "Paul has gone sailing," he admitted. "Justin has reemerged with a new novel in the Ben Abbott series, [*McMansion*, Poisoned Pen Press]. I'm turning the Garrison website into the Garrison/Justin Scott website. It's really nice to be able to meet my editor's face-to-face and have dinner."

Barbara Peters was not alone in recommending Scott for the new series. Peter Lampack and Henry Morrison were old friends, and with Clive's approval, Scott was signed on to write the sequel to *The Chase*. "When we were going through the process," Scott says, "somebody wanted to know if I thought it would be a problem to write in a western voice. I explained I doubt it. I've been reading my father's westerns since I was a kid."

Scott's role as Clive's collaborator has had a major impact on his career. "There were two reasons to accept. Obviously, collaborating with a mega-bestselling writer offered the opportunity to clamber aboard *The New York Times* bestseller list. I had done very well for myself, but when it comes to selling lots and lots of books, he has done it better. Collaborating with Clive is like winning a fellowship to do graduate work at any Ivy League university. He knows how never to be boring - even for one sentence. Every sentence must serve the story and nothing but the story. Clive will go through a scene, identify what Georges Simenon called 'the beautiful sentences,' and skewer them ruthlessly. Entire scenes must also prove their right to exist, as must asides, writer's observations, mental dithering, and authorial thinking out loud - if they serve the story they stay, if they don't, they're out."

Co-writing the Isaac Bell series has made Scott realize he "is more collegial than I thought, and less the gnarly lone wolf I fancied myself to be. Looking back on the early days of my career, I realize editors were still at the center of publishing and there was a lot of collaboration in the writing of books. Clive has revived that atmosphere of making things together, and for that I am grateful."

64
THE HOLY GRAIL

Clive and Janet were married at the Royal Palm Spa in Scottsdale on June 29, 2008. After a simple ceremony, the bride, groom, and fifty family members and friends were directed to an adjacent, elegantly decorated room where they enjoyed dinner and celebrated the couple's union. During the ceremony, the music included *Heaven's Rain*, a song composed by Nils Lofgren. Janet had no idea what to get Clive for a wedding present, so she had asked Lofgren to write a song for the ceremony.

"My wife Amy and I are grateful for Clive and his family's friendship," Lofgren says. "I was honored to work up a tune for the wedding."

"I have always been a fan of Dirk Pitt," Lofgren says "In 1989, I was touring with Ringo Starr's All-Starr Band. In Denver, I did some friendly stalking and invited Clive and his family to the concert. We've been friends ever since."

Lofgren moved to Scottsdale in 2003, and one evening Clive confessed he had, "always wanted to write a corny country song." With Clive providing the vocals, and Lofgren the music, the duo came up with *What Ever Happened to Muscatel?*, a song "with humorous reminiscences to liquors gone by."

Four months after they were married, Clive and Janet flew to Denver for Cussler Con 2008, an event celebrating all things associated with the "Grand Master of Adventure." On the evening of October 5, a crowd gathering in front of the Ramada Plaza Hotel "oohed and aahed" as a dashing 1932 Auburn V-12 Boattail Speedster glided to a stop. At the wheel was Dirk Cussler, accompanied by his sister Dayna. A few moments later, a 1933 American Austin pulled in behind the Auburn. After unfolding his lanky frame from the diminutive car, Clive stood and waved at the cheering throng.

For three days, attendees socialized with Clive and four of his co-writers - Dirk Cussler, Paul Kemprecos, Jack Du Brul, and Grant Blackwood - toured the Cussler Museum, and enjoyed a banquet and address by author Steve Barry. Members lined up afterward to have the authors sign their towering piles of books.

Held annually since 2005, Cussler Con is the highlight for members of the Clive Cussler Collector's Society (CCCS). Founded by Wayne Valero and Bruce Kenfield, the CCCS elevates the author's fandom to another level. Not only does the organization provide its members with a steady stream of facts and news about Clive, the once-a-year convention offers the opportunity to spend a weekend with the author and his associates.

"I read *Raise the Titanic!* in 1976," Wayne Valero said, "and really enjoyed the book. My wife, Cristy, is a big reader and for my birthday she gave me a copy of *Night Probe!* I was hooked." By 1990, Valero, who lived in Denver and worked for the *Denver Post*, had assembled a modest collection of Clive's hardcovers and paperbacks. When he learned Clive was doing a signing for *Dragon* at a local bookstore, Valero, unfortunately, was scheduled to work.

On Friday, he dropped off a stack of his books at the bookstore, along with a note asking Clive to sign them. He also inquired if any of Clive's early books had been published in hardcover since he had only seen them in paperback. Returning to the store, Valero found a note from Clive stuck in one of the books - not only did he have a hardcover copy of *Iceberg*, but Valero was welcome to it.

"Clive was living on Lookout Mountain," Valero said. "I was driving a 1972 Malibu and didn't want to show up in that car, so I borrowed my best friend's brand new Chevy Cavalier. My son came along and after visiting with Clive and Barbara, Clive disappeared in his office and came out with a pristine first edition hardcover copy of *Iceberg*. He inscribed it, '*To Wayne, who is my inspiration for Dirk Pitt. Your pal, Clive Cussler.*' Today, that book is the Holy Grail for Cussler collectors. A pristine copy can sell for $2,000." Asked if Clive was impressed with his borrowed Cavalier, Valero laughed. "I don't think Clive looked to see what kind of car I was driving."

As his collection grew, Valero began to communicate with other Cussler fans on Simon & Schuster's internet forums, a service provided by the publisher for readers to find information about author's bios, news, and upcoming releases. When he found out other fans were collecting Clive's books, Valero wrote, *The Collector's Guide To Clive Cussler*. In his introduction, Paul McCarthy wrote, "Wherever you go in the world of Clive Cussler, take *The Collector's Guide* with you and use it to get even more pleasure and satisfaction from being one of Clive's true fans. That's what I'm doing. Enjoy!"

"The book was published privately in 2002," Valero said. "I was distributing them on the S&S website. Bruce Kenfield bought a dozen copies, sight unseen." When the two men realized they shared the same passion, Kenfield flew to Denver to see Valero's collection, and the CSSS was incorporated in 2002.

Bruce Kenfield owns a construction company in Woodburn, Oregon. He also received his first Cussler book as a birthday present. "It was *Cyclops*," he says. "I've never been what you would call a reader, but I enjoyed Clive's writing and began to look for more books. I had no idea how popular Clive was, and thought I was the only person who knew about him. When I found the Simon & Schuster forum I couldn't believe it. Not only were there thousands of fans, Wayne had written a book about collecting Clive's books. It was exciting to find out there were so many fans out there who liked Clive, but it was more fun when I thought I was the only guy who was reading his books."

Valero wrote two additional books: *From the Mediterranean Caper to Black Wind: A Bibliography of Clive Cussler* and *The Adventure Writing of Clive Cussler*. After a short illness, Wayne Valero died in 2016.

65
SOCIETY OF CUSSLERMEN

Attesting to Clive's remarkable popularity, the Society of Cusslermen (SOC) maintains an internet site providing Clive's fans access to, "pictures, details and information of every book published throughout the US and UK." The SOC's founder, Dave Hyatt, was introduced to Dirk Pitt in 1973. "I stopped into a bookstore on my lunch break and the clerk suggested I might like *The Mediterranean Caper*." Hyatt finished the book that night and went back to the store looking for more, but the clerk informed it was Clive's only book. Two years later, the same clerk called Hyatt to tell him *Iceberg* had just arrived. "I actually ran over to the store and have been reading and collecting his books ever since."

After Hyatt built his website, he met Wayne Valero. "Wayne was a little upset," Hyatt says. "He was in the process of developing his own collector society's website. I went to several CCCS conventions, but ultimately they told me I wasn't welcome." Valero admits there has been some animosity between the

CCCS and SOC. "We've had our run-ins, but ultimately we all share the same interest - Clive and his work. There is room for everybody."

66
A GENEROUS MAN

When Paul McCarthy finished his introduction to Wayne Valero's *The Collector's Guide to Clive Cussler*, he sent a copy to Clive. "A few days later," McCarthy says, "Clive called and told me it was fine, with one exception - I had neglected to call him a 'curmudgeon.'"

It could be the way he looks, the way he walks, perhaps the way he talks. Whatever it is, Clive is often characterized as cantankerous. The Denver newspapers - the same papers that lionized him as the city's "big author" after *Raise the Titanic!* became a bestseller - seem to relish referring to him as "gruff," "grouchy," and a "literary curmudgeon." In the media frenzy surrounding the courtroom battle between Clive and Crusader Entertainment, terms like "crotchety old man . . . grumpy cuss . . . bad tempered" were tossed around by the press.

The name calling is perplexing to those who know Clive, especially his fans. "Anybody who has attended a convention or one of Clive's book signings," Valero states, "cannot help but be impressed by Clive's consideration for his fans and co-writers. Even when it's obvious Clive is tired, he will go out of his way to spend time with everybody present and sign books until I'm afraid his arm will fall off."

CCCS member Tom Gwinn agrees. "Clive has always been accessible. One of my best memories was the Friday evening get-together at the first Denver convention. Clive arrived in a beautiful Locomobile and spent the rest of the night talking to anybody and everybody. It felt more like we were hanging out with an old friend instead of a world-famous author."

During the twenty-plus years Clive has been involved with the Poisoned Pen bookstore, Barbara Peters notes, "Clive can come off as gruff, but I've learned to get along with him, and we have a wonderful relationship. When he does get a little grumpy, or starts to bitch about something, I simply tell him to stop, and he stops. One of the things I admire most is Clive's insistence that his co-authors share in his credit. Clive has always been transparent about his projects, unlike some authors we know who have secret co-authors." She picks up a copy of *The Wrecker* and opens it to the title page, "Clive will not autograph a book for us unless the co-author has also signed - Clive is a very generous man."

If Clive has an Achilles' heel, it may be that he is too generous. "I've never understood assertions my father is a grouch," Dirk says. "Clive will let people into his life who turned out to be nothing but bullshit artists - people who you or I would spend some time with and say this guy is full of it. Maybe Clive just likes a good story, they stroke his ego, or he wants to give them the benefit of the doubt. I don't know, but there's been a series of these jokers."

"I've always been loyal," Clive says, frowning. "To a fault, I suppose. When I became successful, everybody started to come out of the woodwork. First, it was the cleaning lady who hit Barbara up for a thousand bucks and we never saw her again. Next, a friend asked me for $5,000 and he also disappeared. Another gave me a story about how he and his wife wanted to build their retirement log cabin on a lot in Washington State, but some evil corporation was after the land. I sent them $17,000 and that's the last I heard from them."

During the 1980s, Clive hired a publicist he met at one of the car auctions to manage his fan letters, press releases, and interview requests. "Everything worked fine for the first ten years," Clive says. "Then she not only stopped doing the things she was hired to do, there were some money issues. We could have filed criminal charges, but I let her down easy and even gave her a letter stating we had a nice association."

"There was one exception," Clive says, chuckling. "A friend of Dirk's asked me to loan him $800 for his school tuition. I couldn't believe it when, a few months later, he showed up with a check and handed it to me. I told him to keep it. He's the only one who paid me back."

One of the most bizarre scams foisted on Clive involved fabricated cover blurbs. On April 11, 1991, Peter Lampack announced Simon & Schuster had paid a staggering $920,000 to his client, Derek V. Van Arman, for his first novel, *The Killing Time*. Derek V Goodwin (the author's real name) described himself as "a Washington-based communications specialist and investigator in national security who has been employed by numerous federal agencies and maintains sensitive clearances in the United States Government."

When Van Arman originally presented his manuscript, he included ringing endorsements from John Le Carre, Joseph Wambaugh, and Clive Cussler. Two days after Lampack announced the huge payoff, *The New York Times* revealed, "A Spy Novel's Boosters, It Seems Aren't." Le Carre and

Wambaugh both avowed they had never seen the book or had any contact with the author. Le Carre labeled the use of his name, "nothing but straight fraud." Wambaugh said he felt "both angry and bemused that my name had been attached to the scheme."

Unlike Le Carre and Wambaugh, Clive had not only seen the book, but he had a long-standing relationship with the author.

"Barbara and I met Derek and his wife when they lived in Washington," Clive says. "After he and Susan moved to Phoenix, we spent a lot of time socializing. He was a real character and told me all sorts of stories about Washington and the government. During the next ten years, I not only loaned Derek money but when he decided to write a book, I rewrote a few of the chapters. When *The New York Times* came out with the story that Le Carre's and Wambaugh's blurbs were faked, I couldn't believe it. There was no indication Derek was running a scam. Barbara was especially shaken because she thought Derek and Susan were our close friends."

Goodwin claimed he had been "completely duped," and the bogus blurbs were the work of someone with a personal grudge or a former CIA agent. Simon & Schuster did not swallow the yarn and canceled the deal. Lampack eventually sold *The Killing Time* to Dutton for $500,000 (proving the axiom, no publicity is bad publicity). When the book was published in 1992, Clive sent Goodwin a copy with a letter. "I asked him to autograph the book and while he was at it, please send a check for the $143,000 he owed me. We never had to go to court since the royalties came to Peter who signed them over to me." Goodwin sent another manuscript to Lampack, but the agent declared it was unpublishable and Clive has never heard from Goodwin again.

Despite his unfortunate experiences with fair-weather friends and rip-off artists, Clive remains upbeat. "I should be cynical, but I'm not. It's just the way I am. At least I'm not like Babe Ruth, who gave away money to everybody he met."

Dick Klein, Clive's childhood friend and one-time gas station partner, was asked if Clive's success has changed him. "No, he's the same old Clive he was fifty years ago. My wife and I have visited him on various occasions, and we always end up talking about the old days. It's like we're the same young guys who were pumping gas in Alhambra." Klein does have one complaint. "When we go out to dinner, I don't want Clive to think he has to always pick up the check, but we always end up in places I can't afford." Klein laughs, "Maybe one of these days I can convince him to go to Applebee's."

Author Robyn Carr met Clive when they were both scheduled to speak at the Scottsdale Library. "It was twenty-some years ago," Carr remembers. "I thought he was an extremely interesting guy. We were living in Arizona, and my husband and I and Clive and Barbara became good friends. Clive has always tried to put on this gruff exterior, but the truth is, he a wonderful man, always willing to help other writers."

Carr now lives in Henderson, Nevada, and is a major supporter of the local library where she hosts an interview series with authors called *Carr Chat*." "When Clive found out we were planning a fund-raiser for the library," Carr says, "He and Janet showed up without me having to ask. That's the kind of man he is."

"I get infuriated," Janet says, "when somebody calls Clive disagreeable or a curmudgeon. There was a lot of that during the trial from people who have never even met him. When we go to the conventions, book signings, and other events, I am always amazed how kind and gracious Clive is to everyone. He gives so much of himself."

Craftsman Fred Tourneau, the man responsible for the museum quality ship models displayed in Clive's studio, refers to his patron as "a prince." On one occasion, Clive arrived at Tourneau's house to check on a model's progress and was surprised to see a Ferrari with "MD" plates parked in the driveway. The car's owner, it turned out, was picking up a model he had commissioned. While Clive waited, he could hear the two men talking. "The guy was badgering Fred to drop his price," Clive says. "Like most artists, Fred was always getting taken advantage of."

After hearing all he could stand, Clive announced he would like to buy the model in question. Annoyed, the haggler wanted to know who the hell Clive was and why was he getting involved. Clive explained he was one of Tourneau's clients and since it was obvious he did not want the model, Clive would love to add it to his collection. "That did it," Clive says. "He told Fred he would give him a couple hundred more and we went back and forth. By the time we got done, he ended up writing a check for a great deal more than the original price." After the irritated doctor screeched away in his Ferrari, Tourneau looked at the check with a dazed expression. Clive laughed, "Fred, for once, you got paid what it's worth!"

67
THE KEYS TO THEIR FERRARI

A month after *Medusa*, the eighth book in the *NUMA Files* series, was published, Paul Kemprecos's venerable collaboration with Clive came to an end. "We started with *Serpent* in 1999, and finished with *Medusa*, in June 2009," Kemprecos said. "It was a great run. *The Numa Files* have been successful far beyond our expectations, but the task of turning out eight fat books in ten years was catching up with me. Coming up with fresh concepts and the demanding deadlines were having a negative effect on my stress level." Now able to work at his own pace, Kemprecos is concentrating on a series featuring a team of crime fighters led by an undersea robotics engineer and another book based on his original "Soc" Socarides detective series.

Faced with the prospect of replacing Kemprecos, Clive already had somebody in mind. "Janet and I were flying someplace," Clive says. "We were in an airport bookstore, and I bought a novel by Graham Brown. Both of us thought it was outstanding." At Clive's suggestion, Peter Lampack contacted Brown's editor at Random House. "I had just come back from a book signing in Nashville," Brown says. "There was a message from my editor - Peter Lampack, Clive Cussler's agent, would like to get in touch with me." Brown recalls being perplexed. "Why does Cussler want to talk to me? He uses co-writers, I write adventure novels, Clive wants me to work with him. No, I told myself, be realistic. He's simply organizing an event for Arizona authors and wants me to speak. I was going around and around and didn't know what to think."

When Brown called Lampack, the agent explained Clive had read several of his books and was impressed with the dialogue and plots. They were looking for a co-writer and would he be interested? "Would I be interested?" Brown exclaims, "Of course I was interested! Clive was somewhere in Africa, but he would be in touch with me. After I hung up, I sat on my balcony wondering what the hell had just happened."

"I grew up in Connecticut, Illinois, and Pennsylvania," Brown says. "My father worked for British Airways. When the school year started, my friends and I would compare our summers. They went to Disneyland and Great Adventure amusement park. My family had traveled to England or Egypt. At the time I would have preferred Disneyland, but later realized the opportunity to travel inspired me to think of the world as a much bigger place - a major benefit to my writing."

Brown read his first Cussler book on one of his family's trips to Europe. "Walking down the aisle, everybody on that airplane, including me, was reading a book with a ship's stern on the cover. It was *Raise the Titanic!* Brown attended Embry-Riddle Aeronautical School in Prescott, Arizona. "I graduated into a bad economy," Brown explains. "Airlines were laying off pilots. I ended up working at a series of odd jobs and, in my spare time, tried to write a thriller."

When Brown realized it might be a long time before the airlines were hiring, he enrolled in law school at Arizona State. "My plan," he relates, "was to write while I was going to school. I actually finished a draft, but my grades took a nose dive, and I had to put it away." After practicing law for several years, Brown discovered the job required a love for paperwork and arguing with people, two things he dislikes immensely. Moving to California, he spent the next five years working for a health care company.

Brown credits his ex-wife with prodding his stalled writing career. "She suggested I should attend the Mauri Writers Conference," he says. "That was 2006. I figured, even if it proved to be a waste of time, we would have a nice vacation. The conference turned out to be a cross roads for me. It was so exciting to meet like-minded people. That experience inspired me to get serious."

A year later, Brown finished his novel. Looking for an agent, he attended Thrillerfest in New York. "Fortune smiled on me when I met Barbara Poelle with the Irene Goodman Literary Agency. After I gave her my pitch, she told me it was the worst thing she'd heard all week, but for some reason, wanted me to send her ten pages."

Poelle read the ten pages and sent Brown an e-mail. After informing him it could not possibly be the same book he had described in New York, she asked to see the rest of it. "We signed a deal with Random House," Brown says, "*Black Rain* was published in 2010. The plot follows covert government operative Danielle Laidlaw, assisted by a mysterious ex-CIA agent known as Hawker, as they journey to the darkest regions of the Amazon to search for a lost Mayan city.

Brown was working on his third book continuing the adventures of Laidlaw and Hawker when he was contacted by Peter Lampack. "Shortly after I talked to Peter," Brown says,

"Clive called. He was in Morocco, and we had a wonderful conversation. When I asked him how he'd heard about me, he said he picked up my book in an airport. Talk about fate. All my life, I've been picking up Clive Cussler books in the airport."

Working with Clive, Brown explains, "is like someone handing you the keys to their Ferrari - it's fun to drive but don't hit the wall in turn three or you're going to catch hell. In some ways, collaborating with Clive is easier than writing my own books. Not only do Clive and I mix the process up like a creative stew, I know if I get stymied he'll get me back on track." Brown admits he will often end up feeling envious after a brainstorming session. "I end up thinking, damn, why didn't I think of that?"

Early in his relationship with Clive, Brown recalls, "I was shocked when he axed a couple of my precious paragraphs. He noticed my dismay because he laughed and went on to describe a long and detailed scene he wrote in the early days of Dirk Pitt that ended up in the garbage can."

Brown, like Clive's other co-writers, learned one of the fundamental secrets to Clive's success. "Clive is emphatic," Brown explains, "Everything you write has to be interesting to the reader. You can't spend a page describing a streetcar or the interior of a bar. One of his favorite refrains is, 'Keep the action moving. That's what separates the men from the boys - the boy's overwrite.'"

Brown attended his first Cussler Con in 2011. "It was a fantastic experience," he says. "Paul Kemprecos did a fantastic job with the *NUMA Files*, and I realize I've got big shoes to fill. Initially, I noticed some suspicious glances from his many fans, but I think I won them over."

Devil's Gate, Clive and Brown's first collaboration, was published by Putnam on November 14, 2011. Four weeks later, it appeared on *The New York Times* bestseller list, ranked at number five. Reader reviews were overwhelmingly positive. One fan declared, "Cussler and his new co-author Graham Brown have hit a home run with this new adventure. For Cussler fans the fun is back." Another said, "Graham Brown has re-energized the *NUMA Files* with his thrilling collaboration with Cussler - I felt as if I stepped into a time machine and was transported back to Clive at his peak."

68
THE NEXT BIG ADVENTURE

In June 2011, Clive was again faced with the task of finding another co-writer. Shortly after *The Kingdom*, the third novel in the *Fargo* series, was published, Grant Blackwood resigned to concentrate on a new series of his own. As Barbara Peters had done earlier with Justin Scott, she suggested Clive read the work of Thomas Perry.

A native of Tonawanda, New York, Perry earned a B.A. from Cornell University and a Ph.D. in English Literature from the University of Rochester. He is the author of seventeen novels, including *The Butcher's Boy*, awarded an Edgar Award from the Mystery Writers of America for Best First Novel, and *Vanishing Act*, selected as a "100 Favorite Mysteries of the Century" by the Independent Mystery Booksellers Association. Perry and his wife, Jo, have also worked extensively in television both as writers and producers, including stints with *Simon and Simon* and *Star Trek: The Next Generation*.

Clive, impressed with Perry's writing, offered him the job of co-writing the *Fargo* series. "After I talked to Clive," he says, "I read the existing *Fargo* books, not only to find out what was wanted, but if I thought I could do it - or more accurately, learn to do it. When I asked around about Clive, I was amazed by the number of positive reviews. People just love him, and I can see why. Once the business preliminaries were over, I spent two days at his home in Arizona. He is not only wonderful company, I've already started to learn things from him."

On July 15, 2011, Clive's family rented a beach house outside of Puerto Vallarta and celebrated his 80th birthday. On hand for the festivities: Janet, her daughter Whitney, and husband Dale; Dirk and Kerry and their girls Lauren and Bryce; Teri and her children Jason and Amie; Amie's husband Tim, his children Haley and Katie; and Dayna and her boyfriend Brian.

"We managed to get Clive in the ocean to go boogie boarding a time or two," Dirk says. "He also rode a series of zip-lines through the jungle. It was a hoot for everyone and a bit of a challenge for an eighty-year-old guy, but Clive, as always, was game. We cracked open a fifty-year-old bottle of Bordeaux for his birthday dinner, and afterward, my Dad and I spent a lot of time sitting on the patio overlooking the ocean. We drank margaritas, smoked cigars and talked about cars, shipwrecks, and the next big adventure."

Barbara Peters believes Clive will never retire. "He's in good health, and there's nothing else he'd rather do. What would he do if he didn't write? For all his kindness, Clive is not really a social animal. The books allow him to touch people's lives and do other things, like the cars and shipwrecks, but I think Clive's happiest in a world of his own making."

Having represented Clive through both the lean years and his remarkable success, Peter Lampack knows his client as well as anybody. "Clive has never been more alive," Lampack says. "If there are no problems with his health, I see no reason why Clive would want to retire. He has a talented group of writers who are helping to carry the load. This provides Clive and Janet with time to travel. Two years ago he spent a month in Europe. Last year he was in Egypt. He spent a week in Afghanistan in 2011, and was only back for a few weeks, before heading off to India. I'm not sure I could do that."

Clive's trip to Afghanistan was sponsored by the USO. Forsaking the familiar troupe of musicians, comedians, and leggy starlets, "Operation Thriller" sent five authors to the Persian Gulf in November 2011, to meet the troops, discuss their books, and sign autographs. In addition to Clive, Sandra Brown, Kathy Reichs, Mark Bowden, and Andrew Peterson were along for the week-long tour. The flight to the war zone in a C-130 Hercules brought back memories of Clive's experiences during the Korean War. "We were crammed into jump seats," he says, "and had to wear ear plugs because the engines were so loud. During landings and takeoffs, the lights were turned out so we wouldn't attract fire from the ground."

In addition to sharing a b-hut - basically a large plywood box divided into cubicles - with nine soldiers, the five authors were required to wear helmets and body armor. "Our days started at dawn and often ended at midnight," Andrew Peterson recalled. "Most of our time was spent interacting with the troops. Cussler was obviously the most popular and people were coming up right and left with Clive Cussler books."

"During the entire experience," Clive says, "It was obvious we were in a war zone, but it was wonderful to meet and talk to the servicemen and women." In one memorable photograph, a camouflage-clad young lady plants a kiss on Clive's cheek after receiving an autograph.

Seated in his studio, his rangy legs stretched out on his desk,

Clive is surrounded by the books, models, and memorabilia accumulated during his forty-year career as a bestselling author, adventurer, and teacher. Asked if he has any regrets, Clive laughs. "It would be ludicrous of me to give you a long list of things I never got to do. I've had my low points - Barbara's death was a terrible blow - but, I was lucky to meet Janet. Some mornings I still wake up and wonder if all of this is true."

He pauses, "Well, if I really think about it, there are a couple. I've always said, if I found the *Hunley* and the *Bonhomme Richard*, I would die a happy man. We found the *Hunley*, but the *Richard* is still out there. I'm not willing to throw in the towel just yet. Dirk is going to continue the search, and you never know."

Another pause, "Bob Esbenson and I were at a Kruse auction in 1981 when they rolled out a Tucker. I didn't bid, and the car ended up going for somewhere around $35,000. Bob was after me to bid, and I remember, like it was yesterday, telling him, 'Not to worry, another one will come along.' At the 2012 Barrett-Jackson Auction at Monterey, a Tucker sold for $2.9 million. That's a regret!"

69
EPILOGUE

During the sixty-odd years Ellis Island was open for business, more than 15 million immigrants passed through its doors. By the early 1950s, the number of people entering the United States had dwindled to the point where the General Services Administration declared Ellis Island was "surplus to the needs of the federal government" and closed the facility.

For more than twenty years, the island's structures lay fallow. Roofs leaked, pipes burst, machinery and furniture rusted in place, plaster ceilings collapsed, and vandals made off with copper pipes and decorative details. Various schemes to develop the island were floated, but Ellis Island's future remained in limbo until 1982, when Lee Iacocca - whose parents had passed through the island - was chosen to head the Statue of Liberty-Ellis Island Foundation.

Funded by private donations, the Ellis Island Immigration

Museum opened in 1990. When Clive learned an immigrant's name could be memorialized on the Wall of Honor for a donation of $150, he added Eric Cussler's name to the list. Today, the wall, with more than 700,000 names, is one of the museum's most popular exhibits.

In 2004, Clive was in New York for a meeting with his publisher. Finding he had an afternoon free, he decided to visit Ellis Island. While searching for his father's name on the Wall of Honor, Clive struck up a conversation with a National Park Service employee. After Clive told him the story how his father conned his way into America by pretending to be a piano player, the young fellow suggested he should stop by the museum director's office because he was always interested in personal recollections.

After hearing Clive's story, the director thanked him for stopping by and suggested Clive would be remiss if he left without visiting one of the displays on the second floor. Clive climbed the stairs, walked down the hall and entered a room filled with artifacts, including a battered upright piano encased in glass. "I realized why the director sent me up there," Clive says. "That piano was the same one my father played in 1924. I've always wondered what kind of courage, or terror - probably equal parts of each - it took to pull that off. I stood there, crying like a baby."

A few minutes later, Clive turned and walked out of the hall, leaving behind the faded melody of a long forgotten German marching song.

Chairwoman, CEO, and Publisher
Donna Carpenter LeBaron

Chief Financial Officer
Cindy Butler Sammons

Art Director
Matthew Pollock

Senior Editors
**Hank Gilman, Paul Keegan,
Larry Martz, Ken Otterbourg**

Associate Editors
Sherrie Moran, Val Pendergrast

President Emeritus
Helen Rees

Chairwoman Emeritus
Juanita C. Sammons

Made in the USA
Monee, IL
01 December 2020